THE INTERNATIONAL MENU DIABETIC COOKBOOK

CONTEMPORARY
BOOKS, INC.
CHICAGO

Library of Congress Cataloging in Publication Data

Marks, Betty.
    The international menu diabetic cookbook.

    Includes index.
    1. Diabetes—Diet therapy—Recipes.   2. Cookery,
International.   I. Schechter, Lucille Haley.
II. Title.
RC662.M35   1985   641.5'6314   85-15155
ISBN 0-8092-5390-9

Published by Contemporary Books, Inc.
180 North Michigan Avenue, Chicago, Illinois 60601
Manufactured in the United States of America
Library of Congress Catalog Card Number: 85-15155
International Standard Book Number: 0-8092-5390-9

Published simultaneously in Canada by Beaverbooks, Ltd.
195 Allstate Parkway, Valleywood Business Park
Markham, Ontario L3R 4T8 Canada

CONTENTS

ACKNOWLEDGMENTS

Warm thanks to the many friends who accepted our invitation to share these meals and whose comments and criticism helped shape a better book, and to Dr. Gerald Bernstein and Dr. Harold Rifkin for their encouragement and the foreword. Thanks also to Barbara Turro whose nutritional advice was invaluable.

FOREWORD

*"The fault . . . is not in
our stars but in
ourselves."*

This quotation from William Shakespeare might well apply to the problems that affect people with Diabetes Mellitus. The fault in these cases is the failure of the body to provide adequate insulin activity. Either the body puts out too little, or what it does produce is ineffective. A second fault, in Type 2 Diabetes Mellitus, is obesity. This problem is caused by slow burning of calories and the same problem exists for the nondiabetic obese person.

To correct these internal faults, certain external factors need to be applied. For the Type 1 or insulin-dependent diabetic, insulin is supplied by injection and adjusted by self-monitoring techniques. For the Type 2 or noninsulin-dependent diabetic, other forms of therapy, such as exercise and oral hypoglycemic agents, help to improve the effectiveness of whatever insulin is produced. Common to both disorders is the strong need for controlled diet. The internal fault must be controlled by the external milieu. This means restrictions and limitations on the type, amount, and timing of meals and snacks. In the past, these restrictions meant negative experiences. In order to be considered safe, diabetic fare was generally bland and unimaginative. Our society is heavily food oriented today. We are bombarded by words and pictures all meant to make us hungry and want to eat.

The authors of this wonderful and exciting book have blended current knowledge of the metabolic requirements of the person with diabetes together with a sense of true gourmet food. Displaying a vivid love of food, they have presented well-prepared, tasty, balanced meals that are interesting and imaginative. And their book is as much fun to read as it is to use. The culinary pleasure presented in these menus is magnified because foods of so many different nationalities are included.

These international recipes can be understood in terms of the food exchange system, and each is broken down into calories, carbohydrates, protein, fat, and sodium values. Since the Type 1 diabetic is interested in food nutrient breakdown, and the Type 2 diabetic is more concerned with calorie conservation, both groups are well served by this valuable data.

The importance of this unique volume is that compliance on the part of patients, often confined by the temptations society puts before them, can now be achieved without gastronomic sacrifice. Deriving full sensual satisfaction from these meals will allow and indeed encourage further adherence to those external measures that are needed to correct the internal fault. We hope that wide and enthusiastic readership of this book will encourage the restaurant trade to offer similar fare and make intelligent menus available outside the home as well as in it. Our congratulations to the authors for turning a treatment mode into a pleasure mode!

Gerald Bernstein, M.D., F.A.C.P.
Assoc. Clinical Professor of Medicine
Albert Einstein College of Medicine, New York
Attending Physician, Endocrinology and Metabolism,
    Montefiore Medical Center, New York
and
Harold Rifkin, M.D., F.A.C.P.
Clinical Professor of Medicine
Albert Einstein College of Medicine, New York
Professor of Clinical Medicine,
    New York School University School of Medicine, New York
Principal Consultant,
    Diabetes Research and Training Center,
    Albert Einstein College of Medicine—
    Montefiore Medical Center, New York

A WORD ABOUT DIABETES MANAGEMENT

Four major variables affect your blood sugar (glucose): food, exercise, insulin, and stress. I will be focusing on the food aspect, but all four components must be considered if you are going to take charge of your diabetes. The best way to learn and use this information to achieve good control of your diabetes is actually to test your own blood sugar three to seven times per day: before each meal and, if possible, one hour after the meal began. The purpose of this is to see how what you eat changes your blood sugar.

There are some basic principles that are important to know, whether you count carbohydrates (CHO) or use the American Diabetes Association, Inc. (ADA) exchange lists. Carbohydrates provide the major source of energy for our bodies, so we must consume an adequate amount for good health (at least 100 grams per day). Ninety to 100 percent of carbohydrate intake is metabolized into blood sugar. We must face the challenge of selecting an appropriate amount and type of carbohydrate to control diabetes.

Carbohydrates vary in their impact on blood sugar. The two types of carbohydrate to consider are simple sugars (mono- and disaccharides) and complex carbohydrates (polysaccharides). Simple sugars are generally sweet-tasting foods such as fruit and fruit juice (fructose), table sugar (sucrose), and glucose, as well as milk and yogurt (lactose). Some foods may cause blood sugar to rise rapidly, within 15–30 minutes after consumption. The slow acting carbohydrates such as pasta, beans, peas, and corn, take longer to raise the blood sugar. The most significant rise in blood sugar from starchy foods is usually seen between 1 and 1½ hours after consumption. Testing the blood sugar within 1 hour after meals will help you learn how different foods affect your blood sugar.

You might also find that different carbohydrates within the same exchange group will affect your blood sugar differently. For example, ½ cup of cooked pasta may cause less of a rise in blood sugar than a slice of bread. An apple will generally raise the blood sugar less than a banana of equal carbohydrate content.

One more point of interest: Do not be confused by the ADA exchange lists for bread and fruit. One fruit exchange equals 10 grams of carbohydrate and 40 calories; one bread exchange equals 15 grams of carbohydrate and 70 calories. Diabetics often tend to skip the bread exchange and choose a fruit, since it is lower in carbohydrates and calories. Some fruits are larger than one exchange and portion size needs to be measured carefully. I would recommend avoiding eating all of the carbohydrate at the beginning of a meal (unless your blood sugar is below 70 mg/dl); save some of it such as fruit for ½ etc. Based on the quick action of simple sugars, I would recommend avoiding fruit or fruit juice at the beginning of any meal (unless your blood sugar is below 70 mg/dl); save it for ½–1 hour after you *finish* your meal. This is the time when your insulin (whether by injection or from what your pancreas is still producing) is much stronger and better equipped to handle blood sugar rises. Delaying consumption of fruit is especially important for breakfast, since the body can be somewhat resistant to insulin in the early morning hours.

Another way to include your fruit exchanges might be to have fruit (or other dessert) about 15 minutes before an exercise session, since aerobic exercise will also help lower blood sugar. Even a brisk walk after a meal would be beneficial.

Protein is the nutrient necessary to build, maintain, and repair the body. Fifty to 60 percent of protein is also converted into sugar for energy and will appear in the blood about three hours after consumption. Fat, the third major nutrient, has little or no immediate effect on blood sugar. Fat is, however, very high in calories; 1 gram of fat equals 9 calories; 1 gram of protein equals 4 calories; 1 gram of carbohydrate equals 4 calories. Unless fat is used in moderation, it will contribute to weight gain. But be sure to test your blood sugar before exercising.

For each recipe in this book, the nutritional breakdown per serving is as follows: grams carbohydrate (CHO), grams protein (PRO), grams fat (FAT), milligrams sodium (NA), calories (CAL), and ADA exchanges. The serving sizes of the individual recipes can be adjusted to fit your diet plan. For example, in a Brazilian menu, one serving of black bean soup equals one bread exchange, and one serving of rice equals two bread exchanges. If your diet plan allows for only two bread exchanges at dinner, treat yourself to half a serving of rice and one serving of soup; there is no need to deprive yourself of a taste of everything on the menu.

You will find some recipes in which the nutritional breakdown states "Omits 2 fat exchanges." This means that you have 2 extra fat exchanges you can use somewhere else. For example, in the Finnish menu, fillet of sole has much less fat than the lean meat exchange indicates; therefore, you may decide to use the extra fat exchanges in the form of vegetable oil to make up the calories. These calorie calculations are based on the actual composition and not on the exchange value.

It is possible for people with diabetes to eat interesting and varied meals if they understand the interaction among food, exercise, insulin, and stress. The nutritional breakdown provided for each recipe in this cookbook should be part of a comprehensive program to control your blood sugar. Enjoy!

Barbara Turro, Registered Dietician
Formerly of the Diabetes Self Care Program,
New York City

INTRODUCTION

From the time I was grown and out on my own, my greatest pleasure has been travel. Savoring the delicacies of each new place has been an even greater joy. My journeys took me to Mexico, Brazil, Peru, Venezuela, Spain, England, Scotland, Russia, Yugoslavia, Turkey, Morocco, Israel, Canada, Greece, Finland, Holland, Belgium, Luxembourg, Germany, Sweden, Denmark, the Bahamas, the Caribbean, and the United States, of course. I traveled repeatedly through Italy, Switzerland, and France (where I had a small apartment and learned to shop in the neighborhood markets and cook *à la française*).

About eight years ago, during the midst of my peregrinations, I discovered that I had diabetes. Dismayed, I vowed to reconsider the kinds and quantities of food I ate on these junkets. There surely were people with diabetes in all these countries, and certainly they too had to face their individual food problems. I figured that if they could handle their diets and stay in control, so could I when traveling in their lands.

Many modifications were necessary in translating the ingredients of classic foreign foods in order to make them compatible with my nutritional needs. As I covered new territory I began to analyze how substitutions and changes could be made in regional cuisine to keep it authentic yet tailored to a leaner cuisine.

Joining forces with spectacular cook Lucille Schechter, founder of "The Wandering Spoon" (traveling cooking classes throughout Europe and Mexico), I tested and tasted hundreds of recipe adaptations. Never daunted by lack of an ingredient or two, Lucille and I worked together to create nutritionally balanced, authentic, and appealing menus that fit easily into the most up-to-date exchange systems. Boredom in meal planning is not allowed! Restrictive menus can go! The recipes in this introductory compendium of international foods are varied, tasty, and designed for attractive presentation in taste, texture, and color. They are also simply and easily prepared.

Knowing how the dishes of different nations are prepared

xii   INTERNATIONAL MENU DIABETIC COOKBOOK

helps in ordering food when dining in local ethnic restaurants. It also helps in selecting dishes when traveling to foreign lands. It also allows for elegant entertaining at home to the resounding applause of friends and family. In the course of my experiments, I discovered that cooking at home, keeping tight control of ingredients, allowed me to continue to enjoy the gustatory delights of many of the world's great gourmet dishes. Our "diabetic" menus are merely modifications of classic cooking, designed to appeal to everyone. Our menus equal good meals.

Brillat-Savarin, the legendary French chef, once said, "The destiny of nations depends on how they nourish themselves." The same may be said of people with diabetes, whose very lives depend on the quality—and the quantity—of the foods they eat. It is not easy to live with a chronic disease that requires constant monitoring and questioning, especially in an era that puts extraordinary emphasis on eating. But that very challenge and the demand for the right foodstuffs leads directly to general well-being. In a manner of speaking, those with diabetes have a slight edge: Good blood sugar control usually results in the best physical/emotional condition. I feel healthier because I combine good nutrition with a good exercise program. I feel more relaxed about my future since my good control means I may be lucky enough to escape some of the complications diabetes can cause. Those who share my table often ask what differentiates my meals from "normal" repasts. There isn't much difference except that mine are devoid of "junk"—excessive fats and sugars—and mine are made with care as to the freshness and variety of the ingredients and the inventiveness of the recipes and menus.

Good, nourishing, well-balanced meals are easy to prepare. Why not eat well instead of just consuming the ordinary or the bland? Since the prudent person with diabetes is often in better shape than his so-called "healthy" friends or relatives, our culinary voyage around the world will present delicious menus that are the answer to a malady that lingers on: *Eating well is the best revenge!*

Betty Marks
Woodstock, NY
1985

For several years now, I've been devoted to the delightful task of turning my hobby into my profession—cooking. But this has involved more than preparing tasty dishes under a chef's cap and instructing beginners, intermediates, and professionals. Rather, my Wandering Spoon program has been a vehicle for translating years of experience as a working woman with a family preparing celebrated dishes under the pressure of too little time for the kitchen and with a large concern for caloric intake and dietary balance.

Over that time, I have been aware of *cuisine minceur* and have prepared food that looked and tasted good but had minimal calories. This has proved to be a most appropriate background for the discipline needed to write this book. While I do not suffer from diabetes, my years of concentration on such issues as substitution have more than qualified me to create menus that now can be enjoyed by those with this ailment, especially those who feel they have been denied the pleasure of tasty, gourmet dishes for reasons of health and safety.

For example, the years of basic training as a wife-mother-business woman-homemaker (during which time I often had little patience or success with finding exactly what I wanted on supermarket shelves to complete a recipe) were put to excellent use on Wandering Spoon excursions in far stranger territory than the neighborhood store.

One example, the first of many such experiences, will suffice. It was a beautiful, sunny morning on Portugal's Algarve. My first-ever cooking class was to begin in two hours, and the main dish for the day's luncheon—as noted in the student folders I prepared back home—was to be "heavenly cod." I believed this to be an appropriate inaugural dish because cod is the national dish of Portugal.

There were only two problems. The regional fishermen were on strike over some tax dispute, and the only cod available was heavily salted. Now what? Were we to throw away the recipe? Pretend that it never existed, that it was all the slip of some typewriter keys? Certainly not!

The recipe works—for cod or a number of appropriate *substitutes*. I was able to turn this "lemon" into lemonade by candidly telling the class the problems I encountered and substituting another fish.

The opportunity to substitute deftly came up in almost every foreign cooking class. In Crete, the plums were as small as raisins, so we made peach tarts instead of the announced dessert. In some places, the only cream available came in neat little cartons that had remained too long on grocery shelves. I could not trust this product to be whipped and come out properly.

When Betty Marks first discussed this book with me, I immediately saw the usefulness of my experiences in substituting ingredients and how the strict requirements of special diets might be met.

But I also believe that creativity leaves a margin for personal applications. For example, spices allow any individual cook to prepare recipes according to his or her special preference, affording a significant degree of flexibility.

Over the past year, I served these recipes to my guests without prior explanation or apology. Not one person asked, "What is this?" It was a year when I put my theories to the test, when pureed fruits substituted for creamy desserts, when vegetables provided thickness, when lemons and limes did the work of salt, when different herbs were combined to provide intriguing flavors, when butter was reduced in favor of polyunsaturated oils.

It also was a year that confirmed my faith in letting imagination perform wonders at the oven. An entirely new world of splendid tastes awaits anyone daring enough to make sensible substitutions to suit an individual palate.

Another interesting result for me has been that the tasty dishes Betty and I offer in this book have proven to be appropriate not only for people with diabetes, but for everyone concerned with healthful, yet sumptuous, cuisine. These dishes can be enjoyed by anyone, from the standpoint of their appeal to the palate and their kindness to the waistline and digestive system.

As Brillat-Savarin commented, "The discovery of a new dish does more for the happiness of mankind than the discovery of a star." I believe that the application of principles set forth in these pages not only brings happiness through discovery of new dishes, but also can make the person who prepares them a star of the most brilliant magnitude.

Lucille Haley Schechter
New York City
1985

BASIC PRINCIPLES:
WHAT WE WILL AND WHAT WE WON'T

One of the first questions I asked my doctor was, "Am I eating the proper foods?" He assumed so, but to be sure, he sent me to a registered dietitian. Working carefully within the parameters of my lifestyle, my weight, my insulin requirements, and my present food distribution patterns, this nutrition specialist skillfully designed a personal meal plan for me. Based on the exchange system, the plan includes all the nutrients and exchanges vital to a well-balanced, energy-producing and glucose-controlling diet. When I eat something from an ethnic cuisine, I adjust my PMP (Personal Meal Plan) to include the exchange values that are assigned to these special foods. These days, celebrities and ordinary folk alike consult nutritionists. I'd suggest that this is a good idea for everyone. Once a person's daily caloric intake is determined and a Personal Meal Plan is delineated, anyone can arrange to take charge of a wholesome and enticing food regimen.

You should always try to use fresh foods because they are the best foods. Foods lose freshness as they are processed, but in some cases you will have to rely on frozen or canned goods. When this is the case, read the labels carefully so as to avoid the use of foods with dextrose, sucrose, hidden sugars, and chemicals. If a particular vegetable or fruit is not in season when desired, an equivalent can certainly be substituted. We do recommend freezing fresh fruits, berries, and herbs when they are seasonal so that a trip to the freezer will produce these magical ingredients. We want our readers to be flexible and feel free to be inventive and creative in making their own adjustments.

We will be using whole grains, high-fiber foods. Brown rice is preferable to white, as are whole wheat pasta and bread. Pasta made from Jerusalem artichokes is also available. Where such a substitution would alter the dish radically we will recommend white rice or egg noodles.

Wines and ale or other spirits may be used in cooking since the alcohol is burned off in the process. Any carbohydrates remaining have been calculated into the recipes. We do not include uncooked alcohol.

Some cuts of meat are high in fat. Therefore, the meats called for in our recipes are limited to lean beef, lamb, pork, veal, chicken, rabbit, fish, and shellfish. Tofu (soybean curd) is also used.

Only skim milk products will be used: low-fat plain yogurt, low-fat cottage cheese, part skim milk ricotta, nonfat or skim milk, and low-fat cheeses. A list of low-fat cheeses appears in Chapter 20.

Salt is called for only when herbs and spices alone can't do the job, and only a pinch of salt is used in those cases. In Oriental recipes, low-sodium soy sauce is used. It has 47 percent less salt than regular soy, and this may be further reduced by diluting with water.

If fresh herbs are not available, dried herbs may be used, but only in one-fourth the quantity specified for fresh. (We also dry or freeze our own when in season.)

We will give *crossover* recipes when one ingredient is used in multiple cuisines, such as basic chicken or beef stock, and bread and whole wheat pie crust recipes. These recipes are listed in Chapter 19. We recommend cooking and freezing a supply of stocks.

Recipes are also given for Creative Low-Fat Sour Cream, Mayonnaise, Cream Cheese, and Butter in Chapter 19.

We suggest a supply of fine knives for chopping and skinning. Nonstick pots and pans (coated with Teflon or Silverstone) are essential. Woks and steamers are useful for Oriental dishes. A nonstick vegetable spray such as Pam or Mazola is necessary.

To cut down on the need for fats (the most fattening and highest-calorie constituent of foods), recipes call for grilling, broiling, baking, poaching, or sautéing with little or no oil. Poaching fish or chicken in a hot stock will seal in the flavors and vitamins so that they are not lost in the cooking and tossed out with the water. There is no fried food here, and no recipes call for deep frying. Cooking oils such as sunflower seed oil, safflower oil, walnut, and simple corn or vegetable oils are the best.

No sugar, no honey, no molasses, and no maple syrup are used. These only provide empty calories and are anathema to diabetes. Instead, our sweeteners are frozen concentrated fruit juices such as apple, orange, and grape. Fructose may sometimes be included, but in tiny portions.

We hope that this collection of worldwide recipes will turn the tables on the cooks in the family. Rather than a special meal being prepared just for the person with diabetes in the household, our menus will satisfy the entire family. Once the idea of adapting rich recipes to a leaner cuisine becomes habitual, each person can try for personal adaptations.

B.M.

Menu 1
TAJIN
Chicken with Peppers
YAMS UGALI
PEANUT PUDDING

Menu 2
SAFARI LAMB STEW
SEMOLINA
KENYA PUDDING

Menu 3
COUSCOUS
MANGO MANIA

Menu 4
MOINMOIN
Bean Pudding
ETHIOPIAN VEAL STEW
STUFFED ZUCCHINI
EXOTIC FRUITS

1

AFRICA

All regions of the African continent, from the northern cities of Cairo and Casablanca to the villages of the Sahara, have their own unique dishes. Africa is immense, its populace and customs diverse. The available foods depend on climate and cultivation and often on religious practice. Poverty and starvation are the scourge of the land. Traditionally, soups and stews serve to expand a sparse food supply.

In northern Africa, couscous, a fine semolina grain, is the starch of choice. Yams (these are different from our sweet potatoes) and cassava serve that function in the West, and bananas and plantains do so in the rainy regions. French, Spanish, and Near Eastern influences are present. For example, African curries have been borrowed from India. Cinnamon, cumin, and coriander are the spices that enhance African food. Peanuts, beans, red peppers, tomatoes, and okra are popular produce.

In East Africa, locusts and grasshoppers arrive in a seasonal invasion and provide young and old alike with a special treat. We do not include either delicacy in our menus! Tropical fruits such as papaw (papaya), pineapple, and mangoes are West African favorites, both delicious and nutritious. In Swahili, they say *Asante!* (Thanks!)

AFRICA—MENU 1
TAJIN (CHICKEN WITH PEPPERS)
YAMS UGALI
PEANUT PUDDING

TAJIN
(CHICKEN WITH PEPPERS)

1 pound boneless, skinless chicken breasts, cut into 4 pieces
1 teaspoon sunflower seed oil
1 onion, sliced
2 cloves garlic, minced
3 tablespoons finely chopped fresh coriander
Salt and pepper to taste

SAUCE

1 red pepper, roasted
2 green peppers, roasted
1 1-pound can Italian plum tomatoes, drained, chopped
3 tablespoons finely chopped fresh parsley
2 teaspoons sweet paprika
¼ teaspoon salt
Dash pepper
¼ teaspoon ground cumin
3 tablespoons minced fresh coriander

To roast peppers, place under broiler and turn until all sides are charred. Place them in a brown paper bag and let steam until skin is easy to peel. Discard stems, seeds, and ribs. Drain for 5 minutes, then slice into strips. Place the peppers, tomatoes, parsley, paprika, salt and pepper, cumin, and 3 tablespoons coriander in a nonstick skillet and stir over moderate heat about 20 minutes.

In another nonstick skillet quickly brown chicken pieces on both sides. Heat sunflower oil and add onion, garlic, 3 tablespoons coriander, salt, and pepper, and stir for 4 minutes. Transfer chicken to the tomato and pepper sauce and stir together. Cook until tender over low heat, about 15–20 minutes.

Serves 4.

Nutritive values per serving:	CHO (gm)	PRO (gm)	FAT (gm)	NA (mg)	CAL
	14	26.5	10	374	252
Food exchanges per serving:	3 vegetable + 4 lean meat; omits 1 fat				

YAMS UGALI
(SWEET POTATOES)

1 pound yams
Salt to taste
¼ cup skim milk, warmed
1 teaspoon cinnamon
1 teaspoon grated orange rind

Wrap each yam in foil and bake at 350°F until tender, about 1 hour. Peel and mash, adding salt and enough warm milk to make them smooth and creamy. Sprinkle with cinnamon and garnish with orange rind.

Serves 4.

Nutritive values per serving:	CHO (gm)	PRO (gm)	FAT (gm)	NA (mg)	CAL
	14	2	0	594	64
Food exchanges per serving:	1 bread				

PEANUT PUDDING

1 cup evaporated skim milk
4 teaspoons creamy peanut butter (unsweetened)
2 eggs (use only 1 yolk)
¼ teaspoon pure vanilla extract
4 teaspoons chopped roasted peanuts

In a small bowl, mix ½ cup of the milk and the peanut butter until smooth. In another bowl, beat the eggs with a whisk and add remaining milk, the peanut butter mixture, and vanilla. Mix well. Pour into a small ovenproof baking dish. Fill a larger pan with boiling water and place baking dish in it. Bake in preheated 350°F oven for 45 minutes until knife inserted into center of pudding comes out clean. Cool to room temperature, garnish with peanuts, and serve.

Serves 4.

Nutritive values per serving:	CHO (gm)	PRO (gm)	FAT (gm)	NA (mg)	CAL
	12	9	5.5	128	134
Food exchanges per serving:	½ skim milk + ½ vegetable + ⅓ fruit				

AFRICA—MENU 2
SAFARI LAMB STEW
SEMOLINA
KENYA PUDDING

SAFARI LAMB STEW

1¼ **pounds boneless lamb shoulder, cut into bite-size pieces**
2 **pounds fresh tomatoes, peeled and chopped**
½ **pound eggplant, cubed**
1 **zucchini, cut into slices**
4 **small new potatoes, peeled and sliced**
1 **large onion, sliced thin**
1 **teaspoon salt**
½ **teaspoon pepper**
¼ **teaspoon cinnamon**
Dash ground nutmeg
Dash ground cloves
¼ **cup water**

In a large, shallow, ovenproof dish, combine lamb, tomatoes, eggplant, zucchini, potatoes, and onion. Combine all the seasonings and sprinkle over the lamb mixture, tossing gently but thoroughly. Add water and bake, covered with foil, in preheated 350°F oven for 15 minutes. Uncover and bake for 1 hour at 325°F.

Serves 4.

Nutritive values per serving:	CHO (gm)	PRO (gm)	FAT (gm)	NA (mg)	CAL
	13.5	22.5	8	56	216
Food exchanges per serving:	2¾ vegetable + 3 lean meat; omits ½ fat				

SEMOLINA

2 cups water
8 ounces large-grain semolina
Pinch salt

Bring water to boil, add semolina, and return to boil. Cook for 5 minutes or until tender.

Serves 4.

Nutritive values per serving:	CHO (gm)	PRO (gm)	FAT (gm)	NA (mg)	CAL
	25.5	3	0	0	114
Food exchanges per serving:	1¾ bread				

KENYA PUDDING

2 tablespoons fructose
1½ tablespoons arrowroot (mixed with 1½ tablespoons cold water)
½ tablespoon Creative Butter (see index)
4 tablespoons lime juice
½ cup unsweetened evaporated skim milk
½ cup yogurt, drained (see Chapter 19)
½ tablespoon grated lime rind

In a saucepan, mix fructose, arrowroot mixture, butter, lime juice, and evaporated milk. Cook slowly, stirring frequently until thickened. Remove from stove and pour into a glass bowl. Let cool. Stir in yogurt and sprinkle with lime rind. Serve immediately at room temperature. This dessert should not be allowed to sit, as it loses its lime tang.

Serves 4.

Nutritive values per serving:	CHO (gm)	PRO (gm)	FAT (gm)	NA (mg)	CAL
	13.5	4	2	65	88
Food exchanges per serving:	¾ fruit + ½ skim milk + ½ fat				

AFRICA—MENU 3
COUSCOUS
MANGO MANIA

COUSCOUS

1 pound boneless, skinless chicken breasts
1 teaspoon corn oil
1 medium onion, chopped
2 bay leaves
1¼ cups chicken broth (see index)
1 teaspoon turmeric
1 carrot, peeled and sliced thin
1 zucchini, trimmed and sliced
1 cup canned chick-peas, drained
1 cup instant couscous
2 tablespoons Creative Butter (see index)
¼ teaspoon turmeric
1 tablespoon raisins, plumped in hot water and drained

Cut chicken into 4 pieces. Brown in nonstick skillet, then transfer to warm dish. Heat oil in skillet and sauté onions in it. Add bay leaves, chicken broth, 1 teaspoon turmeric, and carrot. Bring to simmer. Add zucchini, chick-peas, and the reserved chicken and cook for 15 minutes.

Meanwhile, prepare couscous: Place grains in a bowl and cover with cold water. Drain immediately. Then put couscous into a fine steamer or a colander lined with cheesecloth. Place over a large kettle of boiling water and let steam, uncovered, for 15 minutes. The colander or steamer should not touch the boiling water. Melt Creative Butter and mix with ¼ teaspoon turmeric and raisins. When couscous is done, turn onto a warm platter, mix in butter mixture, and surround with chicken and vegetables.

Serves 4.

Nutritive values per serving:	CHO (gm)	PRO (gm)	FAT (gm)	NA (mg)	CAL
	36	31.5	17	151	423
Food exchanges per serving:	¼ fruit + 1¾ bread + 1⅓ vegetable + 4½ lean meat				

MANGO MANIA

2 eggs (use only 1 yolk)
1¼ cups skim milk, scalded
1 teaspoon pure vanilla extract
¼ cup unsweetened pineapple juice
Vegetable spray
2 tablespoons fructose
2 mangoes, peeled, sliced, and cut into chunks

Pour eggs, scalded milk, vanilla extract, pineapple juice, and fructose into a small baking dish, lightly coated with vegetable spray. Bake in preheated 350°F oven for 1 hour. Let cool and spoon over mangoes.

Serves 4.

Nutritive values per serving:	CHO (gm)	PRO (gm)	FAT (gm)	NA (mg)	CAL
	29	5.5	2	74	156
Food exchanges per serving:	⅓ skim milk + 2½ fruit + ½ fat				

AFRICA—MENU 4
MOIN MOIN (BEAN PUDDING)
ETHIOPIAN VEAL STEW
STUFFED ZUCCHINI
EXOTIC FRUITS

MOIN MOIN
(BEAN PUDDING)

1 cup dried kidney beans, soaked overnight, drained
1 quart water
1 teaspoon crushed red pepper
1 medium onion, chopped
1 tomato, chopped
Pinch salt
1 tablespoon corn oil, heated
Vegetable spray
1 green pepper, cored and sliced thin

Drain and rinse beans, discarding any shells. Cook in 1 quart water until tender, about 1-1½ hours. Drain off any excess water. In a blender, mix beans, red pepper, onion, tomato, and salt until smooth. Mix in the heated oil. Pour into a small loaf pan coated with vegetable spray and cover tightly with foil. Bake in preheated 350°F oven for 30 minutes and then unmold. Garnish with green pepper slices.

Serves 4.

Nutritive values per serving:	CHO (gm)	PRO (gm)	FAT (gm)	NA (mg)	CAL
	36	12	4	12	228

Food exchanges per serving: 2⅖ bread + 1 vegetable + 1 lean meat; omits ½ fat

ETHIOPIAN VEAL STEW

1 teaspoon sunflower seed oil
1 large onion, chopped
½ teaspoon ground allspice
⅓ teaspoon ground nutmeg
2 cloves garlic, crushed
1 teaspoon peeled and minced gingerroot
1½ teaspoons crushed red pepper
2 teaspoons paprika
1 cup water
1½ pounds lean veal, trimmed of all fat and
    cut into 1-inch cubes
Salt and pepper to taste

In a nonstick skillet, heat oil and sauté onion in it until soft. Add allspice, nutmeg, garlic, ginger, chili pepper, and paprika. Stir for 3 minutes until blended. Add water and veal and bring to a full boil. Add salt and pepper and continue cooking over low heat, covered, for 1½–2 hours, until tender. If the stew looks dry, add more water.

Serves 4.

Nutritive values per serving:	CHO (gm)	PRO (gm)	FAT (gm)	NA (mg)	CAL
	2.5	34	15	157	281
Food exchanges per serving:	½ vegetable + 5 lean meat				

STUFFED ZUCCHINI

4 small zucchini (1 pound)
2 teaspoons turmeric
3 teaspoons curry powder
½ teaspoon cayenne
Pinch salt
Dash pepper
3 garlic cloves, minced
4 tablespoons lemon juice
1 tablespoon walnut oil

Cut tips off zucchini and halve lengthwise but not entirely through. Scoop out seeds. In a small bowl, mix turmeric, curry, cayenne, salt, pepper, garlic, and lemon juice into a paste. Stuff into zucchini and press halves together to close. Heat walnut oil in large nonstick skillet and arrange zucchini in it. Cover and cook over moderate heat until cooked, about 10–15 minutes.

Serves 4.

Nutritive values per serving:	CHO (gm)	PRO (gm)	FAT (gm)	NA (mg)	CAL
	6	1.5	3	2	62
Food exchanges per serving:	1⅓ vegetable + ½ fat				

EXOTIC FRUITS

1 kiwifruit, peeled and sliced
8 medium strawberries, hulled
1 cup black grapes, seeded
1 cup plain low-fat yogurt
¼ cup lemon juice
1 teaspoon grated lemon rind
¼ cup chopped roasted peanuts

Mix yogurt, lemon juice, and lemon rind. Mix fruits together, spoon yogurt over them, and garnish with chopped peanuts.

Serves 4.

Nutritive values per serving:	CHO (gm)	PRO (gm)	FAT (gm)	NA (mg)	CAL
	18	6	5	46	149
Food exchanges per serving:	⅓ skim milk + 1½ fruit + ¾ medium-fat meat				

Menu 1

RADIS AU FROMAGE FRAIS
Red Radishes with Cream Cheese
WATERZOOI DE DINDE
Flemish Turkey and Vegetable Stew
GLACE DE MYRTILLES
Blueberry Ice

Menu 2

COQUILLES ST. JACQUES
Scallops in Sherry
POMMES DE TERRE MONT D'OR
Whipped Potatoes
FROMAGE ET POIRES
Cheese and Pears

Menu 3

SOUPE AUX POIREAUX
Leek Soup
HOMARD ROTI AU BEURRE ROSE
Roast Lobster
ENDIVES BRAISEES
Braised Endive
PETITES TARTES AUX PRUNES
Plum Tart

2
BELGIUM

Some consider Belgian cuisine to be the finest in the world. Perhaps the worst one can do is compare the Belgian's culinary talents with that of his renowned neighbor to the southwest, France.

Belgian dishes are somewhat more robust than those found on French tables. The Flemish *hochepot* is a mélange of meat and vegetables poached in broth, much like the French *pot au feu*. *Waterzooi* can be made with chicken, turkey, or fish, plus fresh vegetables indigenous to Belgium. Belgian vegetables are raised in hothouses and picked in their prime—hence their appellation, *primeurs*. Exported to the United States, these fruits and vegetables are fragile and sold only in the finest gourmet shops. (We make do with the best of more readily available produce.) Belgium is the birthplace of endive, a crisp, delicate salad green used raw in salads, or braised. *Chou de Bruxelles*, Brussel sprouts, are also of Belgian origin.

Belgium's Atlantic coastline nets a catch of shrimp, oysters, scallops, and crayfish. While the use of rich butter and cream sauces is prescribed, we find that milk or yogurt sauces work well and retain the flavor and style of the finest Belgian cuisine. *Eet Smakelyk!*

BELGIUM—MENU 1
RADIS AU FROMAGE FRAIS (RED RADISHES
WITH CREAM CHEESE)
WATERZOOI DE DINDE (FLEMISH TURKEY
AND VEGETABLE STEW)
GLACE DE MYRTILLES (BLUEBERRY ICE)

RADIS AU FROMAGE FRAIS
(RED RADISHES WITH CREAM CHEESE)

12 red radishes
4 tablespoons Creative Cream Cheese (see index)
Sprinkling of kosher salt (optional)
4 lettuce leaves

Trim radishes and slice. Divide into 4 portions and place each in a decorative pattern on a lettuce leaf. Dot each leaf with 1 tablespoon cream cheese and lightly sprinkle with salt, if desired.

Serves 4.

Nutritive values per serving:	CHO (gm)	PRO (gm)	FAT (gm)	NA (mg)	CAL
	15	1	0	15	10
Food exchanges per serving:	⅓ vegetable				

WATERZOOI DE DINDE
(FLEMISH TURKEY AND VEGETABLE STEW)

½ teaspoon corn oil
2 medium onions, chopped
1 1-pound turkey cutlet
2 leeks (white part only), trimmed and diced
4 stalks celery, diced
4 carrots, sliced
2 cups chicken broth
1 bay leaf
¼ cup plain low-fat yogurt
½ teaspoon lemon juice
Pepper to taste
4 new potatoes, parboiled and peeled
2 tablespoons minced parsley

Heat corn oil in large nonstick saucepan and sauté onions in it until tender. Add turkey, leeks, celery, carrots, and chicken broth. Bring to boil and skim off any froth that accumulates. Add bay leaf and simmer gently for 30 minutes. Transfer turkey to cutting board and keep warm. Reduce liquid to 1½ cups and remove bay leaf. Add yogurt and stir, but do not return to the boil. Add lemon juice and pepper. Slice turkey and divide among 4 soup bowls. Add potatoes and ladle sauce and vegetables over each portion. Garnish with parsley.

Serves 4.

Nutritive values per serving:	CHO (gm)	PRO (gm)	FAT (gm)	NA (mg)	CAL
	36.5	35	9	261	367

Food exchanges per serving: 1⅖ bread + 3 vegetable + 4 lean meat; omits ¾ fat

GLACE DE MYRTILLES
(BLUEBERRY ICE)

10 ice cubes
3 cups fresh blueberries
¼ cup water
2 tablespoons concentrated frozen apple juice

Process ice cubes in a blender to shave, add blueberries and water, and puree. Add apple juice and blend. Pour into metal ice tray and place in freezer. Stir after 40 minutes to break up crystals. Refreeze and repeat stirring now and then before serving.

Serves 4.

Nutritive values per serving:	CHO (gm)	PRO (gm)	FAT (gm)	NA (mg)	CAL
	16	.5	.5	1	71
Food exchanges per serving:	1½ fruit				

BELGIUM—MENU 2
COQUILLES ST. JACQUES (SCALLOPS IN SHERRY)
POMMES DE TERRE MONT D'OR (WHIPPED POTATOES)
FROMAGE ET POIRES (CHEESE AND PEARS)

COQUILLES ST. JACQUES
(SCALLOPS IN SHERRY)

1 cup chicken stock
2 scallions, sliced
5 peppercorns
2 sprigs parsley
1½ pounds bay scallops
3 tablespoons sherry
½ cup skim milk
2 tablespoons arrowroot
½ teaspoon lemon juice
Pinch salt
Dash cayenne
Vegetable spray
½ pound mushrooms, sliced
⅓ cup low-fat St. Otho cheese, grated

Bring stock to boil in saucepan and add scallions, pepper-corns, and parsley. Simmer 10 minutes, then strain, reserving liquid. Add scallops. Cover and simmer 3 minutes. Remove scallops and keep warm. Add sherry to saucepan and quickly boil, reducing to 1 cup. In small bowl, mix the milk and arrowroot into a smooth paste and add slowly to the sauce. Add lemon juice, salt, and cayenne.

Coat 4 scallop shells with vegetable spray and spoon equal portions of the scallops and mushrooms into them. Cover with sauce. Top with grated cheese, bake in preheated 350°F oven for 10 minutes, and then place scallop shells on cookie sheet and quickly run under broiler to brown.

Serves 4.

Nutritive values per serving:	CHO (gm)	PRO (gm)	FAT (gm)	NA (mg)	CAL
	16	32	3	837	219
Food exchanges per serving:	⅕ bread + 2½ vegetable + 4 lean meat; omits 2 fat				

POMMES DE TERRE MONT D'OR
(WHIPPED POTATOES)

1 pound potatoes, peeled and quartered
2 tablespoons Creative Butter (see index)
Pinch ground nutmeg
¼ cup skim milk, warmed
Salt and pepper to taste
Pinch ground nutmeg for garnish

Boil potatoes until tender. Transfer to bowl and whip with beater until silky. Add butter and pinch nutmeg and then gradually add milk. Season with salt and pepper. Turn into a flameproof dish and run under broiler until brown. Sprinkle with pinch of nutmeg.

Serves 4.

Nutritive values per serving:	CHO (gm)	PRO (gm)	FAT (gm)	NA (mg)	CAL
	15	5	6	49	134
Food exchanges per serving:	1 bread + 1⅓ fat				

FROMAGE ET POIRES
(CHEESE AND PEARS)

1 low-fat St. Felice cheese (about ¼ pound)
8 walnut halves
2 ripe pears, Bartlett or Bosc, peeled, cored, and sliced

Stud top of the St. Felice cheese with walnuts and bake in low oven until soft, about 10 minutes. Serve each portion with pear slices.

Serves 4.

Nutritive values per serving:	CHO (gm)	PRO (gm)	FAT (gm)	NA (mg)	CAL
	17	8	9	1002	181
Food exchanges per serving:	1¾ fruit + 1¼ medium-fat meat + ½ fat				

BELGIUM—MENU 3

SOUPE AUX POIREAUX (LEEK SOUP)
HOMARD ROTI AU BEURRE ROSE (ROAST LOBSTER)
ENDIVES BRAISEES (BRAISED ENDIVE)
PETITES TARTES AUX PRUNES (PLUM TART)

SOUPE AUX POIREAUX
(LEEK SOUP)

1 cup potatoes, peeled and chopped
2 cups thinly sliced leeks (well washed)
1 quart chicken stock (see index)
¼ cup low-fat yogurt
Pinch salt
Freshly ground pepper
1 tablespoon chopped fresh chives

Simmer potatoes and leeks in chicken stock in covered kettle until tender. Force vegetables through food mill and return to kettle. Stir in yogurt and season with salt and pepper. Serve in individual bowls and sprinkle with chives.

Serves 4.

Nutritive values per serving:	CHO (gm)	PRO (gm)	FAT (gm)	NA (mg)	CAL
	13.5	6	1	43	87
Food exchanges per serving:	½ bread + 1¼ vegetable + ⅓ lean meat				

HOMARD ROTI AU BEURRE ROSE
(ROAST LOBSTER)

ROAST LOBSTER

4 small lobster tails
⅛ teaspoon dried thyme
⅛ teaspoon dried oregano
⅛ teaspoon dried basil
⅛ teaspoon dried marjoram
1 tablespoon Creative Butter (see index)
1 cup Beurre Rose (see recipe below)

Trim lobster tails with kitchen shears and snip through the light shell down the middle; remove the light shell. Sprinkle with mixture of the four herbs. Brush lightly with Creative Butter and roast in preheated 375°F oven until flesh is firm (about 10–12 minutes). Put on individual dishes and serve with Beurre Rose.

BEURRE ROSE

1 cup dry red wine
2 tablespoons minced shallots
½ teaspoon dried thyme
3 tablespoons drained yogurt
2 tablespoons Creative Butter (see index)
1 teaspoon lemon juice
Dash salt
Dash pepper

Combine wine, shallots, and thyme in saucepan and boil. When the mixture is reduced by half, add yogurt and butter. Remove from heat and whisk until thickened. Add lemon juice, salt and pepper to taste, and serve with lobster.

Serves 4.

Nutritive values per serving (including sauce):	CHO (gm)	PRO (gm)	FAT (gm)	NA (mg)	CAL
	6	26	9.5	67	214
Food exchanges per serving:	1 vegetable + 3½ lean meat				

ENDIVES BRAISEES
(BRAISED ENDIVES)

4 endives
1 cup chicken broth (see index)
Vegetable spray

Wash endives and split lengthwise. Pour broth into saucepan and arrange endives in broth. With vegetable spray, coat a round of wax paper or parchment to fit the pan. Place over endives, cover, and braise over low heat until endives are tender, about 10–15 minutes.

Serves 4.

Nutritive values per serving:	CHO (gm)	PRO (gm)	FAT (gm)	NA (mg)	CAL
	2.5	2	0	7	18
Food exchanges per serving:	½ vegetable				

PETITES TARTES AUX PRUNES
(PLUM TARTS)

1½ pounds Italian prune plums
1 teaspoon pure vanilla extract
½ cup apple juice
½-¾ cup water
1 whole wheat pie crust, baked in muffin tins (see index)
4 tablespoons Creative Cream Cheese (see index)

Blanch plums for 1 minute and run under cold water. Peel, remove pits, and slice. Place in saucepan with vanilla and apple juice and simmer until soft, adding water as necessary to keep from burning. When plums are soft, remove from heat and refrigerate. When ready to serve, fill tart shells with plums, top with Creative Cream Cheese, and serve.

Serves 8.

Nutritive values per serving:	CHO (gm)	PRO (gm)	FAT (gm)	NA (mg)	CAL
	30	3	6	85	185
Food exchanges per serving:	1 bread + 1½ fruit + 1 fat				

Menu 1
GALINHA MOQUECA
Poached Ginger Chicken
ARROZ PILAF COM ERZILHAS
Rice with Peas
MANIOC SAO PAULO
Orange Tapioca

Menu 2
SALATA AMAZON
Avacado Salad
VATAPA NANA SA
Shrimp with Peanuts
FAROFA
Farina
BANANAS BRASILIA

Menu 3
SOPA DE FEIJAO
Black Bean Soup
SALMAO COM PIMENTA E LIMAO
Salmon with Pepper and Lime
ARROZ
ESPRESSO MOUSSE

3

BRAZIL

Portuguese prominence in the lush land of Brazil is most evident in its language. But the Portuguese also left a mark in the cooking, which combined with that of the African settlers to create an unusual panoply of foods and flavors. Brazil's climate is tropical, and the land produces a wealth of splendid foods—coconuts, bananas, papaws, yams, cassavas. The thought of Brazil brings the unforgettable memory of being served a dish of tiny translucent quail eggs along with a glass of *cachaça* (a formidable rum concoction!). But that was long ago, and they were exotic!

Shrimp, peanuts, chicken, ginger, and black bean soup ought to compensate for our not including the national Brazilian end-of-the-week specialty, *feijoada* (it's filled with organ meats, sausages, and stuff not of our choosing). A grain like our own farina is delicious with the savory sauces of Brazil. *Dende* oil gives Brazilian food its unique flavor, but it is hard to find (Casa Moneo in New York will send it by mail).

Voodoo is still practiced in some parts of Brazil, where strong beliefs prevail, and ritual meals are sometimes set out to feed the gods. We don't know about the gods, but we do hope you will like our appealing Brazilian offerings. *Bom apetite!*

BRAZIL—MENU 1

GALINHA MOQUECA (POACHED GINGER CHICKEN)
ARROZ PILAF COM ERZILHAS (RICE WITH PEAS)
MANIOC SAO PAULO (ORANGE TAPIOCA)

GALINHA MOQUECA
(POACHED GINGER CHICKEN)

2 whole boneless, skinless chicken breasts, halved
1 tablespoon minced garlic
1 tablespoon peeled and minced fresh gingerroot
1 lemon, sliced thin
1 cup skim milk
1 teaspoon coconut extract
1 cup chopped scallions
½ cup chopped parsley

Sauté chicken lightly in nonstick pan. Remove and set aside in warm dish. Mix remaining ingredients (except scallions and parsley) in saucepan and boil down until sauce is thickened. Add chicken and cook, covered, for 15 minutes. Serve with topping of scallions and parsley.

Serves 4.

Nutritive values per serving:	CHO (gm)	PRO (gm)	FAT (gm)	NA (mg)	CAL
	9	26.5	8.5	124	219
Food exchanges per serving:	¼ skim milk + 1 vegetable + 3 lean meat				

ARROZ PILAF COM ERZILHAS
(RICE PILAF WITH PEAS)

½ teaspoon corn oil
½ cup chopped onion
¾ cup long-grain brown rice
1½ cups chicken broth (see index)
1½ cups green peas

Heat oil in nonstick skillet and sauté onion in it. In oven-proof casserole, mix onions and rice. Stir until rice is coated and add broth. Stir and simmer 10 minutes. Cover and bake in preheated 350°F oven until liquid is absorbed and rice is tender, about 25 minutes. Add peas. Let sit for 10 minutes, then fluff and serve.

Serves 4.

Nutritive values per serving:	CHO (gm)	PRO (gm)	FAT (gm)	NA (mg)	CAL
	17.5	6	1	94	103
Food exchanges per serving:	1 bread + ½ vegetable + ⅓ lean meat				

MANIOC SAO PAULO
(ORANGE TAPIOCA)

2 tablespoons instant tapioca
1½ cups unsweetened orange juice
1 tablespoon lime juice
1 cup orange sections, seeded
Freshly grated nutmeg

In a saucepan, mix tapioca, orange juice, and lime juice. Let stand 5 minutes. Bring to boil, stirring occasionally. Remove from heat and add orange sections. Place in serving bowl and chill. Sprinkle with grated nutmeg.

Serves 4.

Nutritive values per serving:	CHO (gm)	PRO (gm)	FAT (gm)	NA (mg)	CAL
	20	1	0	2	84
Food exchanges per serving:	⅓ bread + 1½ fruit				

BRAZIL—MENU 2
SALATA AMAZON (AVOCADO SALAD)
VATAPA NANA SA (SHRIMP WITH PEANUTS)
FAROFA (FARINA)
BANANAS BRASILIA

SALATA AMAZON
(AVOCADO SALAD)

4 tablespoons walnut oil
1 teaspoon lemon juice
1 teaspoon chopped garlic
1 tablespoon wine vinegar
8 leaves mixed salad greens, washed, dried
2 ripe tomatoes, sliced
½ small avocado, peeled and sliced
1 white of boiled egg, sliced

Combine oil, lemon, garlic, and vinegar and shake well. Divide salad greens among 4 plates and assemble tomatoes, avocado, and egg white over them. Sprinkle with 1 tablespoon of dressing per plate.

Serves 4.

Nutritive values per serving:	CHO (gm)	PRO (gm)	FAT (gm)	NA (mg)	CAL
	6	2.5	18	19	196
Food exchanges per serving:	1 vegetable + ¼ lean meat + 3½ fat				

VATAPA NANA SA
(SHRIMP WITH PEANUTS)

1 tablespoon safflower oil
1 onion, minced
1 hot chili pepper, minced
1 tomato, chopped
1 pound shrimp, shelled and deveined
1 cup skim milk
1 teaspoon coconut extract
½ cup water
1½ tablespoons cornstarch
2 cups water (or less)
½ cup roasted peanuts
1 drop dende oil (optional)

In nonstick pan heat safflower oil. Sauté onion and hot pepper in it. Add tomato and shrimp and cook until shrimp turn pink. Remove from heat. In another saucepan, heat milk and coconut extract with ½ cup water. Mix cornstarch with some water and add a little of the warm milk mixture. Return to pan with milk mixture and stir. Simmer to thicken. Add enough water to make a creamy sauce. Add peanuts and shrimp mixture and heat through. Add dende oil if desired.

Serves 4.

Nutritive values per serving:	CHO (gm)	PRO (gm)	FAT (gm)	NA (mg)	CAL
	18	50	14	355	398
Food exchanges per serving:	⅓ bread + 2 vegetable + ¼ skim milk				

FAROFA
(FARINA)

2 cups skim milk
Pinch salt
⅔ cup farina
½ cup chopped onion
2 tablespoons chopped red pepper
2 tablespoons chopped green pepper
4 tablespoons walnut oil
4 tablespoons wine vinegar

Bring milk and salt to a simmer. Slowly add farina, stirring constantly. Let simmer until thickened, about 11 minutes. In a separate bowl, mix the onion, red and green pepper, oil, and vinegar. Serve separately as condiment for the farina.

Serves 4.

Nutritive values per serving:	CHO (gm)	PRO (gm)	FAT (gm)	NA (mg)	CAL
	32	8	4	67	196
Food exchanges per serving:	⅔ vegetable + ¾ fat				

BANANAS BRASILIA

2 large bananas, peeled and halved lengthwise
4 tablespoons frozen concentrated apple juice
4 tablespoons minced dried apricots

In baking dish, assemble bananas, cover with apple juice, and bake 15 minutes in preheated 325°F oven. Garnish with apricots and serve.

Serves 4.

Nutritive values per serving:	CHO (gm)	PRO (gm)	FAT (gm)	NA (mg)	CAL
	22.5	1	0	3	94
Food exchanges per serving:	2¼ fruit				

BRAZIL—MENU 3

SOPA DE FEIJAO (BLACK BEAN SOUP)
SALMAO COM PIMENTA E LIMAO
(SALMON WITH PEPPER AND LIME)
ARROZ
ESPRESSO MOUSSE

SOPA DE FEIJAO
(BLACK BEAN SOUP)

2 cups dried black beans
3 cups beef stock (see index)
1 onion, chopped
2 stalks celery
1 bay leaf
7 cups water
Pinch salt
Pinch pepper
2 tablespoons sherry
8 lemon slices

Place beans in a pot and add water to cover beans by 1 inch. Soak overnight. Drain. In a large pot, combine beans, stock, onion, celery, bay leaf, water, salt, and pepper and simmer for 3 hours until beans are tender. Remove from pot and puree mixture in blender, a little at a time. Correct seasoning. Add sherry and return to pot to heat through. Serve with lemon slices.

Serves 8.

Nutritive values per serving:	CHO (gm)	PRO (gm)	FAT (gm)	NA (mg)	CAL
	20	8	0	32	112
Food exchanges per serving:	1⅕ bread + ½ vegetable + ¾ lean meat; omits ½ fat				

SALMAO COM PIMENTA E LIMAO
(SALMON WITH PEPPER AND LIME)

4 salmon steaks (1 pound total)
3 hot chili peppers, seeded and chopped
1 onion, sliced
1 clove garlic, minced
½ cup fresh lime juice
Pinch salt

About 1 hour before broiling salmon, puree peppers, on-ion, garlic, and lime juice in a blender. Cover and let steep. Rinse salmon steaks and pat dry. Brush with lime juice mixture. Preheat broiler and place salmon on foil in broiler pan. Broil about 4 inches from heat for 4 minutes. Turn, brush with lime mixture, and broil another 4 minutes until done.

Serves 4.

Nutritive values per serving:	CHO (gm)	PRO (gm)	FAT (gm)	NA (mg)	CAL
	6	33.5	27	202	401
Food exchanges per serving:	¼ fruit + ¾ vegetable + 5 medium fat meat				

ARROZ
(RICE)

¾ cup long-grain brown rice
1½ cups boiling water
1 tablespoon chopped cooked carrots
2 tablespoons toasted almonds

Cover rice with boiling water and cook 30 minutes. Remove from heat and let steam 10 minutes. Add carrots and almonds, fluff, and serve.

Serves 4.

Nutritive values per serving:	CHO (gm)	PRO (gm)	FAT (gm)	NA (mg)	CAL
	31	3.5	3	4	165
Food exchanges per serving:	2 bread + ½ fat				

ESPRESSO MOUSSE

1 package unflavored gelatin
¼ cup cold water
2 cups strong, hot expresso coffee
4 orange slices
4 dollops Creative Cream Cheese (see index)

Soften gelatin in cold water. Dissolve gelatin in boiling coffee and stir. Pour into bowl and place in freezer for 2–3 hours. Stir just before serving. Top each serving with an orange slice and a dollop of Creative Cream Cheese.

Serves 4.

Nutritive values per serving:	CHO (gm)	PRO (gm)	FAT (gm)	NA (mg)	CAL
	4	3.5	0	55	30
Food exchanges per serving:	⅕ fruit + ⅕ skim milk				

Menu 1
WONTON SOUP
STEAMED SEA BASS
BROCCOLI WITH SESAME SEEDS
MANDARIN FRUITS

Menu 2
LEMON CHICKEN
CHINESE VERMICELLI
Rice Sticks
STIR-FRIED VEGETABLES
YANG TAO
Kiwifruit

Menu 3
CHINESE NOODLES WITH SESAME
SAUCE
SNOW PEA SALAD
CANTONESE FRUITS

4

CHINA

Among the most celebrated in the world, Chinese dishes represent a vast array of regional food. Canton, Hunan, Szechwan, and Peking are but a few regions whose food we know in this country. No matter the seasoning, each Chinese meal is composed of many courses—literally from soup to nuts. Since the Chinese never wrote down their recipes, variations and adaptations are frequent and acceptable.

Chicken, fish, shrimp, beef, pork, or scallops combine with fresh vegetables and nuts—cashews, pine nuts, peanuts, and walnuts—and are all tossed into the wok. Food is cut into uniform small pieces, and fast cooking helps it retain flavor, texture, and nutrients. We've lowered the quantities of cooking oils used and also recommended the Chinese method of steaming.

The Chinese feel that one should be quite satisfied after a meal and therefore do not feature desserts. A recent visit to China revealed that a sliced orange was the one dessert served after every meal! We like the Yangtze Valley kiwifruit, too. *Mong yoom!* Enjoy!

CHINA—MENU 1
WONTON SOUP
STEAMED SEA BASS
BROCCOLI WITH SESAME SEEDS
MANDARIN FRUITS

WONTON SOUP

⅛ pound chicken, ground or minced fine
½ tablespoon low-sodium soy sauce
½ teaspoon peeled and minced gingerroot
½ cup chopped fresh spinach
12 wonton wrappers (available in supermarkets, Oriental markets, and natural food stores)
2 quarts water
4 cups chicken stock (see index)
4 tablespoons sliced scallions (green part only)
½ teaspoon sesame oil

Mix together the chicken, soy, ginger, and spinach. Spread out wonton wrappers and place a scant teaspoon of mixture just below the center. Fold lower corner over the filling and tuck edge under it. (Keep unused wonton wrappers damp so they do not dry and break.) Moisten exposed sides of wrapper and roll up, folding ends of the roll over each other. Pinch together tightly. Meanwhile, bring water to a boil. Drop in the filled wontons. Return to a boil, reduce heat, and simmer, uncovered, for 10 minutes. Drain. In another pot, bring chicken stock to a boil. Add wontons, sliced scallions, and sesame oil. Bring back to boil, then serve in soup bowls, 2 wontons per serving.

Serves 6.

Nutritive values per serving:	CHO (gm)	PRO (gm)	FAT (gm)	NA (mg)	CAL
	17	6.5	1.5	50	108
Food exchanges per serving:	1 bread + ½ vegetable + ½ lean meat				

STEAMED SEA BASS

1 whole sea bass, about 3½ pounds, cleaned, scaled,
   head and tail intact
3 cups chicken stock (see index)
1 2-inch piece gingerroot, peeled and sliced
1 carrot, scraped and sliced
1 clove garlic, minced
1 cup sliced mushrooms
½ tablespoon sesame oil
1 red pepper, cored, seeded, and julienned
2 tablespoons low-sodium soy sauce
1 lemon, peeled and sliced thin

Rinse bass under cold water. Score with diagonal slices ¼ inch deep on both sides. In fish steamer, mix stock, half the ginger, the carrot, and the garlic. Bring to boil. Place fish in the steamer basket and cover. Steam until firm, about 15–20 minutes. Chop remaining ginger very fine and sprinkle over fish. Sauté mushrooms lightly in sesame oil. Add red pepper and soy sauce and cook 1 minute. Spoon sauce over the fish and top with lemon slices.

Serves 4.

Nutritive values per serving:	CHO (gm)	PRO (gm)	FAT (gm)	NA (mg)	CAL
	11.5	70	7	505	389
Food exchanges per serving:	½ vegetable + 2¼ lean meat; omits 1 fat				

BROCCOLI WITH SESAME SEEDS

1 pound fresh broccoli, trimmed and cut into flowerets
1 tablespoon sesame seeds, toasted
1 teaspoon sesame oil
1 tablespoon rice wine vinegar
¼ teaspoon red pepper flakes
Juice of ½ lemon

Steam broccoli pieces until tender, about 5 minutes. Combine sesame seeds, oil, vinegar, pepper flakes, and lemon juice. Blend and pour over warm broccoli.

Serves 4.

Nutritive values per serving:	CHO (gm)	PRO (gm)	FAT (gm)	NA (mg)	CAL
	8	5	3.5	17	84
Food exchanges per serving:	1½ vegetable + 1 fat				

MANDARIN FRUITS

2 mandarin oranges or tangerines
1 grapefruit
2 tablespoons chopped toasted pecans

Peel and seed oranges and grapefruit; separate into natural sections. Arrange on individual dishes and sprinkle with pecans.

Serves 4.

Nutritive values per serving:	CHO (gm)	PRO (gm)	FAT (gm)	NA (mg)	CAL
	9	1	3	2	67
Food exchanges per serving:	1 fruit + ½ fat				

CHINA—MENU 2
LEMON CHICKEN
CHINESE VERMICELLI (RICE STICKS)
STIR-FRIED VEGETABLES
YANG TAO (KIWIFRUIT)

LEMON CHICKEN

½ cup fresh lemon juice
1 tablespoon lime juice
1½ tablespoons walnut oil
1½ tablespoons low-sodium soy sauce
2 teaspoons Dijon mustard
Dash cayenne
1 pound skinless, boneless chicken breasts
4 lemon wedges

Combine lemon and lime juice, oil, soy, mustard, and cayenne. Marinate chicken breasts in this for 4 hours or more in a cool place. Cut chicken breasts into 4 pieces and poach in the marinade in a saucepan until tender, about 10 minutes. Transfer chicken to warm platter and reduce marinade until thick. Then spoon over chicken and serve with lemon wedges.

Serves 4.

Nutritive values per serving:	CHO (gm)	PRO (gm)	FAT (gm)	NA (mg)	CAL
	45	27.5	8	284	200
Food exchanges per serving:	½ fruit + 4 lean meat; omits 1 fat				

CHINESE VERMICELLI
(RICE STICKS)

6 ounces rice sticks

Cover rice sticks with boiling water and let soak 15 minutes. Drain and serve with sauce.

Serves 4.

Nutritive values per serving:	CHO (gm)	PRO (gm)	FAT (gm)	NA (mg)	CAL
	34	2	1	5	153
Food exchanges per serving:	⅔ bread				

STIR-FRIED VEGETABLES

1 tablespoon sesame oil
1 tablespoon low-sodium soy sauce
1 teaspoon finely chopped fresh gingerroot
3 cups assorted vegetables (green beans, red or green peppers, broccoli, mushrooms, zucchini, yellow squash, bamboo shoots, water chestnuts, etc.), cut into ½-inch pieces

Mix oil, soy, and ginger in wok or large nonstick skillet. Add vegetables and cook quickly, stirring with chopsticks. Vegetables should be crisp. Cook softest vegetables last. Remove from heat and serve.

Serves 4.

Nutritive values per serving:	CHO (gm)	PRO (gm)	FAT (gm)	NA (mg)	CAL
	6	4	4	141	76
Food exchanges per serving:	1 vegetable + 1 fat				

YANG TAO
(KIWIFRUIT)

4 kiwifruits, peeled and sliced*
1 tangerine, peeled and sectioned
½ teaspoon peeled and finely chopped fresh gingerroot
Fresh mint (optional)

Arrange kiwifruit slices on dessert dishes. Place a few tangerine sections next to them or in center. Garnish with touch of ginger and mint sprig, if desired.

Serves 4.

Nutritive values per serving:	CHO (gm)	PRO (gm)	FAT (gm)	NA (mg)	CAL
	10	1	0	0	44
Food exchanges per serving:	1 fruit				

*Kiwifruit originally came from the Yangtze Valley. They are now cultivated in the United States and New Zealand and are available all year long. They are pretty, tasty, and healthful, high in potassium and vitamin C.

CHINA—MENU 3
CHINESE NOODLES WITH SESAME SAUCE
SNOW PEA SALAD
CANTONESE FRUITS

CHINESE NOODLES WITH SESAME SAUCE

2 cloves garlic, minced
¼ cup tahini or unsweetened peanut butter
½ cup tea
2 tablespoons low-sodium soy sauce
½ teaspoon chili powder
4 tablespoons sesame oil
1 tablespoon concentrated frozen apple juice
1 tablespoon red wine vinegar
8 ounces spinach spaghetti or Chinese egg noodles
¼ cup chopped scallions
¼ cup peeled, seeded, and minced cucumber

For the sauce, place the garlic, tahini or peanut butter, tea, soy sauce, chili powder, 3 tablespoons of the sesame oil, apple juice, and vinegar in blender. Blend until smooth. Bring a large kettle of water to boil and gradually add spaghetti. Boil 14 minutes (less time for egg noodles) until tender. Drain. Toss with 1 tablespoon sesame oil. Place noodles in a bowl and toss with the sauce, adding scallions. Toss again with the minced cucumbers and serve at room temperature.

Serves 6 as main course.

Nutritive values per serving:	CHO (gm)	PRO (gm)	FAT (gm)	NA (mg)	CAL
	32.5	8	14.5	188	293

Food exchanges per serving: 2 bread + ½ vegetable + ½ high-fat meat + 2 fat

SNOW PEA SALAD

2 cups snow peas, trimmed
4 tablespoons rice wine vinegar
1 tablespoon corn oil
1 teaspoon walnut oil
½ cup sliced red pepper

Blanch snow peas in boiling water for 1 minute. Drain and dry. Place in refrigerator to chill. In small bowl, mix vinegar and the oils. Arrange snow peas on individual serving dishes in a circle. Arrange red pepper slices between pea pods for a colorful arrangement. Spoon dressing over each serving.

Serves 4.

Nutritive values per serving:	CHO (gm)	PRO (gm)	FAT (gm)	NA (mg)	CAL
	3	1	8	0	88
Food exchanges per serving:	½ vegetable + 1½ fat				

CANTONESE FRUITS

1 cup kumquats
2 cups water
1 stick cinnamon
6 cloves
2 tablespoons vinegar
1 cup watermelon balls
1 cup cantaloupe (or honeydew melon) balls
1 cup strawberries, hulled and halved, *or* 1 cup red grapes,
    halved and seeded
2 tablespoons pine nuts, toasted

Boil kumquats in 2 cups water with cinnamon stick, cloves, and vinegar for 10 minutes. Refrigerate overnight. Remove kumquats and mix with other fruits, adding a little of the syrup. Chill and serve in individual dessert cups, garnished with pine nuts.

Serves 4.

Nutritive values per serving:	CHO (gm)	PRO (gm)	FAT (gm)	NA (mg)	CAL
	14	1.5	3	12	89
Food exchanges per serving:	1½ fruit + ½ fat				

Menu 1

SALADE D'ENDIVE ET CRESSON
Endive and Watercress Salad

GIGOT D'AGNEAU
Leg of Lamb

LEGUMES ROTIS
Roast Vegetables

MOUSSE DE MYRTILLES
Blueberry Mousse

Menu 2

COQUELOTS AUX CHAMPIGNONS
Cornish Hens with Mushrooms

PETITS POIS AU CITRON
Peas with Lemon

RIZ SAUVAGE
Wild Rice

POIRES POCHEES AU VIN ROUGE
Pears Poached in Red Wine

Menu 3

LAPIN ROTI AUX HERBES
Roast Rabbit with Herbs

CAROTTES PERSILLEES AVEC
CHAMPIGNONS
Parsley Carrots with Mushrooms

POMMES DE TERRE FARCIES
Stuffed Potatoes

SALADE VERTE
Green Salad

TARTELETTES AUX RAISINS
Raisin Tarts

Menu 4

SOUPE A L'OIGNON
Onion Soup

ESPADON POCHE AUX CHAMPIGNONS
Swordfish with Mushrooms

HARICOTS VERTS
Green Beans

PAIN FRANCAIS
French Bread

TARTE AUX FRAISES
Strawberry Tart

Menu 5

ARTICHAUTS VINAIGRETTE
Artichokes with Vinaigrette Dressing

BAR PROVENCAL
Sea Bass with Tomatoes

POMMES DE TERRE
Boiled Potatoes

MELON AU PORTO
Cantaloupe with Port Wine

Menu 6

BOUILLON DE LEGUMES
Vegetable Soup

PAILLARD DIABLE
Chicken Breasts with Tarragon Mustard

POMMES DE TERRE LYONNAISE
Potatoes Lyonnaise

TOMATES FARCIES
Stuffed Tomatoes

PECHES MELBA
Peaches with Raspberry Sauce

5

FRANCE

When one thinks of cuisine—*haute* or *bourgeoise*—one thinks first of *la belle France*. For the French, the enjoyment and the preparation of fine food starts in the home. It endures for a lifetime. Cooking in France is considered a fine art, and eating a civilized pleasure. Traditionally, chefs have followed the great classic recipes of Escoffier, Carème, and Brillat-Savarin with scrupulous fidelity. But today, *cuisine minceur* has parted from those rich ways and proven that cream and butter are not *de rigueur*.

It is always amazing that in France, even after a multi-course meal, one is never "stuffed." Each course is small, one balanced carefully with the other, and elegantly assembled. Light and lovely combinations of fresh vegetables, soups, fish, and roasts comprise our French adaptations. No truffles or *foie gras* appear on our menus, but crusty French bread, crisp salads, mouth-watering entrées, and fresh fruit treats are palate pleasers. Cooking with wine enhances the flavor of many meats—and desserts.

Our selections offer but a small taste of the vast repertoire of superb French edibles. A good number more are readily adaptable by following our basic cooking guidelines of low fat/ no sugar. *Bon appetit à tous!*

FRANCE—MENU 1
SALADE D'ENDIVE ET CRESSON (ENDIVE AND
WATERCRESS SALAD)
GIGOT D'AGNEAU (LEG OF LAMB)
LEGUMES ROTIS (ROAST VEGETABLES)
MOUSSE DE MYRTILLES (BLUEBERRY MOUSSE)

SALADE D'ENDIVE ET CRESSON
(ENDIVE AND WATERCRESS SALAD)

4 medium Belgian endives, sliced into rings ½ inch thick
½ bunch watercress, well washed, thick stems removed
6 tablespoons Vinaigrette Dressing (see index)
2 tablespoons chopped walnuts

Chill endives and watercress and mix together. When
ready to serve, toss with dressing and serve, topped with some
walnuts.

Serves 6.

Nutritive values per serving:	CHO (gm)	PRO (gm)	FAT (gm)	NA (mg)	CAL
	5	2	4.5	51	69
Food exchanges per serving:	1 vegetable + 1 fat				

GIGOT D'AGNEAU
(LEG OF LAMB)

LEGUMES ROTIS
(ROAST VEGETABLES)

1 4- to 5-pound leg of lamb (shank half), trimmed of all fat
White vinegar
¼ cup Dijon mustard
2 tablespoons dried rosemary
1 tablespoon safflower oil
3 cloves garlic, minced
Freshly ground black pepper
2 onions, peeled and quartered
5-6 medium potatoes (about 1½ pounds), peeled and sliced
1 cup beef broth (see index)
4 large carrots, halved lengthwise
Few sprigs watercress

Marinate lamb in vinegar for a few hours. Discard vinegar and pat lamb dry. Mix together mustard, rosemary, safflower oil, minced garlic, and pepper. Coat the lamb with this and let lamb marinate at room temperature for several hours. Place lamb on rack in large roasting pan. Strew onions and potatoes around the lamb and add beef broth. Preheat oven to 450°F. Place lamb in hot oven for 10 minutes. Reduce heat to 350°F, add carrots, and continue roasting for 45 minutes. After this time, lamb will be pink. (Cook 15 minutes more for well done.) Remove lamb and let it sit on a cutting board for about 15 minutes. Continue roasting vegetables until ready to carve meat. Slice meat into thin portions and arrange on warm platter with the watercress sprigs as garnish. Serve with pan vegetables.

Serves 6-10.

Lamb Alone: Nutritive values per 1-oz. serving	CHO (gm)	PRO (gm)	FAT (gm)	NA (mg)	CAL
	0	9	2	26	54

Food exchanges per serving: 1 lean meat
(Choose amount according to your own
diet plan. If, for example, 3 ounces,
calculate by multiplying above by 3.)

Roast Vegetables: serving 6 people	CHO (gm)	PRO (gm)	FAT (gm)	NA (mg)	CAL
	30	5	3.5	169	172
Food exchanges per serving:	1⅓ bread + 2 vegetable + ½ fat				

MOUSSE DE MYRTILLES
(BLUEBERRY MOUSSE)

1½ cups fresh blueberries
¼ cup concentrated frozen apple juice
1 package unflavored gelatin
¼ cup cold water
2 tablespoons plain low-fat yogurt
½ teaspoon ground cinnamon
2 egg whites, beaten stiff

Combine blueberries and apple juice in saucepan and bring to boil. Reduce heat and boil down to 1 cup, mashing berries against side of pan. Remove from heat and chill. Sprinkle gelatin over cold water in a cup, then place in bowl of hot water to dissolve. Stir gelatin into blueberries, setting the bowl over ice. Stir until berries thicken. Fold in yogurt and cinnamon and beat in egg whites. Pour into serving dish and place in freezer for about 1–2 hours, until firm.

Serves 6.

Nutritive values per serving:	CHO (gm)	PRO (gm)	FAT (gm)	NA (mg)	CAL
	10	2.5	0	21	50
Food exchanges per serving:	1 fruit				

FRANCE—MENU 2
COQUELOTS AUX CHAMPIGNONS (CORNISH HENS
WITH MUSHROOMS)
PETITS POIS AU CITRON (PEAS WITH LEMON)
RIZ SAUVAGE (WILD RICE)
POIRES POCHEES AU VIN ROUGE (PEARS
POACHED IN RED WINE)

COQUELOTS AUX CHAMPIGNONS
(CORNISH HENS WITH MUSHROOMS)

2 Rock Cornish hens (about 10 ounces each),
   defrosted if frozen
Several dashes pepper
1 teaspoon Creative Butter (see index)
½ cup chopped mushrooms
½ cup whole wheat bread crumbs
¼ cup finely chopped pecans
1 teaspoon minced shallots
1 clove garlic, minced
½ teaspoon dried tarragon
1-2 tablespoons skim milk
½ cup dry vermouth
Durkee's Imitation Bacon Chips
½ cup minced parsley

Wash and dry hens and remove any excess fat. Sprinkle
with pepper. Heat Creative Butter in nonstick skillet and sauté
chopped mushrooms in it. Add bread crumbs, pecans, shallots,
garlic, pepper, and tarragon. Combine milk and a tablespoon or
so of vermouth; add to stuffing to bind it. Stuff cavities of hens
with mixture and tie legs together. Preheat oven to 350°F.

Place birds breast side up on rack in baking pan. Sprinkle with pepper and place a few pieces of Durkee's Imitation Bacon Chips in the leg creases. Roast at 350°F and baste frequently with the remaining vermouth, turning, for about 45 minutes. Birds are done when juices run clear after leg is pierced with fork. Remove skin from birds before serving, cut in half, spoon sauce over each half, and sprinkle with parsley.

Serves 4.

Nutritive values per serving:	CHO (gm)	PRO (gm)	FAT (gm)	NA (mg)	CAL
	12	33	32	53	468
Food exchanges per serving:	½ bread + 1 vegetable + 4 medium-fat meat + 2 fat				

PETITS POIS AU CITRON
(PEAS WITH LEMON)

2 cups shelled fresh peas *or* 1 10-ounce package frozen peas
1 teaspoon Creative Butter (see index)
Grated rind of 1 large lemon
1 slice lemon, curled, for garnish

Bring to boil 1 cup water. Place peas in steamer basket, cover, and cook until tender, just a few minutes. If using frozen peas, cook with ½ cup water for 3–4 minutes, until heated. Drain and toss with Creative Butter and lemon rind. Garnish with lemon slice.

Serves 4.

Nutritive values per serving:	CHO (gm)	PRO (gm)	FAT (gm)	NA (mg)	CAL
	11	4	1	8	69
Food exchanges per serving:	¾ bread + ⅓ fat				

RIZ SAUVAGE
(WILD RICE)

¾ cup wild rice
1½ quarts boiling water
½ teaspoon Creative Butter (see index)
2 tablespoons minced carrots
2 tablespoons minced celery
2 tablespoons minced onion
1½ cups chicken stock (see index)
1 bay leaf
½ teaspoon dried thyme
Pepper to taste

Drop rice into boiling water. Let boil 5 minutes, uncovered, then drain. Heat Creative Butter in ovenproof nonstick casserole. Add carrots, celery, and onions and cook for 5–10 minutes. Add drained rice and stir to mix. Add chicken stock, bay leaf, thyme, and pepper and bring to boil. Cover casserole and bake in preheated 350°F oven for 30–40 minutes, until rice is tender. If liquid is absorbed before rice is cooked, add more. Discard bay leaf, fluff rice, and serve.

Serves 4.

Nutritive values per serving:	CHO (gm)	PRO (gm)	FAT (gm)	NA (mg)	CAL
	17.5	14	1	12	95
Food exchanges per serving:	1 bread + ½ vegetable + ¼ fat				

POIRES POCHEES AU VIN ROUGE
(PEARS POACHED IN RED WINE)

2 ripe pears
1 cinnamon stick
2 cups dry red wine
4 cloves
1 tablespoon grated orange rind

Peel pears and core from bottom up, leaving stems intact. Place in enamel or stainless steel saucepan and add cinnamon, wine, and cloves. Cover and cook until tender, about 30 minutes. When tender, remove pears but continue cooking liquid until slightly thickened. Cut pears in half lengthwise, place in dessert dishes, and spoon on some of the sauce. Sprinkle with orange rind.

Serves 4.

Nutritive values per serving:	CHO (gm)	PRO (gm)	FAT (gm)	NA (mg)	CAL
	18	1	0	5	76
Food exchanges per serving:	2 fruit				

FRANCE—MENU 3

LAPIN ROTI AUX HERBES (ROAST RABBIT WITH HERBS)
CAROTTES PERSILLEES AVEC CHAMPIGNONS (PARSLEY
CARROTS WITH MUSHROOMS)
POMMES DE TERRE FARCIES (STUFFED POTATOES)
SALADE VERTE (GREEN SALAD)
TARTELETTES AUX RAISINS (RAISIN TARTS)

LAPIN ROTI AUX HERBES
(ROAST RABBIT WITH HERBS)

1 rabbit (about 3½ pounds cleaned weight), cut into pieces
Freshly ground pepper
1½ teaspoons rosemary, pulverized
2 cloves garlic, minced
2 tablespoons minced shallots
¼ cup dry white wine
¾ cup chicken stock (see index)
1 tablespoon Dijon mustard
1 tablespoon Creative Butter (see index)
¼ cup chopped parsley

MARINADE

½ cup dry white wine
Juice of 1 lemon
1 bay leaf
1 clove garlic, minced
Pinch rosemary
1 inch gingerroot, peeled and sliced

Wash rabbit and remove any fat. Mix marinade ingredients together and marinate rabbit for several hours or a day or so, as desired. Turn several times. (The longer the marination, the better the flavor.) When ready to roast, pat rabbit dry, sprinkle with pepper and rosemary, and place in a baking dish. Preheat oven to 450°F.

Bake rabbit for 30 minutes on middle rack of oven. Turn

pieces over, sprinkle with garlic and shallots, and bake another 5 minutes. Add wine and chicken stock. Continue baking another 20 minutes, turning. When meat is tender, remove. Stir Dijon mustard and Creative Butter into the baking dish and mix with liquid in dish. Spoon sauce over rabbit, garnish with parsley, and serve.

Serves 4.

Nutritive values per serving:	CHO (gm)	PRO (gm)	FAT (gm)	NA (mg)	CAL
	6	55	22	151	442
Food exchanges per serving:	1 vegetable + 7 lean meat + ½ fat				

CAROTTES PERSILLEES AVEC CHAMPIGNONS
(PARSLEY CARROTS WITH MUSHROOMS)

1 pound carrots, scraped, trimmed, and julienned
1 teaspoon fructose
½ cup seltzer
1 tablespoon Creative Butter (see index), divided
Few grinds black pepper
1 cup sliced mushrooms
2 tablespoons minced parsley

Place carrots in enamel or nonstick saucepan with fructose, seltzer, ½ tablespoon Creative Butter, and pepper. Bring carrots to boil, cover, and simmer 30 minutes, until tender. Add mushrooms and cook a few minutes longer. Drain off any remaining liquid. When ready to serve, add remaining Creative Butter and parsley. Heat, toss, and serve.

Serves 4.

Nutritive values per serving:	CHO (gm)	PRO (gm)	FAT (gm)	NA (mg)	CAL
	13.5	2	3	84	89
Food exchanges per serving:	2½ vegetable + ½ fat				

POMMES DE TERRE FARCIES
(STUFFED POTATOES)

4 small baking potatoes, well scrubbed
2 tablespoons grated onion
1 tablespoon Creative Butter (see index)
½ cup skim milk
Freshly ground pepper
1 egg white, beaten stiff
¼ cup grated skim-milk mozzarella cheese
Paprika

Bake potatoes in 450°F oven for 1 hour, pricking once with a fork after 30 minutes. Meanwhile, sauté onion in butter in a nonstick skillet. When potatoes are cooked, remove from oven, slice in half, and scoop out pulp, keeping shells intact. Mash potatoes with onions, milk, fresh pepper. Fold beaten egg white into potato mixture and stuff into the shells. Top with sprinkling of mozzarella and paprika. Return to oven until tops are golden.

Serves 4.

Nutritive values per serving:	CHO (gm)	PRO (gm)	FAT (gm)	NA (mg)	CAL
	19	6	4	91	136
Food exchanges per serving:	1⅓ bread + ½ fat-high meat				

SALADE VERTE
(GREEN SALAD)

1 head Boston lettuce *or* 2 heads Bibb lettuce

VINAIGRETTE DRESSING

3 tablespoons red wine vinegar
1 tablespoon Dijon mustard
Freshly ground black pepper
1 clove garlic, minced
½ teaspoon dried tarragon
¼ teaspoon dried dill
1 tablespoon safflower oil
2 tablespoons fresh lemon juice

Wash lettuce leaves in cold water and trim into small pieces. If leaves are small, leave whole. Dry.

Make Vinaigrette Dressing: In a jar, mix vinegar, mustard, pepper, garlic, tarragon, and dill; shake to blend. Add oil and lemon juice and shake again. Chill.

Toss lettuce with dressing and serve immediately.

Serves 4.

Nutritive values per serving:	CHO (gm)	PRO (gm)	FAT (gm)	NA (mg)	CAL
	5	2	4	59	64
Food exchanges per serving:	1 vegetable + 1 fat				

TARTELETTES AUX RAISINS
(RAISIN TARTS)

½ cup raisins
¼ cup port wine or marsala
1 cup part-skim ricotta cheese
1 tablespoon grape juice
2 teaspoons grated lemon rind
Pinch salt
½ teaspoon pure vanilla extract
¼ cup chopped walnuts
1 batch **Whole Wheat Pie Crust dough** (see index)

Plump raisins in the wine for about 2 hours. Place in saucepan and reduce until liquid is evaporated, about 5 minutes. Mix ricotta cheese with grape juice, lemon rind, salt, vanilla. Stir in cooled raisins and walnuts. Meanwhile, mix Whole Wheat Pie Crust dough. Roll thin and cut into pieces to fit an 8-cup muffin tin. Preheat oven to 350°F and bake crust for 20–30 minutes, until brown. Remove from oven and let cool. Stuff with ricotta-raisin mixture and return to oven for 10–15 minutes. Let cool, remove from muffin tins, and serve.

Serves 8.

Nutritive values per serving:	CHO (gm)	PRO (gm)	FAT (gm)	NA (mg)	CAL
	20	6	8	78	176
Food exchanges per serving:	⅔ bread + 1 fruit + ½ medium-fat meat + 1 fat				

FRANCE—MENU 4
SOUPE A L'OIGNON (ONION SOUP)
ESPADON POCHE AUX CHAMPIGNONS (SWORDFISH WITH
MUSHROOMS)
HARICOTS VERTS (GREEN BEANS)
PAIN FRANCAIS (FRENCH BREAD)
TARTE AUX FRAISES (STRAWBERRY TART)

SOUPE A L'OIGNON
(ONION SOUP)

2 cups thinly sliced onions
2 tablespoons Creative Butter (see index)
6 cups beef broth
½ cup dry white wine
1 bay leaf
2 tablespoons Dijon mustard
¼ teaspoon cayenne
1 slice whole wheat toast, quartered, topped with sapsago or
    Romano cheese (optional)

Heat Creative Butter in nonstick saucepan and sauté onions in it, covered, until tender, about 20–25 minutes. Add beef broth, wine, bay leaf, mustard, and cayenne. Bring to boil and then reduce heat and let simmer, covered, for at least 1 hour. Remove bay leaf and serve soup with a piece of toast and grated cheese, if desired.

Serves 4.

Nutritive values per serving (without toast and cheese):	CHO (gm)	PRO (gm)	FAT (gm)	NA (mg)	CAL
	10	6.5	6	143	120
Food exchanges per serving:	2 vegetable + 1 fat + ½ lean meat				

ESPADON POCHE AUX CHAMPIGNONS
(SWORDFISH WITH MUSHROOMS)

1 teaspoon Creative Butter (see index)
1 pound fresh swordfish (or tuna)
1 cup dry white wine
1 bay leaf
Pinch pepper
Pinch dried thyme
½ teaspoon dried tarragon
1 cup sliced mushrooms
1 tablespoon Dijon mustard
¼ cup chopped parsley
1 lemon, sliced thin
4 parsley sprigs

In large nonstick saucepan, heat Creative Butter and brown fish in it on both sides. Add wine, bay leaf, pepper, thyme, and tarragon and bring to boil. Cover, reduce heat, and let simmer 10–20 minutes, until fish is tender. After 5 minutes of cooking time has elapsed, add mushrooms and continue cooking. Transfer fish to warm platter. Mix mustard and chopped parsley into the sauce. Serve and spoon sauce over fish. Top with lemon slices and parsley sprigs.

Serves 4.

Nutritive values per serving:	CHO (gm)	PRO (gm)	FAT (gm)	NA (mg)	CAL
	6.5	23	6	77	172
Food exchanges per serving:	½ fruit + ½ vegetable + 3 lean meat; omits ½ fat				

HARICOTS VERTS
(GREEN BEANS)

1½ pounds fresh string beans
1 tablespoon Creative Butter (see index)
2 tablespoons lemon juice
1 tablespoon minced scallion (white part only)
Pepper to taste
2 tablespoons minced parsley

Wash and trim beans, removing any strings. Bring large kettle of water to boil. Drop beans into water a handful at a time and bring back to boil. Cook 10–15 minutes, until beans are tender but still crunchy. Drain, turn into heavy saucepan, and toss with butter, lemon juice, scallions, and pepper. Heat, covered, just to warm. Serve with sprinkling of parsley.

Serves 4.

Nutritive values per serving:	CHO (gm)	PRO (gm)	FAT (gm)	NA (mg)	CAL
	13.5	5.5	3	34	95
Food exchanges per serving:	2¾ vegetable + ½ fat				

PAIN FRANCAIS
(FRENCH BREAD)

See Chapter 19, "Basics."

TARTE AUX FRAISES
(STRAWBERRY TART)

1 Whole Wheat Pie Crust (see index)
2 cups fresh strawberries, hulled
1 envelope unflavored gelatin
¼ cup concentrated frozen apple juice
1 cup diet ginger ale or fruit-flavored no-calorie soda

Fill baked shell with berries. Sprinkle gelatin over apple juice in a glass measuring cup. Dissolve by placing cup in a bowl of boiling water. Mix with ginger ale or no-calorie soda. Let set partially and then spoon over berries to glaze. Refrigerate and serve.

Serves 6.

Nutritive values per serving:	CHO (gm)	PRO (gm)	FAT (gm)	NA (mg)	CAL
	21.5	3	5	50	143
Food exchanges per serving:	¾ fruit + 1 bread + fat				

FRANCE—MENU 5
ARTICHAUTS VINAIGRETTE (ARTICHOKES
WITH VINAIGRETTE DRESSING)
BAR PROVENCAL (SEA BASS WITH TOMATOES)
POMMES DE TERRE (BOILED POTATOES)
MELON AU PORTO (CANTALOUPE WITH PORT WINE)

ARTICHAUTS VINAIGRETTE
(ARTICHOKES WITH VINAIGRETTE DRESSING)

4 globe artichokes
Juice of ½ lemon
1 tablespoon vinegar
Salt
Vinaigrette Dressing (see index)
1 teaspoon capers, rinsed and chopped
1 tablespoon minced chives
1 tablespoon minced parsley

Combine vinaigrette with capers, chives, and parsley and blend thoroughly. Refrigerate until ready to use.

Snap stems off the artichokes and break off any small leaves at the base. Trim the bottoms so that artichokes will stand upright. With a sharp knife, cut an inch off tops and also trim points of remaining leaves using scissors. Rinse well in cold water. Rub cut leaves with lemon juice and immerse artichokes in bath of vinegar and water until ready to cook. Bring 4–5 quarts of water to a boil in a large saucepan with a little salt. Drop in artichokes, cover with 2 layers of cheesecloth, and boil, uncovered, for 40–45 minutes, until leaves pull off easily. Drain upside down in colander. Serve each, warm or cold, with 1–2 tablespoons vinaigrette.

Serves 4.

Nutritive values per serving:	CHO (gm)	PRO (gm)	FAT (gm)	NA (mg)	CAL
	15	4	4	86	112
Food exchanges per serving:	3 vegetable + ¾ fat				

BAR PROVENCAL
(SEA BASS WITH TOMATOES)

Juice of 1 lemon
2 tablespoons plus 1 teaspoon safflower oil
Dash cayenne
1½ pounds sea bass fillets or fillets of other firm white fish
1 cup chopped onions
2 green peppers, cored, seeded, and cut into strips
2 cloves garlic, minced
1 pound tomatoes, peeled, seeded, and chopped
Pinch fennel seeds
Pinch dried thyme
4 peppercorns
1 tablespoon fresh oregano or ¼ tablespoon dried
¼ cup chopped parsley
1 lemon, sliced

Mix lemon juice and 2 tablespoons safflower oil with cayenne. Wash fish and pat dry. Place fish in oil/lemon mixture, cover, and refrigerate several hours. Drain, but reserve liquid. Heat 1 teaspoon oil in nonstick saucepan and sauté onions until soft. Then add peppers and garlic and cook 5–10 minutes. Add tomatoes, fennel seeds, thyme, peppercorns, oregano, and half the parsley and cook until all vegetables are tender. Broil fish about 4 inches from heat source, brushing with marinade and turning. Cooking time depends on thickness of fish, but fish is ready when it flakes when pierced with fork. Remove fish from broiler and place in center of a warm serving platter. Spoon vegetables alongside fish on the platter. Top with lemon. Sprinkle fish with remaining parsley.

Serves 4.

Nutritive values per serving:	CHO (gm)	PRO (gm)	FAT (gm)	NA (mg)	CAL
	15	36.5	10.5	136	301

Food exchanges per serving: ¼ fruit + 2½ vegetable + 5 lean meat; omits 1 fat

POMMES DE TERRE
(BOILED POTATOES)

1 pound small new potatoes

Scrub potatoes well and boil in their jackets until tender. When ready to serve, cut a ribbon of the peel from the center of each potato.

Serves 4.

Nutritive values per serving:	CHO (gm)	PRO (gm)	FAT (gm)	NA (mg)	CAL
	14.5	2	0	3	66

Food exchanges per serving: 1 bread

MELON AU PORTO
(CANTALOUPE WITH PORT WINE)

4 slices ripe cantaloupe, peeled, cut ¼ inch thick
1 cup port wine
1 stick cinnamon
2 cloves
2 slices lemon
¼ cup fresh blueberries

Remove seeds and pulp from center of melon slices and discard. Place melon slices in enamel saucepan with the wine, cinnamon, cloves, and lemon. Bring to boil and cook 5 minutes. Let cool and serve melon slices with wine sauce. Place 1 tablespoon of blueberries in center of each slice.

Serves 4.

Nutritive values per serving:	CHO (gm)	PRO (gm)	FAT (gm)	NA (mg)	CAL
	14	1	0	4	60
Food exchanges per serving:	1½ fruit				

FRANCE—MENU 6
BOUILLON DE LEGUMES (VEGETABLE SOUP)
PAILLARD DIABLE (CHICKEN BREASTS
WITH TARRAGON MUSTARD)
POMMES DE TERRE LYONNAISE (POTATOES LYONNAISE)
TOMATES FARCIES (STUFFED TOMATOES)
PECHES MELBA (PEACHES WITH RASPBERRY SAUCE)

BOUILLON DE LEGUMES
(VEGETABLE SOUP)

1 tablespoon thinly sliced shallot
4 cups chicken stock (see index)
1 carrot, scraped and julienned
½ cup finely chopped celery
½ cup green peas
2 teaspoons chopped fresh basil (optional)
2 teaspoons chopped parsley

Cook shallot for 5 minutes, until softened. In a large saucepan, bring to boil the stock and add carrot, celery, shallot, and peas. Simmer 15 minutes. Sprinkle with fresh basil and parsley and serve.

Serves 4.

Nutritive values per serving:	CHO (gm)	PRO (gm)	FAT (gm)	NA (mg)	CAL
	8	5	1	32	61
Food exchanges per serving:	⅕ bread + 1 vegetable + ⅓ lean meat				

PAILLARD DIABLE
(CHICKEN BREASTS WITH TARRAGON MUSTARD)

1 pound skinless, boneless chicken breasts, cut into 4 pieces
1 teaspoon dried tarragon
1 teaspoon fresh lemon juice
Pepper
¼ cup good-quality Dijon mustard
1 lemon, sliced
1 tablespoon chopped parsley

Place chicken breasts between 2 sheets of wax paper and pound with mallet (or a heavy pot) to flatten them.

Mix together the tarragon, lemon juice, pepper to taste, and mustard into a mayonnaise-type consistency and coat the chicken pieces. Preheat broiler and place paillards about 4 inches from heat source. Broil until mustard begins to bubble, about 5–6 minutes, turn, and grill other side. Remove before mustard begins to burn. Top each piece with lemon sprinkled with parsley.

Serves 4.

Nutritive values per serving:	CHO (gm)	PRO (gm)	FAT (gm)	NA (mg)	CAL
	4	28	3.5	253	160
Food exchanges per serving:	⅓ fruit + 4 lean meat; omits 1½ fat				

POMMES DE TERRE LYONNAISE
(POTATOES LYONNAISE)

1 pound new potatoes, parboiled
1 tablespoon Creative Butter (see index), divided
1 onion, sliced thin
1 tablespoon chopped parsley
¼ teaspoon freshly ground black pepper

Peel potatoes and cut into ¼-inch slices. Heat half of Creative Butter in nonstick skillet and add potatoes. Cook over medium heat for about 20 minutes, shaking pan every 5 minutes or so. In another nonstick skillet, heat remaining Creative Butter and sauté onions in it until translucent. Add a little water if necessary. Turn onions into the potato pan, combine, and cook until potatoes are tender. Sprinkle with parsley and pepper and serve.

Serves 4.

Nutritive values per serving:	CHO (gm)	PRO (gm)	FAT (gm)	NA (mg)	CAL
	17	2	3	25	103
Food exchanges per serving:	⅓ vegetable + 1 bread + ½ fat				

TOMATES FARCIES
(STUFFED TOMATOES)

4 medium tomatoes
Salt
¼ cup whole wheat bread crumbs
½ teaspoon dried basil (or oregano)
1 teaspoon freshly ground pepper
1 tablespoon dried mustard
2 tablespoons minced parsley
1 tablespoon chopped scallion
1 teaspoon Creative Butter (see index)

Cut tops off tomatoes and carefully scoop out pulp. Salt insides of tomato shells and set upside down to drain for 15 minutes. Meanwhile, mix tomato pulp with half the bread crumbs, the basil or oregano, pepper, mustard, parsley, and scallions. Stuff the drained tomato shells with this mixture. Top each with remaining bread crumbs and a dab of Creative Butter. Place in preheated 350°F oven and cook for 15–20 minutes.

Serves 4.

Nutritive values per serving:	CHO (gm)	PRO (gm)	FAT (gm)	NA (mg)	CAL
	12	2.5	3	36	85
Food exchanges per serving:	⅓ bread + 1½ vegetable + ½ fat				

PECHES MELBA
(PEACHES WITH RASPBERRY SAUCE)

4 large ripe peaches
1 cup raspberries
½ cup part-skim ricotta cheese
1 tablespoon grape juice

Blanch peaches by dropping them into boiling water for 30 seconds. Remove and run under cold water; the skins will then peel off easily. Cut in half, discard pits, and place 2 peach halves on each of 4 individual dessert dishes. Puree raspberries with ricotta cheese and grape juice, reserving 2 tablespoons whole berries for topping. Spoon puree over the peaches, top with a few berries, and serve cold.

Serves 4.

Nutritive values per serving:	CHO (gm)	PRO (gm)	FAT (gm)	NA (mg)	CAL
	22	5	3	41	135
Food exchanges per serving:	2 fruit + 1 lean meat				

Menu 1
SAUERBRATEN
Braised Beef
CHAMPAGNEKRAUT
Red Cabbage
KARTOFFELKLOSSE
Potato Dumplings
MELONE MIT LIMONADE
Melon with Raspberry Fizz

Menu 2
SCHELLFISCH
Haddock Pudding
SELLERIESALAT
Celery Root Salad
ROTE FRUCHTE SCHLAGEN
Red Fruit Froth

Menu 3
STEINPILZE
Marinated Mushrooms
KAISERFLEISCH
Pork Roast with Sauerkraut
KARTOFFEL PFANNKUCHEN
Potato Pancake
BIRNEN EIS
Pear Sherbet

6

GERMANY

If one were to conduct a survey of most German dishes, it might seem surprising that more people don't perish of heart disease and overweight! Peeking into food shop windows, and observing restaurant patrons, one would see a myriad of sausages draped in butcher shop displays and plates on tables heaped high with potatoes, dumplings, sauerkraut, and *wursts*. Cakes and cookies are dearly loved, and *schlag*, whipped cream, is everywhere. But times are changing, and Germany's health-conscious are trying to cut back the calories.

Germany relies on such cold-weather vegetables as cabbage, turnips, lentils, split peas. Today desserts are apt to be mixed fruit and nuts or cheese and fresh bread. Rabbit, veal, pork, and fish are much enjoyed, and when it comes to potatoes no one is more inventive than the German chef. We've eliminated the heavy cream and butter and the sausages, but we have included some dumplings and presented a representative—but pared down—version of some typical German repasts. *Guten appetit!*

GERMANY—MENU 1
SAUERBRATEN (BRAISED BEEF)
CHAMPAGNEKRAUT (RED CABBAGE)
KARTOFFELKLOSSE (POTATO DUMPLINGS)
MELONE MIT LIMONADE (MELON WITH RASPBERRY FIZZ)

SAUERBRATEN
(BRAISED BEEF)

3 pounds boned rump, all fat removed
1½ tablespoons arrowroot
½ tablespoon Creative Butter (see index)
1 lemon, sliced thin
Pinch fructose
¼ cup low-fat yogurt
Parsley sprigs for garnish

MARINADE

2 cups ale
2 cups water
½ lemon
1 bay leaf
1 onion, sliced
1 clove
1 small tomato, chopped
Few sprigs parsley
2 peppercorns

Mix marinade ingredients and pour over meat. Cover and refrigerate 2 days, turning the meat several times. Remove meat from marinade, strain, and save liquid. Dry meat and pat on arrowroot. Brown in Creative Butter. Add 1 cup of marinade liquid, lemon, and fructose. Cook, covered, over low heat on top of stove for 2½ hours or until meat is tender.

Transfer meat to warm platter. Strain sauce and skim off any fat. Add yogurt to sauce and blend. Slice the meat, arrange on platter, and spoon sauce over it. Garnish platter with parsley sprigs.

Serves 6.

Nutritive values per serving:	CHO (gm)	PRO (gm)	FAT (gm)	NA (mg)	CAL
	9.5	40.5	13	113	317
Food exchanges per serving:	⅓ bread + ⅕ fruit + ½ vegetable + 5½ lean meat; omits ⅔ fat				

CHAMPAGNEKRAUT
(RED CABBAGE)

½ teaspoon corn oil
1 medium onion, chopped
1 small head red cabbage (about 1 pound), sliced thin
½ teaspoon lemon juice
¼ cup hot water
¼ teaspoon fructose
¼ cup white wine

Heat oil in large nonstick skillet and sauté onion in it until soft. Add cabbage, lemon juice, water, and fructose. Cover and cook 20 minutes. Add wine and cook, uncovered, 5 minutes. Serve when cabbage is tender and liquid absorbed.

Serves 4.

Nutritive values per serving:	CHO (gm)	PRO (gm)	FAT (gm)	NA (mg)	CAL
	10.5	2.5	1	32	61
Food exchanges per serving:	2 vegetable				

KARTOFFELKLOSSE
(POTATO DUMPLINGS)

¾ pound potatoes, cooked
½ cup all-purpose unbleached flour
1 egg, beaten (use only ½ yolk)
Pinch salt
4 cups beef broth (see index)
1 tablespoon minced fresh parsley

Peel potatoes and mash. Work in flour, egg, salt. Knead until stiff and shape into balls 1½ inches in diameter. Bring broth to boil in a large kettle and drop potato dumplings in one at a time. When they rise to the top, cook another 5 minutes. Remove from broth with slotted spoon, garnish with fresh parsley, and serve.

Serves 4.

Nutritive values per serving:	CHO (gm)	PRO (gm)	FAT (gm)	NA (mg)	CAL
	26	9	1.5	59	154
Food exchanges per serving:	1½ bread + ½ vegetable + ½ lean meat				

MELONE MIT LIMONADE
(MELON WITH RASPBERRY FIZZ)

¾ **cup seltzer**
½ **teaspoon fresh lemon juice**
1 cup unsweetened raspberry juice
4 cups honeydew or cantaloupe melon balls

Mix seltzer with lemon and raspberry juices and pour over the melon balls. Refrigerate 1 hour before serving. Spoon melon balls into dessert glasses, adding a bit more seltzer for added fizz.

Serves 4.

Nutritive values per serving:	CHO (gm)	PRO (gm)	FAT (gm)	NA (mg)	CAL
	19.5	1.5	.5	31	89
Food exchanges per serving:	2 fruit				

GERMANY—MENU 2
SCHELLFISCH (HADDOCK PUDDING)
SELLERIESALAT (CELERY ROOT SALAD)
ROTE FRUCHTE SCHLAGEN (RED FRUIT FROTH)

SCHELLFISCH
(HADDOCK PUDDING)

1½ pounds haddock fillets
2 small potatoes, parboiled and peeled
½ teaspoon corn oil
1 onion, sliced
Vegetable spray
2 eggs, beaten (use only 1 yolk)
½ cup low-fat yogurt
¼ cup skim milk
Salt and pepper to taste
4 tablespoons toasted whole wheat bread crumbs

Wash haddock and slice the peeled potatoes. Heat corn oil in nonstick skillet and lightly sauté onion in it. Layer slices of haddock, onion, and potatoes in a vegetable-sprayed, oven-proof casserole. In separate bowl, mix the eggs, yogurt, milk, salt, and pepper and pour over the fish. Top with bread crumbs. Preheat oven to 350°F and bake, uncovered, 30 minutes.

Serves 4.

Nutritive values per serving:	CHO (gm)	PRO (gm)	FAT (gm)	NA (mg)	CAL
	20	40	3	172	267
Food exchanges per serving:	1 bread + ½ vegetable + ⅓ skim milk + 5 lean meat; omits 2½ fat				

SELLERIESALAT
(CELERY ROOT SALAD)

3 celery roots, peeled and sliced
1 tablespoon walnut oil
1½ tablespoons vinegar
½ teaspoon fructose
Salt and pepper to taste

Parboil celery root until tender but still crunchy. Drain and chill. In small bowl, mix oil, vinegar, fructose, salt, and pepper. Pour over chilled celery root and serve.

Serves 4.

Nutritive values per serving:	CHO (gm)	PRO (gm)	FAT (gm)	NA (mg)	CAL
	1.5	0	3.5	16	38
Food exchanges per serving:	⅓ vegetable + ½ fat				

ROTE FRUCHTE SCHLAGEN
(RED FRUIT FROTH)

1½ teaspoons arrowroot
1 cup plus 3 tablespoons unsweetened cranberry juice
8 red plums, pitted
1 tablespoon lemon juice
1 teaspoon fructose

In saucepan, mix arrowroot and 2 tablespoons cranberry juice. When blended, slowly add remaining cranberry juice and bring to a boil, stirring. In blender, puree plums, lemon juice, and enough cranberry juice to make a custardlike sauce. Blend this with the arrowroot and cranberry mixture. Chill until ready to serve.

Serves 4.

Nutritive values per serving:	CHO (gm)	PRO (gm)	FAT (gm)	NA (mg)	CAL
	23	.5	0	3	94
Food exchanges per serving:	2⅓ fruit				

GERMANY—MENU 3
STEINPILZE (MARINATED MUSHROOMS)
KAISERFLEISCH (PORK ROAST WITH SAUERKRAUT)
KARTOFFEL PFANNKUCHEN (POTATO PANCAKE)
BIRNEN EIS (PEAR SHERBET)

STEINPILZE
(MARINATED MUSHROOMS)

1 pound mushrooms
1 quart water
1 tablespoon fresh lemon juice
1 cup tarragon vinegar
¼ cup safflower oil
¼ cup water
4 peppercorns, crushed
1 bay leaf
Pinch salt
⅛ teaspoon dried thyme
1 tablespoon minced fresh parsley

Trim stems off mushrooms and wipe clean. Bring 1 quart water to boil in large kettle and add lemon juice. Blanch mushrooms in it for 3 minutes and drain. Set aside. In another saucepan, bring to boil the vinegar, oil, ¼ cup water, peppercorns, bay leaf, salt, and thyme. Pour this marinade over mushrooms and chill in covered dish. Remove bay leaf, drain, and serve mushrooms with garnish of parsley.

Serves 4.

Nutritive values per serving:	CHO (gm)	PRO (gm)	FAT (gm)	NA (mg)	CAL
	11	2	14.5	11	183
Food exchanges per serving:	2 vegetable + 3 fat				

KAISERFLEISCH
(PORK ROAST WITH SAUERKRAUT)

2½ pounds center-cut pork loin
1 clove garlic, peeled
3 cups sauerkraut, drained
1 teaspoon juniper berries
1 Granny Smith apple, cored, quartered

Trim fat off pork loin and rub meat with garlic clove. Place on rack in baking pan. Mix drained sauerkraut with juniper berries and apple quarters. Arrange in a foil "cradle" alongside the meat. Insert meat thermometer into pork, being sure it doesn't touch the bone. Preheat oven to 400°F and roast pork for 1 hour. Reduce heat to 375°F and roast another hour until meat is tender. Thermometer should read 185°F. Let roast rest 10 minutes before slicing. Serve with sauerkraut.

Serves 6.

Nutritive values per serving:	CHO (gm)	PRO (gm)	FAT (gm)	NA (mg)	CAL
	7	33	15	300	295
Food exchanges per serving:	1½ vegetable + 5½ lean meat; omits 1 fat				

KARTOFFEL PFANNKUCHEN
(POTATO PANCAKE)

1 pound potatoes, parboiled and peeled
1 teaspoon caraway seeds
1 tablespoon Creative Butter (see index), divided

Let potatoes cool in refrigerator for 1 hour. Grate on medium (tear-shaped) side of grater. Add caraway seeds and ½ tablespoon Creative Butter. Melt remaining Creative Butter in 8" nonstick skillet and turn in potatoes. Brown on one side, turn, and brown the other side.

Serves 4.

Nutritive values per serving:	CHO (gm)	PRO (gm)	FAT (gm)	NA (mg)	CAL
	14.5	2	3	22	93
Food exchanges per serving:	1 bread + ½ fat				

BIRNEN EIS
(PEAR SHERBET)

1 egg white, beaten until stiff
⅓ cup nonfat dry milk
⅓ cup cold water
2 large ice cubes, shaved in blender
2 teaspoons pure vanilla extract
2 tablespoons unsweetened pear juice
2 ripe pears, cored, peeled, and sliced

To the beaten egg white add all the remaining ingredients except the sliced pears. Beat until thick. Pour into ice tray and place in freezer 1–2 hours, until ready to serve. Spoon over sliced pears.

Serves 4.

Nutritive values per serving:	CHO (gm)	PRO (gm)	FAT (gm)	NA (mg)	CAL
	16	3	0	40	76
Food exchanges per serving:	⅕ skim milk + 1½ fruit				

Menu 1

ZOLDBAB LEVES
String Bean Soup

CSIRKE PAPRIKAS
Chicken Paprikash

TARHONYA
Egg Barley

UBORKASALATA
Cucumber Salad

LEKVAROSHAP
Prune Whip

Menu 2

GOMBA LEVES
Mushroom Soup

BORJUSULT CITROMOS
UBORKAMARTAS
Roast Veal with Lemon-Cucumber Sauce

RUTABAGA PUREE

TUROS GOMBOC
Cheese Dumplings

Menu 3

ECETES SALATA
Wilted Lettuce Salad

MARHA GULYAS
Beef Goulash

PALACSINTA/LEKVAR
Pancakes with Apricot Puree

Menu 4

KOMENY MAGOS LEVES
Caraway Seed Soup

SULTHAL BURGONYAVAL
Baked Haddock with Potatoes

KARALABE
Browned Kohlrabi

ALMAKOMPOT MASMODON
Stewed Apples

7

HUNGARY

My grandmother was Hungarian. To watch her cook and bake was a culinary lesson without compare. Her *strudel* (tissue-paper thin, stuffed with goodies) was a weekly happening. Her goulash was spectacular, to say nothing of her *paprikash!* The Hungarian tradition in food was gleaned from many cultures—the little land was invaded by hordes of Mongols and then the Turks, who brought along their peppers. Paprika is thus the most distinctive mark of Hungarian cuisine, providing flavor from mild to fiery hot and a warm rose color wherever it is used.

Mixed grills were adapted from the Transylvanians, but today Hungary is best known for its stews and soups. In former days the family stewpot always hung over the fire. Dill, poppy seed, and caraway are popular. Sour cream is an integral part of Hungarian cooking, but plain yogurt (drained a few hours) is as good. *Spaetzle* or *nockerdli*, little dumplings, are delicious, and so are egg noodles in all shapes and sizes. *Tarhonya* (egg barley) is a traditional accompaniment. Onions (they must be "burned"), potatoes, and green peppers are the base of any good *gulyas*. Kohlrabi, squash, cabbage, and turnips are used widely. For a special dessert, the *palacsinta*, or crepe stuffed with apricots or prunes (*lekvar*) and some nuts, is justly celebrated. *Jo etvagyat kivanok!*

HUNGARY—MENU 1

ZOLDBAB LEVES (STRING BEAN SOUP)
CSIRKE PAPRIKAS (CHICKEN PAPRIKASH)
TARHONYA (EGG BARLEY)
UBORKASALATA (CUCUMBER SALAD)
LEKVAROSHAP (PRUNE WHIP)

ZOLDBAB LEVES
(STRING BEAN SOUP)

4 cups chicken broth (see index)
½ pound fresh string beans, sliced diagonally
into 1-inch pieces
1 onion, chopped fine
2 cloves garlic, minced
1 tablespoon Hungarian paprika
1 tablespoon arrowroot, dissolved in 2 tablespoons
cold water
2 tablespoons vinegar
4 tablespoons chopped parsley

Heat broth and add washed beans and onion. Simmer 20 minutes. In small nonstick skillet, cook garlic for 5 minutes. Blend the paprika and dissolved arrowroot with the garlic. Add enough cold water to make a paste and then stir this into the soup. Simmer 5 minutes more, then add vinegar and parsley.

Serves 6.

Nutritive values per serving:	CHO (gm)	PRO (gm)	FAT (gm)	NA (mg)	CAL
	10	4	.5	10	61
Food exchanges per serving:	2 vegetable				

CSIRKE PAPRIKAS
(CHICKEN PAPRIKASH)

1 pound skinless, boneless chicken breast, cut into
  ½-inch slices
1 medium onion, chopped
1 tablespoon Hungarian sweet paprika
½ cup chicken broth (see index)
1 tablespoon tomato paste
1 small green pepper, cored, seeded and chopped
½ cup low-fat yogurt
Freshly ground pepper to taste

Stir-fry the chicken pieces in nonstick skillet on both sides for 1–2 minutes. Remove from pan and set aside. Heat onion in skillet until browned and then stir in the paprika. Add broth and tomato paste. Bring to boil for 5 minutes. Add the chicken and green pepper. Cover and cook 10 minutes. Uncover and cook another 5 minutes. Mix in yogurt and stir (do not let boil or yogurt will separate). Season with pepper and serve.

Serves 4.

Nutritive values per serving:	CHO (gm)	PRO (gm)	FAT (gm)	NA (mg)	CAL
	6	29	3	84	167
Food exchanges per serving:	1 vegetable + 4 lean meat; omits 2 fat				

TARHONYA
(EGG BARLEY)

1 tablespoon Creative Butter (see index)
¾ cup egg barley
2 cups hot water
1 small onion
Salt and pepper to taste

In nonstick saucepan melt Creative Butter. Add barley and brown over moderate heat. Slowly add water. Add onion and sprinkle with salt and pepper. Cover and cook 15 minutes over low heat. If necessary, add water to keep from burning. Cook for another 5–10 minutes, until barley is tender. May be kept warm in double boiler. Remove onion and serve.

Serves 4.

Nutritive values per serving:	CHO (gm)	PRO (gm)	FAT (gm)	NA (mg)	CAL
	32	3.5	3	23	169
Food exchanges per serving:	2 bread + ½ fat				

UBORKASALATA
(CUCUMBER SALAD)

1 large cucumber, peeled and sliced thin
1 teaspoon salt
1 small red onion, sliced
1 clove garlic, chopped
3 tablespoons vinegar
2 tablespoons cold water
Pepper to taste
½ teaspoon Hungarian sweet paprika

Combine cucumber slices and salt in small bowl. Refrigerate at least ½ hour. Drain off liquid and squeeze out remaining moisture with paper towels. In serving bowl, combine onion, garlic, vinegar, cold water, and cucumber slices. Season with pepper and paprika.

Serves 4.

Nutritive values per serving:	CHO (gm)	PRO (gm)	FAT (gm)	NA (mg)	CAL
	4	.5	0	493	18
Food exchanges per serving:	1 vegetable				

LEKVAROSHAP
(PRUNE WHIP)

16 pitted prunes
3 small pieces lemon rind
1½ cups water
2 egg whites, beaten until stiff
1 teaspoon lemon juice

Soak prunes and lemon rind in water for 1 hour. Simmer for 20–30 minutes, until fruit is soft. If necessary, add more water. Let cool. Puree in blender. Fold beaten egg whites into prune puree. If prune puree is too stiff, add more water before folding in. Add lemon juice. Chill for at least 1 hour. Serve in individual dishes.

Serves 6.

Nutritive values per serving:	CHO (gm)	PRO (gm)	FAT (gm)	NA (mg)	CAL
	18.5	2	0	18	82
Food exchanges per serving:	2 fruit				

HUNGARY—MENU 2
GOMBA LEVES (MUSHROOM SOUP)
BORJUSULT CITROMOS UBORKAMARTAS (ROAST VEAL WITH
LEMON-CUCUMBER SAUCE)
RUTABAGA PUREE
TUROS GOMBOC (CHEESE DUMPLINGS)

GOMBA LEVES
(MUSHROOM SOUP)

4 cups chicken stock (see index)
½ pound mushrooms, sliced thin
1 carrot, diced
1 small onion, chopped
1 small green pepper, chopped
2 teaspoons Cream of Wheat (farina)
1 teaspoon Hungarian sweet paprika
¼ cup low-fat yogurt

Heat chicken broth in saucepan. Add all vegetables and simmer for 20 minutes. Add farina and cook another 5 minutes. Blend paprika with yogurt and stir into soup. Warm gently for 5 minutes, but do not boil. Stir and serve.

Serves 6.

Nutritive values per serving:	CHO (gm)	PRO (gm)	FAT (gm)	NA (mg)	CAL
	9	4	.5	22	57
Food exchanges per serving:	2 vegetable				

BORJUSULT/CITROMOS UBORKAMARTAS
(ROAST VEAL WITH LEMON-CUCUMBER SAUCE)

3 pounds boneless veal, rolled and tied, trimmed of all fat
Pepper to taste
1 tablespoon lemon juice
3 cloves garlic, slivered
1 teaspoon Durkee's Imitation Bacon Chips
1 cup chicken broth
1 bunch watercress, rinsed well
Lemon-Cucumber Sauce (see recipe below)

Season veal with pepper and lemon juice, turning. Make several slits in meat and insert garlic and bacon chips. Place veal in small roasting pan and pour half the broth over it. Roast in preheated 325°F oven for 2 hours, basting every 15 minutes with remaining broth. Be careful not to let roast burn. A meat thermometer should read 160–165°F when meat is done. Remove roast from oven and let rest 15 minutes. When ready to serve, slice thin and arrange on bed of watercress on warm serving platter. Spread lemon-cucumber sauce in a ribbon over the meat.

Serves 6.

Nutritive values per serving:	CHO (gm)	PRO (gm)	FAT (gm)	NA (mg)	CAL
	1	45	20.5	183	369
Food exchanges per serving:	6½ lean meat				

LEMON-CUCUMBER SAUCE

2 medium cucumbers, peeled, quartered, and seeded
1 tablespoon Creative Butter (see index)
1 tablespoon Cream of Wheat (farina)
½ cup chicken broth (see index)
White pepper
Grated rind of 1 lemon
2 tablespoons lemon juice, strained
½ cup low-fat yogurt

Dice seeded cucumbers. Cook in boiling water 3 minutes. Drain and pat dry. Heat Creative Butter in nonstick saucepan and cook cucumbers a minute or 2, until lightly browned. Stir in farina, broth, pepper, lemon rind, and lemon juice and simmer 5 minutes. Stir in yogurt but do not boil. Pour over veal slices.

Serves 6.

Nutritive values per serving:	CHO (gm)	PRO (gm)	FAT (gm)	NA (mg)	CAL
	8	3	3	43	71
Food exchanges per serving:	1 vegetable + ⅓ bread + ½ fat				

RUTABAGA PUREE

1 rutabaga (about 1 pound), peeled and diced
1 medium potato, peeled and diced
¼ teaspoon cayenne
½ teaspoon freshly grated nutmeg
3 tablespoons chopped parsley

Place rutabaga and potato pieces in saucepan and cover with water. Bring to boil and let simmer, covered, for about 30 minutes, until tender. Drain. Place in food mill and grind into bowl (or puree in blender). Add cayenne and nutmeg and stir. Rewarm a few minutes in saucepan before serving. Serve with garnish of parsley.

Serves 8.

Nutritive values per serving:	CHO (gm)	PRO (gm)	FAT (gm)	NA (mg)	CAL
	7.5	1	0	4	34
Food exchanges per serving:	½ fruit + ⅕ bread				

TUROS GOMBOC
(CHEESE DUMPLINGS)

6 ounces low-sodium farmer cheese
2 small eggs (use only 1 yolk)
¼ cup matzo meal
1½ quarts cold water
1 tablespoon Creative Butter (see index)
½ cup Nutri Grain cereal, crushed
1 tablespoon fructose, mixed with 1 tablespoon cinnamon

Mash farmer cheese in a bowl with a potato masher. Mash in eggs. Gradually mix in matzo meal until dough becomes firm. Let chill for 2 hours. When ready to cook, bring water to boil in a large pot. Form cheese into little round dumplings about ¾ inch in diameter. Lower into the simmering water and cook, uncovered, for 30 minutes or until the dumplings rise to the surface and roll over. Remove one at a time as they turn themselves, using a slotted spoon. Drain in colander. Heat Creative Butter in nonstick skillet. Add crushed cereal flakes and then the dumplings. Cover pan and shake back and forth to coat with crumbs. Serve on warm plates and sprinkle with cinnamon mixture.

Serves 8.

Nutritive values per serving:	CHO (gm)	PRO (gm)	FAT (gm)	NA (mg)	CAL
	14	14	12	0	204
Food exchanges per serving:	⅔ bread + ⅓ fruit + 2 medium-fat meat				

HUNGARY—MENU 3
ECETES SALATA (WILTED LETTUCE SALAD)
MARHA GULYAS (BEEF GOULASH)
PALACSINTA/LEKVAR (PANCAKES AND APRICOT PUREE)

ECETES SALATA
(WILTED LETTUCE SALAD)

½ cup white vinegar
½ teaspoon fructose
½ cup water
1 tablespoon minced onion
Freshly ground black pepper
2 small heads Boston lettuce
1 tablespoon sunflower seed oil

To make dressing, mix together vinegar, fructose, water, onion, and pepper. Let stand 30 minutes at room temperature. Wash lettuce and separate leaves, discarding hard core. Pat dry. Mix with dressing and refrigerate. Just before serving, sprinkle each serving with a drop or 2 of sunflower seed oil.

Serves 4.

Nutritive values per serving:	CHO (gm)	PRO (gm)	FAT (gm)	NA (mg)	CAL
	4	1	4	8	56
Food exchanges per serving:	1 vegetable + ⅔ fat				

MARHA GULYAS
(BEEF GOULASH)

1 pound boneless chuck steak, all fat removed, cut into
    1-inch cubes
1 medium onion, minced
1 clove garlic, minced
1 tablespoon Hungarian sweet or hot paprika
1 cup water or enough to cover meat
1 bay leaf
1 small ripe tomato, quartered and seeded
¼ teaspoon caraway seeds
Pepper to taste
4 medium potatoes, peeled and diced
1½ cups carrots, scraped and cut into 1-inch rounds
1 small green pepper, cored, seeded and quartered

In nonstick skillet, cook beef little by little until browned
on all sides. Remove meat and set aside. Cook onion and garlic
for 3 minutes, then return beef to skillet. Add paprika so that it
coats beef. Then add the water, bay leaf, tomato, caraway, and
season with pepper. Cover and simmer over low heat for 2
hours. Remove bay leaf.

Parboil potatoes and carrots for 10 minutes, drain, and
add to meat with green peppers. Cook for 30 minutes until
vegetables are tender. This dish tastes even better if made a
day ahead. Before reheating, spoon off any fat.

Serves 4.

Nutritive values per serving:	CHO (gm)	PRO (gm)	FAT (gm)	NA (mg)	CAL
	30	26	18	107	386
Food exchanges per serving:	2 vegetable + 1½ bread + 3 medium-fat meat				

PALACSINTA/LEKVAR
(PANCAKES AND APRICOT PUREE)

PALACSINTA (PANCAKES)

2 eggs (use only 1 yolk)
½ cup plus 2 tablespoons buckwheat flour
½ cup skim milk
1 teaspoon fructose
Pinch salt
½ cup seltzer
½ cup Creative Cream Cheese (see index)
Lekvar (Apricot Puree) (see recipe below)
¼ cup walnuts
Cinnamon

Mix eggs, flour, milk, fructose, and salt. Mix to make a smooth batter and then set aside for 2 hours. Stir in seltzer just before cooking. Heat a 6″ nonstick skillet. Test for correct heat by sprinkling a drop of water on the pan: When water dances, the skillet is at the right heat. It may be necessary to discard the first few pancakes until they turn out just right!

Pour a small ladle of batter into the pan. It should be thin but should cover the whole 6″ pan. When holes begins to appear on top of pancake, turn it over and cook another few seconds. Remove as they are done and serve on warm dessert dishes with 2 tablespoons Creative Cream Cheese, 2 teaspoons apricot puree (or other sugar-free conserve), 1 tablespoon walnuts and sprinkling of cinnamon per serving. (Sugar/honey-free fruit conserves are available from several sources. See back of book or check local natural food stores.) Extra pancakes may be frozen, wrapped in individual wax paper packets.

Serves 4 (2 pancakes per person).

LEKVAR (APRICOT PUREE)

½ cup dried apricots
½ cup water
1 teaspoon lemon juice

Soak apricots in ½ cup water for 2 hours. Bring to boil and simmer 10 minutes. Puree in blender with 1 teaspoon lemon juice. Serve on pancakes with Creative Cream Cheese and walnuts.

Serves 4.

Nutritive values per serving:	CHO (gm)	PRO (gm)	FAT (gm)	NA (mg)	CAL
	27	9.5	11	152	245
Food exchanges per serving:	1½ fruit + 1 bread + 1 medium-fat meat + 1 fat				

HUNGARY—MENU 4
KOMENY MAGOS LEVES (CARAWAY SEED SOUP)
SULTHAL BURGONYAVAL (BAKED HADDOCK WITH POTATOES)
KARALABE (BROWNED KOHLRABI)
ALMAKOMPOT MASMODON (STEWED APPLES)

KOMENY MAGOS LEVES
(CARAWAY SEED SOUP)

5 teaspoons caraway seeds
5 cups boiling water, divided
1 tablespoon Creative Butter (see index)
1½ tablespoons Cream of Wheat (farina), mixed with
    ¼ cup hot water
1 tablespoon Hungarian sweet paprika
1 egg (use only ½ yolk)
1 slice whole wheat toast
1 clove garlic, peeled

Place caraway seeds in 3 cups boiling water and simmer, covered, for 30 minutes. Strain, reserve liquid, and discard seeds. Heat Creative Butter in saucepan and stir in Cream of Wheat mixture. Add paprika, caraway water, and remaining boiling water. Stir until smooth and cook another 5 minutes. Meanwhile, beat the egg and add to it ½ cup of the soup. Return this to the soup pot and warm, but do not bring back to a boil. Rub garlic clove over the whole wheat toast on both sides and cut into croutons. Garnish soup with the croutons.

Serves 4.

Nutritive values per serving:	CHO (gm)	PRO (gm)	FAT (gm)	NA (mg)	CAL
	7.5	3	4	64	78
Food exchanges per serving:	½ bread + 1 fat				

SULTHAL BURGONYAVAL
(BAKED HADDOCK WITH POTATOES)

4 medium potatoes, peeled
1 onion, sliced thin
1 green pepper, seeded and cut into rings
Vegetable spray
2 tablespoons Creative Butter (see index)
Pepper to taste
¼ teaspoon dried thyme
1½ pounds haddock, cod, or other firm white fish
2 tomatoes, sliced thin
1 teaspoon Durkee's Imitation Bacon Chips
½ cup plain low-fat yogurt
1 tablespoon Hungarian sweet paprika

Parboil potatoes for 20 minutes. Drain and cut into thin slices. Parboil onion and green pepper for 5 minutes. Drain. Coat a 10-inch baking dish with vegetable spray. Heat oven to 400°F. Layer half the potatoes in the dish, then half the onion. Dot with Creative Butter and some pepper and thyme. Arrange fish on top of these layers and cover with green pepper, tomatoes, and remaining potatoes. Season again with pepper and top with bacon chips. Cover with aluminum foil and bake 20 minutes. Remove foil. Mix the yogurt and paprika and spread half on top of the potatoes. Replace foil and continue cooking 10 minutes more. Cover again with remaining yogurt and paprika and cook another 5 minutes, uncovered.

Serves 4.

Nutritive values per serving:	CHO (gm)	PRO (gm)	FAT (gm)	NA (mg)	CAL
	29	40	18	229	438

Food exchanges per serving: 1½ bread + 1½ vegetable + 5 lean meat + ½ fat

KARALABE
(BROWNED KOHLRABI)

1 tablespoon Creative Butter (see index)
1 pound kohlrabi (about 6 knobs), peeled and diced
½ teaspoon fructose
4 tablespoons chopped parsley
½ cup chicken broth (see index)

In a nonstick skillet, melt butter and stir in kohlrabi, fructose, parsley. Cover and cook over low heat 25 minutes, until kohlrabi is tender. Add chicken stock if necessary to keep from burning.

Serves 4.

Nutritive values per serving:	CHO (gm)	PRO (gm)	FAT (gm)	NA (mg)	CAL
	9	3	3	32	75
Food exchanges per serving:	2 vegetable + ½ fat				

ALMAKOMPOT MASMODON
(STEWED APPLES)

1½ cups water
3 tablespoons concentrated frozen apple juice
1 cinnamon stick
4 cooking apples, peeled, quartered, and cored
Rind of 1 lemon, sliced
½ cup dry white wine
¼ cup chopped almonds

In saucepan, combine water, apple juice concentrate, and cinnamon stick. Boil for 5 minutes. Add apples, lemon rind, and wine. Cover and simmer 10–15 minutes until apples are tender. Discard cinnamon and lemon rind and serve apples in glass dishes with almonds sprinkled on top.

Serves 6.

Nutritive values per serving:	CHO (gm)	PRO (gm)	FAT (gm)	NA (mg)	CAL
	20	1	3.5	2	116
Food exchanges per serving:	2 fruit + ¾ fat				

Menu 1

CHICKEN KORMA
Curried Coconut Chicken
KADDOO KI CHAT
Butternut Squash and Pepper Salad
PEAS PULAO
Rice with Green Peas
WATERMELON SORBET

Menu 2

TOMATO SHORBA
Tomato Soup
TAJ
Stuffed Sea Bass
STIR-FRIED EGGPLANT
PEACH PUDDING

Menu 3

TAMATOR KOOT
Tomatoes with Garlic and Mustard
LAMB KEBABS WITH SPINACH
ALOO KARI
Curried Potatoes
PAPAYA WITH TOASTED ALMONDS
AND GINGER

8

INDIA

India encompasses a land of wide variety and its cooking styles are no exception. In the northern Himalayan region, the climate provides abundant meat, milk products, and wheat. Breads of all kinds—griddle-baked, fried, leavened, and unleavened—contribute the carbohydrates. To the south, rice takes its place. As temperatures soar near the equator, hot spices help to keep people cool.

Beyond the climate, India's food patterns are often governed by religion. The majority practice Hinduism, and these people are vegetarians. Vegetables, therefore, compose simple to very intricate dishes. Where wealth is scarce, meat is not eaten except on rare feast days. Muslims eat meat but not pork. Dishes in this group called "Mogul-inspired" might be quite elaborate. In Pakistan, there is a dish prepared for a holy day made of vermicelli soaked in milk and covered with finely beaten silver leaf!

But the Indians also like fish and shrimp and chicken, seasoned with a combination of many perfumed spices. *Tandoori* cooking is a method of dry baking. *Dals* are made of dried beans, lentils, and chick-peas and are often meals in themselves. *Basmati* rice has a special nutty flavor and is the best of many types. Mangoes, papayas, watermelon, pineapples, and bananas are but a few of the Indian fruits and, with almonds, pistachios, semolina and rice puddings, provide dessert options.

The Indians use *ghee,* a clarified butter, for frying. We use vegetable oils that work as well. Tea is served at most meals. When Indians sit down at the table, they merely say, "Let's eat." But, when finished, they say, *"Khana achha tha!"* Thank you!

INDIA—MENU 1

CHICKEN KORMA (CURRIED COCONUT CHICKEN)
KADDOO KI CHAT (BUTTERNUT SQUASH AND
PEPPER SALAD)
PEAS PULAO (RICE WITH GREEN PEAS)
WATERMELON SORBET

CHICKEN KORMA
(CURRIED COCONUT CHICKEN)

1 pound boneless, skinless chicken breasts, cut into 4 pieces
1 teaspoon corn oil
1½ cups water, divided
1 tablespoon peeled and minced fresh gingerroot
2 teaspoons minced garlic
3 tablespoons unsalted, roasted cashews

STEP 1

Sauté chicken in oil in nonstick skillet. In blender, mix ½ cup water with ginger, garlic, and cashews. Add to chicken. Cover with 1 cup water and simmer for 15 minutes. Remove chicken and keep warm. Reduce sauce to 1 cup.

STEP 2

1 garlic clove, peeled
2 teaspoons peeled and minced fresh gingerroot
1 tablespoon corn oil
¼ teaspoon turmeric
2 cups water

In blender, mix garlic, ginger, oil, and turmeric at high speed. Add water. Transfer to saucepan and simmer until thickened.

STEP 3

¼ cup water (or more)
3 whole cloves
¼ teaspoon ground cinnamon
¼ teaspoon peppercorns
7 tablespoons finely chopped onion
¾ tablespoon poppy seeds
½ cup plain low-fat yogurt
¼ cup skim milk
¼ teaspoon coconut extract

In blender, mix at high speed ¼ cup water with cloves, cinnamon, peppercorns, onion and poppy seeds. Transfer to saucepan and add sauces from Step 1 and Step 2. Stir together. If too thick, add ¼ cup more water. Return chicken to sauce. Stir in yogurt, skim milk, and coconut extract. Heat but do not boil.

Serves 4.

Nutritive values per serving:	CHO (gm)	PRO (gm)	FAT (gm)	NA (mg)	CAL
	10	28	19	140	323
Food exchanges per serving:	⅓ skim milk + 1⅓ vegetable + 4 lean meat + 1 fat				

KADDOO KI CHAT
(BUTTERNUT SQUASH AND PEPPER SALAD)

1 small butternut or acorn squash
1 tablespoon concentrated frozen orange juice
⅓ cup fresh lime juice
¼ cup minced fresh mint
3 bell peppers, seeded and sliced (use combination of red,
**   yellow, and green peppers if available)**
2 tablespoons roasted almonds

Cut squash in half and steam until tender enough to peel readily. Seed and cut into ½-inch slices. Mix orange and lime juices with mint. Toss vegetables with sauce and garnish with almonds.

Serves 4.

Nutritive values per serving:	CHO (gm)	PRO (gm)	FAT (gm)	NA (mg)	CAL
	23	4	2.5	9	131
Food exchanges per serving:	¾ bread + 1½ vegetable + ⅓ fruit + ½ fat				

PEAS PULAO
(RICE WITH GREEN PEAS)

1½ cups chicken stock (see index)
¾ cup Basmati rice, well washed until water runs clear
1½ cups fresh or frozen peas

Bring stock to boil. Add rice. Cover and simmer over low heat for 30 minutes. Remove cover and add peas. Let rest 10 minutes, covered. Fluff and serve.

Serves 4.

Nutritive values per serving:	CHO (gm)	PRO (gm)	FAT (gm)	NA (mg)	CAL
	38	7	.5	15	185
Food exchanges per serving:	2½ bread + ¼ lean meat				

CHAPATTI*

¾ cup whole wheat flour
¼ teaspoon salt
1 tablespoon corn oil
¼ cup cold water

Sift flour and salt into a bowl and gradually add oil and water to make a soft, elastic dough. Roll into a ball after kneading 4–5 times, cover, and refrigerate for 30 minutes. Divide into 8 pieces and roll into little balls. Roll out each ball as thin as possible between 2 sheets of wax paper—each should be about 6 inches in diameter. Remove upper sheet of paper and cover with damp towel for 20 minutes. Bake 1 or 2 at a time on ungreased griddle, turning frequently until browned. Push down edges so that chapatti puff up in the middle. Cover to keep warm and serve.

Serves 4.

Nutritive values per serving:	CHO (gm)	PRO (gm)	FAT (gm)	NA (mg)	CAL
	16	2	3.5	123	104
Food exchanges per serving:	1 bread + ¾ fat				

---

*This is a typical Indian bread and may be used if extra bread exchange is desired.

WATERMELON SORBET

4 cups watermelon, peeled, seeded and cubed
4 ice cubes
2 tablespoons concentrated frozen apple juice

Puree watermelon in blender with ice cubes and apple juice concentrate. Pour into a metal ice tray and place in freezer. After 30 minutes, stir to break up crystals and return to freezer. Repeat process until ready to serve, then stir once again.

Serves 4.

Nutritive values per serving:	CHO (gm)	PRO (gm)	FAT (gm)	NA (mg)	CAL
	13	1	0	2	56
Food exchanges per serving:	1⅓ fruit				

INDIA—MENU 2
TOMATO SHORBA (TOMATO SOUP)
TAJ (STUFFED SEA BASS)
STIR-FRIED EGGPLANT
PEACH PUDDING

TOMATO SHORBA
(TOMATO SOUP)

6 tomatoes, peeled, seeded and chopped
2 cups skim milk
1 teaspoon ground cumin
¼ teaspoon ground coriander
1 teaspoon chopped fresh parsley

Blend together first 4 ingredients (don't puree!). Chill. Garnish with parsley and serve.

Serves 4.

Nutritive values per serving:	CHO (gm)	PRO (gm)	FAT (gm)	NA (mg)	CAL
	17	6.5	1	71	103
Food exchanges per serving:	½ skim milk + 2 vegetable				

TAJ
(STUFFED SEA BASS)

1 whole sea bass (about 3½ pounds), cleaned,
   head and tail intact
Salt
4 tablespoons fresh lemon juice
Vegetable spray
½ cup chopped onion
½ cup chopped blanched almonds
2 tablespoons peeled and chopped fresh gingerroot
½ teaspoon crushed mustard seed
¼ teaspoon freshly ground pepper
3 cups chopped cooked spinach
1½ teaspoons ground cinnamon
1 teaspoon ground cardamom
⅛ teaspoon coconut extract
4 slices lemon

Rinse bass in cold water and lightly salt cavity. Pat dry and marinate in lemon juice for 1 hour. Meanwhile, in a nonstick pan lightly coated with vegetable spray, sauté onion until translucent. Add almonds, ginger, mustard seed, and pepper. Mix together and heat. Add chopped spinach, cinnamon, cardamom, and coconut extract. If mixture is too dry, add a tablespoon of water. Remove fish from marinade, pat dry, and stuff with mixture. Place lemon slices over fish, cover with foil, and bake in preheated 325°F oven for 45 minutes. Fish is done if it flakes when pierced with a fork.

Serves 4.

Nutritive values per serving:	CHO (gm)	PRO (gm)	FAT (gm)	NA (mg)	CAL
	13	75	17	315	505
Food exchanges per serving:	2½ vegetable + 10 lean meat; omits 2½ fat				

STIR-FRIED EGGPLANT

1 large eggplant (1 pound)
1 teaspoon turmeric
1 teaspoon minced garlic
¼ teaspoon red pepper flakes
1 tablespoon corn oil

Cut eggplant into strips. Mix together turmeric, garlic, and red chili pepper. Moisten eggplant with water and toss with spices. Over high heat, heat oil in nonstick pan, quickly stir in eggplant, and cook until tender.

Serves 4.

Nutritive values per serving:	CHO (gm)	PRO (gm)	FAT (gm)	NA (mg)	CAL
	7	1.5	4	5	70
Food exchanges per serving:	1½ vegetable + ½ fat				

PEACH PUDDING

1 package unflavored gelatin
¼ cup cold water
2 cups peeled and mashed fresh peaches
1 cup plain low-fat yogurt
1 teaspoon pure vanilla extract
4 teaspoons concentrated frozen orange juice
1 tablespoon grated orange rind

Sprinkle gelatin over cold water. Stir over gentle heat until dissolved. Cool. Mix all remaining ingredients except orange rind, and then add cooled gelatin. Cover bowl and place in freezer until firm but not frozen solid, about 1–2 hours. Serve in individual dessert glasses garnished with orange rind.

Serves 4.

Nutritive values per serving:	CHO (gm)	PRO (gm)	FAT (gm)	NA (mg)	CAL
	16	5	1	41	93
Food exchanges per serving:	⅓ skim milk + 1¼ fruit + ⅓ lean meat				

INDIA—MENU 3

TAMATOR KOOT (TOMATOES WITH GARLIC AND MUSTARD)
LAMB KEBABS WITH SPINACH
ALOO KARI (CURRIED POTATOES)
PAPAYA WITH TOASTED ALMONDS AND GINGER

TAMATOR KOOT
(TOMATOES WITH GARLIC AND MUSTARD)

1 tablespoon corn oil
1 chili pepper, minced
5 garlic cloves, minced
1 tablespoon Dijon mustard
8 small plum tomatoes, seeded and cut into wide strips

In a nonstick skillet heat oil and sauté chili pepper and garlic until limp. Then add mustard and stir. Add tomatoes and heat. Serve at room temperature.

Serves 4.

Nutritive values per serving:	CHO (gm)	PRO (gm)	FAT (gm)	NA (mg)	CAL
	11	2	4	24	88
Food exchanges per serving:	2 vegetable + ¾ fat				

LAMB KEBABS WITH SPINACH

1½ pounds lean lamb, cut into cubes, all fat removed
2 tablespoons corn oil
3 tablespoons lemon juice
¼ cup tarragon vinegar
1 tablespoon garlic, crushed, divided
2 cups very finely chopped cooked spinach
¼ tablespoon minced onion
1 tablespoon peeled and minced fresh gingerroot
1 cup plain low-fat yogurt
1-2 tablespoons skim milk

Marinate the lamb cubes in the oil, lemon juice, vinegar, and ½ tablespoon garlic for 3 hours. Thread lamb cubes on skewers and broil for 5 minutes, turning. In the meantime, heat spinach in a saucepan and add ½ tablespoon garlic, onions, and ginger. Mix in the yogurt and enough of the milk to make a sauce of medium consistency. Heat but do not boil. Pour over the lamb and serve.

Serves 4.

Nutritive values per serving:	CHO (gm)	PRO (gm)	FAT (gm)	NA (mg)	CAL
	8	34.5	12	186	278
Food exchanges per serving:	1½ vegetable + 4½ lean meat; omits ⅓ fat				

ALOO KARI
(CURRIED POTATOES)

½ teaspoon corn oil
1 teaspoon black mustard seeds
1 pound new potatoes, boiled in their jackets until tender
2 teaspoons curry powder

Coat a nonstick skillet with oil. Fry mustard seeds until they stop popping. Cut the potatoes into thick slices. Add to pan with 2 teaspoons of curry and toss until warmed.

Serves 4.

Nutritive values per serving:	CHO (gm)	PRO (gm)	FAT (gm)	NA (mg)	CAL
	15	2	1.5	3	82
Food exchanges per serving:	1 bread + ⅓ fat				

PAPAYA WITH TOASTED ALMONDS AND GINGER

2 cups fresh papaya or cantaloupe, peeled, seeded, and cut
    into chunks
4 tablespoons toasted almonds
1 cup seedless green grapes
½-inch piece of gingerroot, peeled and chopped
1 tablespoon lime juice

Mix all ingredients together, chill, and serve.

Serves 4.

Nutritive values per serving:	CHO (gm)	PRO (gm)	FAT (gm)	NA (mg)	CAL
	16	1.5	5.5	1	120
Food exchanges per serving:	1⅔ fruit + 1 fat				

Menu 1
BAYEM CHA
Spinach Broth (Java)
TAHN TELOR/SAMBAL KACONG
Tofu Omelet with Spicy Peanut Sauce (Java)
BAHMI GORENG
Indonesian Fried Noodles
PAPAYA ICE

Menu 2
GADO GADO
Indonesian Vegetable Salad
BAKED BANANAS

Menu 3
BANGKO IKAN LAUT
Steamed Seafood Envelopes
OSENG OSENG
Spicy Squash Saute
KETIMUM BISTEK
Cucumber Steak
KOLAK
Sweet Potato and Banana Pudding

9

INDONESIA

The Indonesian cook employs ingredients and cooking techniques similar to those of the Chinese and Indians. The *sambals,* or side dishes, are indispensable and unite rich assortments of herbs, spices, and grasses that grow in Southeast Asia. Pepper, chili, garlic, ginger, cinnamon, cloves, and curry are used in profusion. Coconut milk is an important ingredient, but here we must be wary. The coconut is high in saturated fat. Our alternative combines skim milk with coconut extract, retaining the taste but eliminating the fat factor.

The climate of the Indonesian islands yields an abundance of rice, soybeans, fruits, and vegetables. The Indonesians have amalgamated foods that were brought to the islands by myriads of settlers, most notably the Dutch. We have not offered all the splendors of the famous national feast, *rijsttafel,* for that in itself would take an entire book! But we have served up several interesting meals, and we wish you *trimakasi!*

INDONESIA—MENU 1

BAYEM CHA (SPINACH BROTH) (JAVA)
TAHN TELOR/SAMBAL KACONG (TOFU OMELET WITH SPICY
PEANUT SAUCE) (JAVA)
BAHMI GORENG (INDONESIAN FRIED NOODLES)
PAPAYA ICE

BAYEM CHA
(SPINACH BROTH)

½ teaspoon corn oil
3 cloves garlic, crushed
3 cups chicken broth (see index)
1 teaspoon concentrated frozen apple juice
¼ teaspoon freshly ground pepper
½ pound fresh spinach, washed well
1 scallion, chopped (white part only)

Heat corn oil in nonstick skillet and brown garlic in it. Add chicken broth, apple juice, and pepper and bring to a boil. Add spinach with water that clings to leaves and stir until leaves are wilted. Serve in warm bowls, topped with scallions.

Serves 4.

Nutritive values per serving:	CHO (gm)	PRO (gm)	FAT (gm)	NA (mg)	CAL
	5.5	4	1	41	47
Food exchanges per serving:	1 vegetable + 1 lean meat				

TAHN TELOR
(TOFU OMELET)

8 ounces tofu (bean curd), cubed
4 eggs (use only 2 yolks), beaten
1 tablespoon chopped parsley
2 scallions, sliced
1 teaspoon low-sodium soy sauce
¼ teaspoon corn oil
Sambal Kacong (Spicy Peanut Sauce) (see following recipe)

Dry the tofu and mix with beaten eggs, parsley, scallions, and soy sauce. Heat oil in large nonstick skillet. Pour mixture into skillet and cook about 2 minutes, until set. Fold or roll the omelet over and brown on other side. Remove from heat, divide into 4 portions, and serve with Sambal Kacong.

Serves 4.

Nutritive values per serving:	CHO (gm)	PRO (gm)	FAT (gm)	NA (mg)	CAL
	3	10	6	104	106
Food exchanges per serving:	½ vegetable + 1 medium-fat meat + ½ fat				

SAMBAL KACONG (SPICY PEANUT SAUCE)

2 tablespoons crunchy peanut butter
2 tablespoons water
1 clove garlic, crushed
2 tablespoons low-sodium soy sauce
2 teaspoons lemon juice
2 teaspoons concentrated frozen apple juice
1 teaspoon dried red pepper flakes

Stir peanut butter and water together to form a paste. Add remaining ingredients and mix together.

Serves 4.

Nutritive values per serving:	CHO (gm)	PRO (gm)	FAT (gm)	NA (mg)	CAL
	4	2.5	4	275	62
Food exchanges per serving:	½ fruit + 1 fat				

BAHMI GORENG
(INDONESIAN FRIED NOODLES)

8 ounces rice stick noodles (Chinese vermicelli)
1 teaspoon sunflower seed oil
1 onion, chopped fine
2 cloves garlic, crushed
1-inch piece fresh gingerroot, peeled and minced
1 teaspoon dried chili powder
½ teaspoon dried shrimp paste (optional)
1 large stalk celery, sliced
2 leaves Chinese or white cabbage, shredded
2 tablespoons low-sodium soy sauce
2 scallions, chopped
1 tablespoon chopped peanuts

Cook noodles in boiling water until tender, 3–5 minutes. Drain, rinse under cold water, and set aside. In nonstick skillet, heat sunflower seed oil and in it sauté onion, garlic, ginger, and dried red pepper flakes for about 3 minutes. Stir in shrimp paste and sauté 2 more minutes. Add celery and cabbage and stir-fry another 2 minutes. Then add noodles and stir together, cooking for 2–3 minutes more. Add soy sauce and serve with garnish of scallions and peanuts.

Serves 4.

Nutritive values per serving:	CHO (gm)	PRO (gm)	FAT (gm)	NA (mg)	CAL
	34	4	1	133	105
Food exchanges per serving:	1 bread + 1 vegetable + 1 lean meat				

PAPAYA ICE

1 ripe papaya, peeled, seeded
6 ice cubes
¼ teaspoon pure vanilla extract
1 tablespoon lemon juice

Cut papaya into chunks and reserve seeds. Place ice cubes in blender and process to shave. Add papaya and puree with ice. Add vanilla and lemon juice. Pour into ice tray and place in freezer for about an hour or so. Break up crystals periodically with fork. Repeat before serving in individual glass dessert dishes. (If desired, use reserved seeds as topping.)

Serves 4.

Nutritive values per serving:	CHO (gm)	PRO (gm)	FAT (gm)	NA (mg)	CAL
	8	.5	0	2	34
Food exchanges per serving:	¾ fruit				

INDONESIA—MENU 2
GADO GADO (INDONESIAN VEGETABLE SALAD)
BAKED BANANAS

GADO GADO
(INDONESIAN VEGETABLE SALAD)

In this quintessentially Indonesian salad, any combination of fresh vegetables may be used. The following are traditional:

½ cup fresh string beans, trimmed
½ cup carrots, scraped and cut into rounds
½ cup cauliflower flowerets
1 cup shredded cabbage
1 cup bean sprouts
1 cup sliced cooked potatoes
½ cup peeled and sliced cucumber

GARNISH

8 ounces tofu, cubed and lightly browned
2 scallions, chopped
1 tomato, sliced
2 small hard-boiled eggs, sliced

Blanch string beans, carrots, and cauliflower separately for 3 minutes each. Run under cold water, then drain in colander. Blanch shredded cabbage and sprouts separately for 2 minutes each, then drain. Arrange cooked vegetables in layers in a deep serving dish, placing cabbage on the bottom. Next, arrange the beans, cauliflower, carrots, potatoes, and cucumber and top with cooked sprouts. Brown tofu cubes in nonstick skillet and strew over the sprouts. Then sprinkle scallions on top. Around the borders of the serving dish, alternate tomato and egg slices for a colorful presentation.

DRESSING

1 clove garlic
1 fresh green chili, sliced and seeded (wear gloves to prevent burns)
1 teaspoon low-sodium soy sauce
¾ cup skim milk, mixed with 1 teaspoon coconut extract
⅛ teaspoon shrimp paste (optional)
4 tablespoons chunky peanut butter
2 teaspoons fresh lemon juice
1-inch-square piece lemon zest

Crush garlic and chili pepper with mortar and pestle. Place in blender with soy sauce, coconut milk, shrimp paste, peanut butter, and lemon juice. Blend into sauce. Pour this into small saucepan with the lemon zest and cook over medium heat for 10 minutes until sauce thickens. Remove from heat but keep warm. Pour over vegetables and serve.

Serves 4.

Nutritive values per serving:	CHO (gm)	PRO (gm)	FAT (gm)	NA (mg)	CAL
	23	17.5	12.5	136	275
Food exchanges per serving:	⅓ milk + 2½ vegetable + ½ bread + 2 medium-fat meat				

BAKED BANANAS

1 tablespoon Creative Butter (see index)
1 teaspoon fructose
¼ teaspoon ground cloves
2 tablespoons fresh orange juice
1 teaspoon fresh lemon juice
1-inch piece fresh gingerroot, peeled and minced
2 small ripe bananas, peeled and halved lengthwise
Vegetable spray

Mix Creative Butter with fructose and beat in cloves, orange and lemon juices, and ginger. Place bananas on vegetable-sprayed baking dish and spread sauce over them. Bake in preheated 375°F oven for 15 minutes, until bananas are cooked through and sauce bubbles. Remove from oven and serve at once.

Serves 4.

Nutritive values per serving:	CHO (gm)	PRO (gm)	FAT (gm)	NA (mg)	CAL
	24	1	3	21	127
Food exchanges per serving:	2½ fruit + ½ fat				

INDONESIA—MENU 3
BONGKO IKAN LAUT (STEAMED SEAFOOD ENVELOPES)
OSENG OSENG (SPICY SQUASH SAUTE)
KETIMUM BISTEK (CUCUMBER STEAK)
KOLAK (SWEET POTATO AND BANANA PUDDING)

BONGKO IKAN LAUT
(STEAMED SEAFOOD ENVELOPES)

1 pound fish fillets such as flounder or sole
½ pound large shrimp
2 tablespoons sliced onion
1 clove garlic, chopped
½ cup sliced tomatoes
1 teaspoon dried red pepper flakes
1 teaspoon fructose
½ teaspoon turmeric
4 teaspoons fresh lime juice
2 teaspoons peeled and chopped fresh gingerroot
1 lemon, quartered

Cut fish into 3-inch pieces. Shell and devein shrimp. Mix remaining ingredients except lemon and add fish and shrimp. Divide mixture into 2 equal portions and place on 2 15-inch squares of aluminum foil. Fold ends toward the center and seal by twisting together. Place in steamer basket and cook over hot water for about 20 minutes. Open envelopes and serve in foil with lemon wedges.

Serves 4.

Nutritive values per serving:	CHO (gm)	PRO (gm)	FAT (gm)	NA (mg)	CAL
	7	29	1	295	153
Food exchanges per serving:	½ vegetable + ⅓ fruit + 4 lean meat; omits 2 fat				

OSENG OSENG
(SPICY SQUASH SAUTE)

¼ teaspoon corn oil
¼ cup sliced onion
1 clove garlic, minced
1 teaspoon low-sodium soy sauce
¼ teaspoon freshly ground pepper
1 pound yellow squash, cut into chunks
¼ cup chopped tomatoes
¼ cup water
½ cup cellophane noodles, soaked in hot water for 10
    minutes and drained.

Heat corn oil in nonstick skillet and sauté onion and garlic in it. Add soy sauce and pepper and stir for 2 minutes. Add squash, tomatoes, water, and drained noodles. Stir over medium heat for 5 minutes, until squash is tender but still crunchy.

Serves 4.

Nutritive values per serving:	CHO (gm)	PRO (gm)	FAT (gm)	NA (mg)	CAL
	20	4	1	133	105
Food exchanges per serving:	1⅕ bread + ½ vegetable				

KETIMUM BISTEK
(CUCUMBER STEAK)

2 large cucumbers, peeled, halved lengthwise, and seeded
1 teaspoon salt
½ teaspoon Creative Butter (see index)
¼ cup sliced onion
½ green chili, seeded and diced (wear rubber gloves to
     prevent burns)
1 clove garlic, chopped
¾ cup water
1 tablespoon rice wine vinegar
1 tablespoon low-sodium soy sauce
¼ teaspoon freshly ground nutmeg
¼ teaspoon ground cloves
¼ teaspoon freshly ground black pepper

Prick cucumbers in a few places and rub with salt. Place in covered bowl and let stand 10 minutes. Drain off water and rub off salt. Cut into ½-inch-thick slices. Heat butter in nonstick skillet and sauté cucumbers in it until soft. Remove from pan. Meanwhile, blend remaining ingredients into a sauce and cook down in small saucepan until liquid is reduced by half. Pour warm sauce over cucumbers and serve.

Serves 4.

Nutritive values per serving:	CHO (gm)	PRO (gm)	FAT (gm)	NA (mg)	CAL
	4	1	1.5	137	25
Food exchanges per serving:	1 vegetable				

KOLAK
(SWEET POTATO AND BANANA PUDDING)

½ **pound sweet potatoes, peeled and cut into ½-inch cubes**
¼ **cup water**
2 **ripe bananas, peeled and cut into ¼-inch pieces**
¾ **cup skim milk, mixed with ½ teaspoon coconut extract**
1 **stick cinnamon (about 1 inch)**
1 **tablespoon concentrated frozen orange juice**
¼ **teaspoon pure vanilla extract**
6 **pecan halves**

Boil sweet potatoes in water for 20 minutes, until tender. If water has not evaporated, drain off any excess. Add bananas, coconut milk, cinnamon stick, and orange juice. Cook about 15 minutes or until thick. Remove cinnamon stick and add vanilla. Puree in blender and serve warm or chilled, each serving topped with a pecan half.

Serves 6.

Nutritive values per serving:	CHO (gm)	PRO (gm)	FAT (gm)	NA (mg)	CAL
	23	2	.5	3	105
Food exchanges per serving:	1 bread + 1 fruit				

Menu 1

ANTIPASTO FREDDO
Cold Antipasto

POLLO ALLA CACCIATORA
Chicken Hunter's Style

PANCROCINO
Garlic Bread

MELECOTTE
Baked Apples

Menu 2

CONCHIGLIE ALLA FIORENTINO
Pasta Shells with Spinach and Ricotta

SCALLOPINI DE VITELLO AL MADERO
Veal in Madeira Sauce

INSALATA VERDE
Mixed Green Salad

GRANITA DE CAFFE
Coffee Ice

Menu 3

POLENTA CON FUNGHI
Cornmeal Pudding with Mushrooms

SPADA ALLA GRIGLIA
Grilled Swordfish

FAGIOLINI CON PIGNOLI
Green Beans with Pine Nuts

MELONE CON FORMAGGIO
Melon with Cheese

Menu 4

STRACCIATELLA
Roman Egg Soup

SCAMPI
Shrimp

INSALATA DI BROCCOLI
Broccoli Salad

CREMA D' ANANASSO
Pineapple Cream

Menu 5

UMIDO DI CONIGLIO
Rabbit Stew

SCAROLA
Escarole

PERE PIPIERE
Stuffed Pears

Menu 6

OSTRICE OREGANATA
Oysters in Oregano Sauce

LASAGNA
Noodle Pudding

TUTTI FRUTTI
Fresh Fruit

Menu 7

ZUPPA DI POLLO CON SCAROLA
Chicken and Escarole Soup

MELANZANA PARMIGIANA
Eggplant Parmesan

ZITI CON BASILICO
Macaroni with Basil

GELATO VERDE E ROSSO
Kiwifruit and Grape Ice

10

ITALY

The *cucina* of Italy is one of the oldest in all Europe. Historically, food was one of the few pleasures available to the ancient Italian families. Meals had to be prepared quickly to prevent spoilage and to nourish many hungry hard-workers. Whatever the ingredients and however different the regional fillips, the meals were always tasty and abundant. *Abbondanza!* Celebrate! Good eating is the byword from Abruzzi to Venice, and the password everywhere is *mangia!*

The basic recipes of traditional Italian cookery endure, although many have been embellished. Flavor and color play an important part in the presentation of an Italian meal. Fish, veal, and cheese are the preferred proteins. Fresh vegetables, herbs, and fruits provide nutritious accompaniments. Rice and noodles—the ever-popular pasta—provide the carbohydrates, as do the fresh, nourishing Italian breads. While Italian chefs prefer olive oil and butter, our meals are lighter, cooked with vegetable oils. The Italians do not demand sweet desserts except on special occasions. They prefer, as do we, fresh fruits. *Buon apetito!*

ITALY—MENU 1

ANTIPASTO FREDDO (COLD ANTIPASTO)
POLLO ALLA CACCIATORA (CHICKEN HUNTER'S STYLE)
PANCROCINO (GARLIC BREAD)
MELECOTTE (BAKED APPLES)

ANTIPASTO FREDDO
(COLD ANTIPASTO)

6 leaves romaine lettuce or chicory, washed
1 large ripe tomato, sliced thin
2 stalks celery, sliced diagonally
2 stalks fennel, sliced diagonally
12 radishes, cut into roses (see Chapter 21)
½ cup chick-peas, drained if using canned garbanzos
½ cup red kidney beans, drained if using canned beans
1 red pepper, cored and cut into strips
1 green pepper, cored and cut into thin strips
6 black olives
6 green olives
1 tablespoon capers, drained and rinsed
½ cup diced skim-milk mozzarella cheese
Italian Dressing (see recipe below)

Arrange lettuce on large platter. Make small mounds of each vegetable around the platter. Strew the vegetables with olives, capers, and mozzarella. Other vegetables may be used as desired. Serve with Italian Dressing.

Serves 6.

Nutritive values per serving:	CHO (gm)	PRO (gm)	FAT (gm)	NA (mg)	CAL
	15.5	8	5	305	139
Food exchanges per serving:	1 bread + 1 medium-fat meat				

ITALIAN DRESSING

1 clove garlic, crushed
6 tablespoons balsamic vinegar
Juice of 1 lemon
¼ teaspoon freshly ground black pepper
2 tablespoons virgin olive oil
¼ teaspoon dried oregano
¼ teaspoon dried basil

Mix garlic, vinegar, and lemon juice with pepper. Shake well. Add olive oil and herbs. Shake again before serving.

Makes about ⅔ cup (1-2 tablespoons per serving, as desired).

Nutritive values per serving:	CHO (gm)	PRO (gm)	FAT (gm)	NA (mg)	CAL
	1	.5	3	0	33
Food exchanges per serving:	¾ fat				

POLLO ALLA CACCIATORA
(CHICKEN HUNTER'S STYLE)

1 3-pound frying chicken, skinned and cut into pieces
1 teaspoon paprika
2 cloves garlic, minced
2 cups Italian plum tomatoes in puree
2 tablespoons fresh oregano or 1 teaspoon dried
1 teaspoon pepper
½ cup chopped parsley
½ teaspoon olive oil
1 medium onion, sliced
½ pound mushrooms, sliced

Season chicken pieces with paprika. Sprinkle with garlic pieces. Brown a few minutes on each side under broiler. While chicken is browning, combine tomatoes with oregano and pepper. Transfer chicken and add with parsley to this sauce. Cook, covered, over low heat for 30 minutes, until chicken is tender. Meanwhile, in a nonstick skillet, heat olive oil and sauté onion in it. Add mushrooms and cook until they are lightly browned and onions are transparent. Add to chicken and tomatoes, stir together, and serve. Reduce if sauce is too thin by cooking down, uncovered.

Serves 4.

Nutritive values per serving:	CHO (gm)	PRO (gm)	FAT (gm)	NA (mg)	CAL
	12	55	11	281	387
Food exchanges per serving:	2½ vegetable + 7 lean meat; omits 1½ fat				

PANCROCINO
(GARLIC BREAD)

1-day-old French Bread/Italian Bread (see index)
6 cloves garlic, peeled
Pepper
1 tablespoon olive oil
1 tablespoon finely chopped parsley

Slice bread into twelve pieces. The pieces should be about ½ inch thick. Brown both sides of each piece under the broiler. When toasted, remove from heat and rub both sides of bread with garlic cloves. Sprinkle with pepper. Mix the olive oil with parsley. When ready to serve, paint some of this on the bread slices with a pastry brush.

Serves 6 (2 slices per serving).

Nutritive values per serving:	CHO (gm)	PRO (gm)	FAT (gm)	NA (mg)	CAL
	23	3.5	2	165	124
Food exchanges per serving:	1½ bread + ⅖ fat				

MELECOTTE
(BAKED APPLES)

2 firm, large baking apples (Rome)
2 tablespoons raisins, plumped in ½ cup red wine
4 whole cloves
½ teaspoon ground allspice
½ teaspoon ground cinnamon
½ teaspoon freshly ground nutmeg

TOPPING

¼ cup part-skim ricotta cheese
1 tablespoon concentrated frozen apple juice
1 tablespoon grape juice

Wash and core apples. Cut away skin ½ inch from the top of each apple and prick sides with a fork. Place close together in a baking dish. Remove raisins from wine, reserving wine, and drop a few into each apple along with 2 cloves. Mix spices together and sprinkle over the apples. Pour wine over apples and bake in preheated 350°F oven for 40 minutes, until apples are soft and puffy. Baste several times during cooking and again before serving.

Beat topping ingredients together until smooth. Cut apples in half, and pass bowl of topping when serving apples.

Serves 4.

Nutritive values per serving:	CHO (gm)	PRO (gm)	FAT (gm)	NA (mg)	CAL
	15.5	1.5	1.5	17	82
Food exchanges per serving:	1½ fruit + ⅓ fat				

ITALY—MENU 2

CONCHIGLIE ALLA FIORENTINO (PASTA SHELLS WITH
SPINACH AND RICOTTA)
SCALLOPINI DE VITELLO AL MADERO (VEAL IN
MADEIRA SAUCE)
INSALATA VERDE (MIXED GREEN SALAD)
GRANITA DI CAFFE (COFFEE ICE)

CONCHIGLIE ALLA FIORENTINO
(PASTA SHELLS WITH SPINACH AND RICOTTA)

½ **pound fresh spinach, washed well**
⅛ **cup part-skim ricotta cheese**
⅛ **cup grated sapsago or Romano cheese**
5 ounces spinach noodle shells
Pepper

Detach stems from spinach and discard. Rinse well under
cold water to remove all sand. Squeeze out excess water and
place spinach in saucepan with just the water remaining on
leaves. Cover and cook over medium heat until tender, about
10 minutes. Drain well in sieve. When cool, chop fine and set
aside. Mix with ricotta and grated cheese. Meanwhile, cook
shells for 12–14 minutes in boiling water until tender but still
firm. When cooked, drain in colander. Transfer to warm bowl.
Add spinach, cheese mixture, and pepper to taste. Stir well and
serve.

Serves 4

Nutritive values per serving:	CHO (gm)	PRO (gm)	FAT (gm)	NA (mg)	CAL
	29	10	3	136	183
Food exchanges per serving:	1¾ bread + ½ vegetable + 1 lean meat				

SCALLOPINI DI VITELLO AL MADERO
(VEAL IN MADEIRA SAUCE)

1 teaspoon virgin olive oil
1 medium onion, chopped fine
1 pound veal scallopini, sliced very thin
2 cloves garlic, minced
2 tablespoons chopped Italian parsley
¼ teaspoon freshly ground pepper
½ cup Madeira wine
1 cup sugarless tomato juice
1 lemon, scored and sliced thin, for garnish (see note below)
6 sprigs parsley for garnish

Heat oil in large nonstick skillet. Brown onion and then remove from pan and set aside. Brown veal slices quickly on each side. Add garlic, chopped parsley, cooked onion, and pepper, then the wine. Cook for 2 minutes over high heat and add tomato juice. Simmer to reduce over low heat for about 5 minutes. If sauce needs further reduction, remove the veal and cook sauce until thick. Serve veal with sauce at once, with slices of lemon and parsley sprigs as garnish.

Note: To score lemons, slice about ⅛ inch along the long sides and discard the slivers. When the lemon is sliced into rounds, the effect will be a decorative scalloped edge.

Serves 4.

Nutritive values per serving:	CHO (gm)	PRO (gm)	FAT (gm)	NA (mg)	CAL
	9	24	11.5	206	236
Food exchanges per serving:	2 vegetable + 3½ lean meat				

INSALATA VERDE
(MIXED GREEN SALAD)

1 bunch arugula (if not available, use watercress)
2 endives, bottoms cut off, leaves opened
4 leaves chicory, broken into small pieces
6-8 tablespoons Italian Dressing (see index)

Wash greens well and pat dry. Toss greens together with dressing and serve chilled.

Serves 4.

Nutritive values per serving:	CHO (gm)	PRO (gm)	FAT (gm)	NA (mg)	CAL
	4	2	6	19	78
Food exchanges per serving:	1 vegetable + 1 fat				

GRANITA DI CAFFE
(COFFEE ICE)

**3 cups Italian espresso coffee (decaffeinated may be
  substituted if desired)**
3 drops almond extract
1 drop pure vanilla extract
2 tablespoons chopped almonds
1 tablespoon grated lemon rind

Mix coffee with almond and vanilla extracts and pour into
metal ice tray. Place in freezer compartment about 2 hours
before serving. Every 20 minutes or so, stir with a fork to break
up crystals. Repeat just before serving. Divide among 4 sherbet
glasses. Top with crushed almonds and lemon zest.

Serves 4.

Nutritive values per serving:	CHO (gm)	PRO (gm)	FAT (gm)	NA (mg)	CAL
	1	—	—	—	4
Food exchanges per serving:	free				

ITALY—MENU 3
POLENTA CON FUNGHI (CORNMEAL PUDDING
WITH MUSHROOMS)
SPADA ALLA GRIGLIA (GRILLED SWORDFISH)
FAGIOLINI CON PIGNOLI (GREEN BEANS WITH PINE NUTS)
MELONE CON FORMAGGIO (MELON WITH CHEESE)

POLENTA CON FUNGHI
(CORNMEAL PUDDING WITH MUSHROOMS)

1 teaspoon olive oil
1 pound mushrooms, cleaned, trimmed and sliced
2 cups canned Italian plum tomatoes
¼ teaspoon freshly ground pepper
4 cups water, divided
1 cup yellow cornmeal
4 tablespoons grated sapsago or Romano cheese

Heat olive oil in nonstick skillet. Brown mushrooms in oil.
Slowly stir in tomatoes and pepper. Simmer 20–30 minutes
over low heat. Meanwhile, bring 3 cups of water to the boil in a
saucepan. Mix cornmeal with 1 cup of cold water and gradually
stir this into the hot water in saucepan. Bring back to a boil and
cook until thick, stirring constantly. Cover and lower heat.
Cook slowly for 10–15 minutes. Transfer cooked cornmeal to
warm platter, top with tomato sauce, sprinkle with grated
cheese, and serve.

Serves 4.

Nutritive values per serving:	CHO (gm)	PRO (gm)	FAT (gm)	NA (mg)	CAL
	40	10.5	6	838	256
Food exchanges per serving:	2 bread + 2 vegetable + 1 fat				

SPADA ALLA GRIGLIA
(GRILLED SWORDFISH)

1 pound swordfish steak
2 tablespoons virgin olive oil
Juice of 2 large lemons
2 teaspoons chopped fresh oregano or ½ teaspoon dried
1 teaspoon chopped fresh mint or ¼ teaspoon dried
Freshly ground pepper to taste
1 tablespoon chopped basil or 1 teaspoon dried
1 tablespoon capers, rinsed and drained
6 sprigs parsley
1 lemon, scored and sliced into rounds (see note below)

Have fish sliced 1 inch thick. Wash and pat dry. Blend together oil, lemon juice, oregano, mint, pepper, basil. Brush fish with this sauce and preheat broiler. Place fish on broiler pan about 4 inches under broiler. Broil about 5 minutes and then turn and brush again with sauce. Return to broiler until fish is cooked, about 7 minutes more. Brush again with dressing before serving, strew with capers, and garnish with parsley sprigs and lemon slices. Serve on warm platter.

Note: To score lemons, slice about ⅛ inch along the long sides and discard the slivers. When the lemon is sliced into rounds, the effect will be a decorative scalloped edge.

Serves 4.

Nutritive values per serving:	CHO (gm)	PRO (gm)	FAT (gm)	NA (mg)	CAL
	4.5	22.5	11.5	36	212
Food exchanges per serving:	3 lean meat + ½ fruit + ½ fat				

FAGIOLINI CON PIGNOLI
(GREEN BEANS WITH PINE NUTS)

1 pound green beans or Italian beans
2 cups cold water
¼ cup pine nuts, toasted
2 tablespoons chopped Italian parsley
1 clove garlic, minced
Juice of 2 lemons
Freshly ground pepper

Cut ends off beans and wash thoroughly. Leave whole. Bring 2 cups of water to boil in saucepan. Place beans in steamer basket over boiling water and cover. Cook over medium heat about 8–10 minutes or until beans are bright green but still crisp. Meanwhile, place pine nuts in small skillet and toast until brown. Shake so that they do not burn. Wrap in paper towel before using to absorb any oils. Chop parsley and garlic together. Mix with lemon juice and a grind or 2 of fresh pepper. When beans are ready, drain in colander, place in warm bowl, and toss with lemon mixture. Garnish with pine nuts and serve.

Serves 4.

Nutritive values per serving:	CHO (gm)	PRO (gm)	FAT (gm)	NA (mg)	CAL
	11.5	7	7	45	137
Food exchanges per serving:	2 vegetable + ½ lean meat + 1⅓ fat				

MELONE CON FORMAGGIO
(MELON WITH CHEESE)

1 ripe cantaloupe
¼ pound New Holland low-fat cheese
1 lemon, cut into wedges

Slice melon into wedges about 2 inches wide at center. Remove seeds. Divide cheese and place a bit of it next to each serving. Top melon slices with lemon wedges.

Serves 4.

Nutritive values per serving:	CHO (gm)	PRO (gm)	FAT (gm)	NA (mg)	CAL
	10.5	8	6.5	1013	133
Food exchanges per serving:	1 fruit + 1¼ medium-fat meat				

ITALY—MENU 4
STRACCIATELLA (ROMAN EGG SOUP)
SCAMPI (SHRIMP)
INSALATA DI BROCCOLI (BROCCOLI SALAD)
CREMA D' ANANASSO (PINEAPPLE CREAM)

STRACCIATELLA
(ROMAN EGG SOUP)

4 cups chicken broth (see index)
1 tablespoon chopped fresh oregano or ½ teaspoon dried
1 cup cooked penne or other small pasta
2 eggs (use only 1 yolk)
1 teaspoon finely chopped Italian parsley
⅛ teaspoon white pepper
1 tablespoon lemon juice
1 tablespoon grated sapsago or Romano cheese

Bring chicken broth and oregano to a boil in saucepan. Add cooked pasta to the broth. Stir. Bring back to boil. Lightly beat together the eggs, parsley, pepper, lemon juice, and cheese. Add to this ¼ cup of the hot broth. Just before serving, whisk this mixture back into the soup. Serve in warm bowls.

Serves 4.

Nutritive values per serving:	CHO (gm)	PRO (gm)	FAT (gm)	NA (mg)	CAL
	11	4.5	2	16	80
Food exchanges per serving:	⅔ bread + ½ medium-fat meat				

SCAMPI
(SHRIMP)

4 cloves garlic, minced
1 teaspoon dry mustard
¼ teaspoon freshly ground black pepper
2 tablespoons finely chopped parsley
3 tablespoons fresh lemon juice
3 tablespoons sunflower seed oil
1 pound jumbo shrimp, shelled, deveined, and washed
Lemon wedges

To make marinade, combine all ingredients but shrimp and lemon wedges. Place cleaned raw shrimp and marinade in bowl, cover, and refrigerate for about 2 hours. Remove shrimp from marinade, reserving marinade. Heat large, nonstick skillet. Place shrimp with a little of the marinade in the skillet and quickly cook over high heat until shrimp is pink on all sides, about 2–3 minutes. (Shrimp get tough if overcooked!) Serve at once with lemon wedges.

Serves 4.

Nutritive values per serving:	CHO (gm)	PRO (gm)	FAT (gm)	NA (mg)	CAL
	3.5	22	11.5	161	206
Food exchanges per serving:	3 lean meat + 1 fat				

INSALATA DI BROCCOLI
(BROCCOLI SALAD)

1 pound broccoli
3 tablespoons virgin olive oil
3 tablespoons lemon juice
1 clove garlic, sliced
⅛ teaspoon pepper

Trim stalks and break broccoli into small flowerets. Bring water to boil in large saucepan and place broccoli in a steamer basket. Cover and cook 3–4 minutes, until bright green. Broccoli should not be overcooked or limp. Remove and run under cold water to stop cooking process. Drain. Chill in refrigerator. Mix together the remaining ingredients. Spoon over chilled broccoli and serve.

Serves 4.

Nutritive values per serving:	CHO (gm)	PRO (gm)	FAT (gm)	NA (mg)	CAL
	8	4	11	17	147
Food exchanges per serving:	2 vegetable + 2 fat				

CREMA D' ANANASSO
(PINEAPPLE CREAM)

1 cup canned, unsweetened pineapple chunks, drained
8 ounces unsweetened evaporated skim milk
Juice of 1 lime
1 teaspoon pure vanilla extract
1 envelope unflavored gelatin
2 tablespoons cold water
1 teaspoon grated lemon rind

In blender, combine pineapple chunks, milk, lime juice, and vanilla extract and puree in blender. Reserve 4 tablespoons pineapple chunks for topping. Sprinkle gelatin over cold water in a cup. Let stand a few minutes to gel and then place cup in a bowl of hot water to dissolve. Remove, let cool, and add to pineapple mixture, blending. Mix in lemon rind and pour into dessert dishes. Refrigerate or place in freezer until set. Garnish with reserved pineapple chunks.

Serves 4.

Nutritive values per serving:	CHO (gm)	PRO (gm)	FAT (gm)	NA (mg)	CAL
	14	6.5	0	74	82
Food exchanges per serving:	1 fruit + ½ skim milk				

ITALY—MENU 5
UMIDO DI CONIGLIO (RABBIT STEW)
SCAROLA (ESCAROLE)
PERE PIPIERE (STUFFED PEARS)

UMIDO DI CONIGLIO
(RABBIT STEW)

1 rabbit (about 3½ pounds) skinned, cleaned, and
  cut into pieces
1 cup red wine
3 bay leaves
5 cloves
1 chili pepper, sliced, seeds removed
1 tablespoon vegetable oil
2 medium onions, chopped
1 cup canned Italian plum tomatoes, drained
2 cloves garlic, minced
½ teaspoon red pepper flakes
4 medium potatoes, peeled and quartered
½ teaspoon rosemary
½ pound mushrooms, sliced
2 carrots, sliced

Wash rabbit pieces and place in bowl. Cover with wine and
add bay leaves, cloves, and chili pepper. Cover and let marinate
in refrigerator overnight or up to 2 days, turning rabbit several
times. When ready to cook, remove rabbit pieces from marinade but reserve liquid. Discard spices. In large, nonstick
vessel, heat oil and in it sauté onions, then the rabbit for about
20 minutes, turning. Add tomatoes, garlic, and pepper flakes.
Cover and cook slowly for 30–40 minutes. Add potatoes, rosemary, mushrooms, carrots, and 1 cup of marinade. Continue
cooking, covered, over low heat for 1 hour or until rabbit and
potatoes are tender. If sauce is too thin, reduce by cooking a bit
longer, uncovered.

Serves 4.

Nutritive values per serving:	CHO (gm)	PRO (gm)	FAT (gm)	NA (mg)	CAL
	36.5	59	23	168	589
Food exchanges per serving:	1½ bread + 3 vegetable + 7 lean meat + ⅓ fat				

SCAROLA
(ESCAROLE)

1½ pounds escarole
½ cup cold water
1 medium onion, chopped
1 teaspoon pepper
1 lemon, cut into wedges

Discard tough outer ribs of escarole. Break leaves into small pieces. Rinse well to remove sand. Place in large saucepan with water, onion, and pepper. Bring to boil, then reduce heat. Cook over low heat 20 minutes. If liquid is not evaporated, raise heat and cook until it is. Serve with lemon wedges.

Serves 4.

Nutritive values per serving:	CHO (gm)	PRO (gm)	FAT (gm)	NA (mg)	CAL
	11.5	4	0	27	62
Food exchanges per serving:	2⅓ vegetable				

PERE PIPIERE
(STUFFED PEARS)

2 large, ripe pears, Bartlett or Bosc
1 tablespoon grated orange rind
1 tablespoon grated lemon rind
¼ cup ground almonds
¼ teaspoon almond extract
½ cup dry sherry

Peel pears and cut in half lengthwise. Scoop out cores, leaving a well. Mix orange and lemon rinds, almonds and almond extract, and stuff into pear halves. Place stuffed pears in a baking dish and pour sherry over them. Bake in preheated 350°F oven for 15–20 minutes or until pears are warm. Baste with sauce. Serve warm or chilled.

Serves 4.

Nutritive values per serving:	CHO (gm)	PRO (gm)	FAT (gm)	NA (mg)	CAL
	18	2	4	1	116
Food exchanges per serving:	2 fruit + 1 fat				

ITALY—MENU 6

OSTRICE OREGANATA (OYSTERS IN OREGANO SAUCE)
LASAGNA (NOODLE PUDDING)
TUTTI FRUTTI (FRESH FRUIT)

OSTRICE OREGANATA
(OYSTERS IN OREGANO SAUCE)

1 pint shucked oysters, drained (reserve liquid)
2 cloves garlic, minced
1 tablespoon grated sapsago or Romano cheese
Dash cayenne
1 tablespoon chopped fresh oregano or 1 teaspoon dried
Freshly ground pepper
¼ cup chopped fresh parsley
4 tablespoons fresh lemon juice
1 tablespoon sunflower seed oil
2 tablespoons whole wheat bread crumbs

These can be served in single scallop shells or baked in a casserole and divided into 4 portions.

Place an equal amount of drained oysters in each scallop shell or place all oysters in casserole. Combine garlic, cheese, cayenne, oregano, pepper, and parsley with enough of the reserved oyster liquid to bind. Spread this over the oysters. Drizzle lemon juice and sunflower seed oil over oysters and top with bread crumbs. Bake in preheated 375°F oven for 10–15 minutes, until tops are golden.

Serves 4.

Nutritive values per serving:	CHO (gm)	PRO (gm)	FAT (gm)	NA (mg)	CAL
	10	11.5	6	113	140
Food exchanges per serving:	½ bread + ¼ fruit + 1 lean meat + 1 fat				

LASAGNA
(NOODLE PUDDING)

½ medium onion, chopped
¼ cup chopped green pepper
5 ounces tomato sauce (sugarless)
¼ cup sliced mushrooms
2 cloves garlic, minced
1 tablespoon chopped fresh basil or 1 teaspoon dried
1 tablespoon chopped oregano or 1 teaspoon dried
5 ounces curly lasagna noodles
Vegetable spray
½ cup part-skim ricotta cheese
½ cup grated skim-milk mozzarella cheese
2 tablespoons grated sapsago or Romano cheese

In nonstick skillet, sauté onion and green pepper. Add tomato sauce, sliced mushrooms, garlic, and herbs. Simmer for 20 minutes until sauce is reduced and vegetables cooked. Meanwhile, bring to boil a large kettle of water. Drop in the pieces of lasagna, one at a time, being careful not to break them. Cook for 12–13 minutes, until noodles are tender but not soggy. Drain in colander. Coat a baking dish with vegetable spray. Place layer of drained noodles in dish. Spread some ricotta cheese over them, then some tomato sauce, then the mozzarella. Repeat the layering several times, until ingredients are used up. Sprinkle with sapsago or Romano cheese and bake in preheated 350°F oven for 40 minutes, until browned.

Serves 4.

Nutritive values per serving:	CHO (gm)	PRO (gm)	FAT (gm)	NA (mg)	CAL
	33	13	5.5	823	317
Food exchanges per serving:	2 bread + 1 vegetable + 1 medium-fat meat				

TUTTI FRUTTI
(FRESH FRUIT)

1 cup blueberries, washed
1 cup fresh strawberries, hulled and sliced
1 kiwifruit, peeled and sliced
¼ cup fresh orange juice
½ teaspoon freshly grated nutmeg
½ banana, sliced

Mix all fruits except banana in a bowl with the orange juice and nutmeg. Add banana just before serving so that it doesn't turn brown. Refrigerate and serve chilled in glass dessert dishes.

Note: Any combination of fresh fruit may be used in exchange proportions. We like the above when in season.

Serves 4.

Nutritive values per serving:	CHO (gm)	PRO (gm)	FAT (gm)	NA (mg)	CAL
	16	1	.5	1	73
Food exchanges per serving:	1¾ fruit				

ITALY—MENU 7
ZUPPA DI POLLO CON SCAROLA (CHICKEN AND
ESCAROLE SOUP)
MELANZANA PARMIGIANA (EGGPLANT PARMESAN)
ZITI CON BASILICO (MACARONI WITH BASIL)
GELATO VERDE E ROSSO (KIWIFRUIT AND GRAPE ICE)

ZUPPA DI POLLO CON SCAROLA
(CHICKEN AND ESCAROLE SOUP)

1 bunch escarole or chicory (about 1 pound)
4 cups chicken stock (see index)
½ teaspoon peeled and minced fresh gingerroot
1 tablespoon dry sherry
Dash pepper
1 slice whole wheat toast
1 clove garlic, crushed
1 tablespoon grated sapsago or Parmesan cheese

Tear chicory or escarole leaves into small pieces. Bring stock to boil with the ginger. Add chicory. Simmer 20 minutes. Add sherry and pepper and cook another 5 minutes. Rub toast with garlic and cut into croutons. Serve in individual soup bowls with croutons and grated cheese as garnish.

Serves 4.

Nutritive values per serving:	CHO (gm)	PRO (gm)	FAT (gm)	NA (mg)	CAL
	10	6.5	5	54	111
Food exchanges per serving:	1½ vegetable + 1 medium-fat meat				

MELANZANA PARMIGIANA
(EGGPLANT PARMESAN)

1 eggplant (about 1½ pounds)
1 teaspoon corn oil
1 cup chopped onion
1 cup chopped green pepper
10 ounces tomato sauce (sugarless)
1 cup chopped mushrooms
Dash cayenne
Vegetable spray
3 tablespoons chopped fresh oregano or 2 teaspoons dried
½ pound skim-milk mozzarella, cut into thin slices (fresh
    mozzarella tastes better than packaged)
¼ cup grated sapsago or Romano cheese

Cut eggplant crosswise into ¼-inch slices. To make tomato sauce, heat corn oil in nonstick skillet and sauté onion in it. Add green pepper, tomato sauce, and mushrooms and bring to boil. Reduce heat and let simmer 20 minutes. Add cayenne pepper and stir.

Place half of eggplant slices in a layer in an 8″ × 8″ baking dish lightly coated with vegetable spray. Then layer half oregano, mozzarella, tomato sauce, and grated sapsago or Romano cheese. Repeat layering until all ingredients are used up. Bake, covered, in a preheated 350°F oven for 30–40 minutes, until cheese is melted and eggplant is tender.

Serves 4.

Nutritive values per serving:	CHO (gm)	PRO (gm)	FAT (gm)	NA (mg)	CAL
	23	22.5	15	823	317
Food exchanges per serving:	4 vegetable + 3 medium-fat meat				

ZITI CON BASILICO
(MACARONI WITH BASIL)

8 ounces ziti
2 cloves garlic, chopped
¼ cup water
2 tablespoons chopped fresh basil or 1 teaspoon dried
2 tablespoons Creative Butter (see index)
Freshly ground pepper

Bring to boil a large kettle of water and drop in ziti gradually. Stir to prevent ziti from sticking to the pot. Cook 12–14 minutes, until tender. Drain and return to pot. Meanwhile, heat garlic in ¼ cup water. Toss into pot with drained ziti, along with basil and Creative Butter. Toss well, sprinkle with fresh pepper, and serve.

Serves 6.

Nutritive values per serving:	CHO (gm)	PRO (gm)	FAT (gm)	NA (mg)	CAL
	28.5	5	4	27	170
Food exchanges per serving:	2 bread + ⅔ fat				

GELATO VERDE E ROSSO
(KIWIFRUIT AND GRAPE ICE)

10 ice cubes
**2 kiwifruit, peeled, or 1 cup peeled and chopped honeydew
  melon**
2 tablespoons lemon juice
½ teaspoon pure vanilla extract
1 cup unsweetened grape juice
Blueberries or raspberries for garnish (optional)

In blender or food processor, shave ice cubes. Divide in half. Blend half of shaved ice with the peeled kiwifruit or melon. Add 1 tablespoon lemon juice and ¼ teaspoon vanilla. Pour into ice tray and place in freezer until ready to serve, about 1–2 hours. Blend grape juice and remainder of ice in the same manner and add 1 tablespoon lemon juice and ¼ teaspoon vanilla extract. Pour into ice tray and freeze 1–2 hours. Break up crystals periodically and again before serving each ice in dessert dishes. Top with a few blueberries or raspberries, if available.

Serves 4.

Nutritive values per serving:	CHO (gm)	PRO (gm)	FAT (gm)	NA (mg)	CAL
	15	.5	0	1	62
Food exchanges per serving:	1½ fruit				

Menu 1
MISO SOUP
Soybean Paste Soup
TORI SUKI
Chicken Sukiyaki
SUKIYAKI ORANGE SLICES

Menu 2
SAKE NO ISOBEYAKI
Grilled Salmon
SOBA
Buckwheat Noodles
KYURI TO MOYASHI NO GOMA-AE
Bean Sprouts and Cucumber with Sesame Seeds
HONEYDEW MELON LADDER

Menu 3
WAKADORI NO NANBAN YAKI
Cold Cornish Hens
HIYAMUGI NOODLES
Chilled Noodle Salad
PINEAPPLE STARS

Menu 4
TAIRAGAI NO SANSHO YAKI
Sea Scallops with Japanese Pepper
KURI GOHAN
Chestnut Rice
ASPARAGUS NO MISO-AE
AWAYUKI KAN
Strawberry Whip

11

JAPAN

The Japanese combine healthful fresh ingredients in a sensible and beautiful manner. Their goal is harmony of texture, color, flavor, and form. Because foods are cut into small pieces, actual cooking time is brief, chopsticks are the utensils, and the food is usually served in individual bowls, always with rice (or noodles) and tea. Dessert is usually a fresh fruit.

Low-sodium *shoyu* (soy sauce) has 47 percent less salt than ordinary soy and is recommended for our meals. Kikkoman makes such a low-sodium sauce. For those watching salt carefully, water can be used to dilute soy further.

One-pot meals such as *sukiyaki* are called *nabemono*. *Terriyaki* is broiled, marinated meat, chicken, or fish. Small portions are the rule, and, happily, the Japanese cuisine is low in fat. Buddhism accounts for vegetarianism.

Decorative garnishes distinguish Japanese presentation. Overlapping lemon slices, a fan of sliced mushrooms, carved carrots or turnips, scallion brushes, thin red radish slices pierced with parsley, a pile of tiny slivers of lemon peel ("pine needles") or ginger help decorate a dish. And whether you sit on the floor, shoes off, as do the Japanese, or at your dining table, we wish you *itadakimasu!*

JAPAN—MENU 1
MISO SOUP (SOYBEAN PASTE SOUP)
TORI SUKI (CHICKEN SUKIYAKI)
SUKIYAKI ORANGE SLICES

MISO SOUP
(SOYBEAN PASTE SOUP)

4 cups Dashi (see recipe below) or chicken stock
4 tablespoons red miso paste (soybean paste)
2 mushrooms, sliced
4 scallions, sliced into rings (white parts only)

Pour Dashi into a saucepan and heat. Spoon miso into a measuring cup and gradually stir into it a tablespoon of the broth. Continue this process until bean paste is dissolved in a cup of the soup. Then stir dissolved miso into remainder of Dashi stock and add mushroom slices. Heat to simmering point and remove from heat. Serve in bowls, garnished with scallions.

DASHI

1 sheet kombu (seaweed)
5 cups cold water
½ cup dried bonito flakes

Cut seaweed into 4 pieces and slash around the sides. Place in bottom of 2-quart kettle. Add water and gradually bring to simmer. Lift out seaweed before the water boils. Add bonito flakes and bring back to boil. Strain over a bowl and discard flakes. Use Dashi for Miso Soup, above.

Serves 4.

Nutritive values per serving:	CHO (gm)	PRO (gm)	FAT (gm)	NA (mg)	CAL
	4	3	1	422	37
Food exchanges per serving:	⅓ bread + ⅓ lean meat				

TORI SUKI
(CHICKEN SUKIYAKI)

Called *nabemono,* this is a one-pot meal, popular throughout Japan.

1 pound skinless, boneless chicken breasts or turkey cutlets
1 teaspoon sesame oil
1 cup thinly sliced bamboo shoots
1 cup thinly sliced fresh mushrooms
1 cup spinach, well washed, stems removed
2 carrots, sliced and parboiled
8 ounces tofu, cut into 1-inch cubes
3½ ounces shirataki (cellophane noodles)
¼ cup low-sodium soy sauce
½ cup water
2 tablespoons dry sherry
4 scallions, julienned, chilled in ice water
1 teaspoon peeled and grated fresh gingerroot

Several hours before starting this dish, place chicken breasts in freezer and remove just before they are frozen. Slice paper-thin with sharp knife or cleaver. Heat sesame oil in deep, nonstick saucepan and quickly brown chicken slices (not too many at a time). Add bamboo shoots, mushrooms, spinach, carrots, and tofu and mix well. Meanwhile, break the noodles into 2-inch pieces and soak in boiling water for 10 minutes. Drain and rinse with warm water. Stir into skillet and cook about 2 minutes more. Combine soy, water, and sherry. Pour over chicken and vegetables and simmer 5 minutes. Top with julienned scallions and ginger. Serve in soup bowls.

Serves 4.

Nutritive values per serving:	CHO (gm)	PRO (gm)	FAT (gm)	NA (mg)	CAL
	15	30	6	464	234
Food exchanges per serving:	½ bread + 1½ vegetable + 4 lean meat; omits 1⅓ fat				

SUKIYAKI ORANGE SLICES

2 tablespoons fresh lemon juice
1 tablespoon sake or dry sherry
3 small oranges, peeled and sliced
1 tablespoon sesame seeds
4 small sprigs parsley

Heat lemon juice and sake or sherry in a small skillet. Add orange slices and heat 1 minute, stirring carefully. Remove and divide among 4 dessert dishes. Toast sesame seeds in small pan until they begin to jump. Sprinkle over the oranges, then top each serving with parsley sprig for color.

Serves 4.

Nutritive values per serving:	CHO (gm)	PRO (gm)	FAT (gm)	NA (mg)	CAL
	11	1	2	2	66
Food exchanges per serving:	1 fruit + ½ fat				

JAPAN—MENU 2
SAKE NO ISOBEYAKI (GRILLED SALMON)
SOBA (BUCKWHEAT NOODLES)
KYURI TO MOYASHI NO GOMA-AE (BEAN SPROUTS AND
CUCUMBER WITH SESAME SEEDS)
HONEYDEW MELON LADDER

SAKE NO ISOBEYAKI
(GRILLED SALMON)

¾ pound fresh salmon fillets
3 tablespoons low-sodium soy sauce
3 tablespoons sake or dry sherry
1 sheet nori (dried seaweed)
1 inch fresh gingerroot, peeled and julienned
4 thin slices lemon
4 small sprigs parsley, stems removed

Cut salmon into 4 slices on a 30-degree angle. Combine soy
and sake and marinate salmon in this for ½ hour. Remove fish.
Pour marinade into a saucepan, warming gently. Dip salmon
into marinade and then place 4 inches under preheated broiler
for 2 minutes. Turn and brush again and repeat process. Do not
overcook; 5–7 minutes should be sufficient. Transfer fish to
warm plates. Meanwhile, toast seaweed for a few minutes by
holding over burner until both sides are ready to crumble.
Sprinkle nori cumbs over salmon. Garnish fish with a little
heap of ginger, lemon slices, and parsley.

Serves 4.

Nutritive values per serving:	CHO (gm)	PRO (gm)	FAT (gm)	NA (mg)	CAL
	3.5	17	13.5	426	204
Food exchanges per serving:	½ vegetable + 2½ medium-fat meat				

SOBA
(BUCKWHEAT NOODLES)

12 ounces soba noodles
3 scallions, trimmed and sliced
4 mushrooms, cleaned and sliced

In saucepan, boil 2 cups water. Add noodles and bring back to boil. Add 1 cup cold water and bring back to boil, cooking until noodles are tender—about 6 minutes. Drain and rinse under hot water. Mix with scallions and mushrooms and toss with any remaining fish marinade.

Serves 6.

Nutritive values per serving:	CHO (gm)	PRO (gm)	FAT (gm)	NA (mg)	CAL
	15	2	0	0	68
Food exchanges per serving:	1 bread				

KYURI TO MOYASHI NO GOMA-AE
(BEAN SPROUTS AND CUCUMBER WITH SESAME SEEDS)

2 cups bean sprouts (fresh or canned), rinsed
1 cucumber, peeled if waxed, halved lengthwise, and seeded
Salt
1 tablespoon rice vinegar
1 tablespoon sesame oil
2 tablespoons low-sodium soy sauce
1 tablespoon sesame seeds, toasted
Five-spice powder

Boil water in a saucepan and cook sprouts for 2 minutes. Drain and cool. Cut cucumber halves into thin slices. Place in bowl and sprinkle with salt. Cover with heavy dish. Squeeze gently after 15 minutes to release water. Rinse. Meanwhile, mix vinegar, sesame oil, and soy sauce together. Add sprouts and cucumber slices. Sprinkle toasted sesame seeds over vegetables and serve in small bowls with a dash of five-spice powder.

Serves 6.

Nutritive values per serving:	CHO (gm)	PRO (gm)	FAT (gm)	NA (mg)	CAL
	4	2	4	176	60
Food exchanges per serving:	¾ vegetable + 1 fat				

HONEYDEW MELON LADDER

1 small honeydew melon
6 slices lemon, scored
6 small radishes, trimmed and sliced thin

Cut melon wedges about 2 inches wide at center. Remove seeds. With grapefruit cutter or knife, separate meat from rind. Cut melon into 1-inch slices and move them in and out of the rind so that they alternate in a ladder pattern. Chill and serve each slice topped with a lemon slice and a fan of radish slices for color.

Serves 6.

Nutritive values per serving:	CHO (gm)	PRO (gm)	FAT (gm)	NA (mg)	CAL
	20	2	1	3	97
Food exchanges per serving:	2 fruit				

JAPAN—MENU 3
WAKADORI NO NANBAN YAKI (COLD CORNISH HENS)
HIYAMUGI NOODLES (CHILLED NOODLE SALAD)
PINEAPPLE STARS

WAKADORI NO NANBAN YAKI
(COLD CORNISH HENS)

2 cornish game hens, split, backbones removed
½ cup sake or dry sherry
2 tablespoons light soy sauce
¼ teaspoon white pepper
Vegetable spray
1 tablespoon sesame seeds, toasted

Wash hens and pat dry, removing any fat. Combine sake, soy sauce, and pepper in saucepan and bring to a boil. Cook over low heat for 5 minutes. Cool and marinate hens in this mixture for 4 hours or overnight. When ready to cook, drain hens but reserve marinade. Preheat broiler and place hen halves on lightly sprayed broiling pan, skin side down. Broil 10 minutes on each side, brushing with marinade. Remove from broiler, skin birds, and baste with marinade. Run under broiler for another few minutes. Serve warm or let cool. Sprinkle with toasted sesame seeds.

Serves 4.

Nutritive values per serving:	CHO (gm)	PRO (gm)	FAT (gm)	NA (mg)	CAL
	4	22.5	9	317	187
Food exchanges per serving:	⅓ fruit + 3 lean meat				

HIYAMUGI NOODLES
(CHILLED NOODLE SALAD)

1 cup Dashi (see index) or chicken stock
2 tablespoons low-sodium soy sauce
2 tablespoons concentrated frozen apple juice
¼ cup sake or dry sherry
8 ounces spinach spaghetti
1 scallion, sliced
½ medium cucumber, peeled and sliced thin on diagonal
2 carrots, cut into thin diagonal slices and blanched
½ pound green beans, trimmed, blanched, and chilled
1 tomato, peeled, cut into 4 slices, seeds poked out
2 hard-boiled eggs, quartered (discard yolks)
1 large radish, cut into a rose (see Chapter 20)
Five-spice powder or dash of cayenne

Combine Dashi, soy sauce, apple juice, and sake in a saucepan and bring to a boil. Remove from heat and let cool. Chill and pour into small glass bowls. Set aside for dipping.

Drop noodles into large kettle of boiling water and cook 12–14 minutes. Drain and run under cold water. Add a few ice cubes to chill.

Meanwhile, chop scallions and place in cold water to crisp. Drain and squeeze dry. Place in small side dish. Arrange cucumber pieces, carrots, and string beans around rim of drained cold noodles placed in the center of a large bowl. Alternate with tomato slices for color contrast. Arrange egg white quarters in a flower pattern on top of noodles. Place radish rose in its center. (Add more ice cubes to keep chilled, if necessary.) Serve with dipping sauce. Sprinkle with scallions and pepper.

Serves 6.

Nutritive values per serving:	CHO (gm)	PRO (gm)	FAT (gm)	NA (mg)	CAL
	39.5	8.5	1	209	201
Food exchanges per serving:	2 bread + 2 vegetable				

PINEAPPLE STARS

1 pineapple, peeled and cut into thin rounds
8 whole strawberries or red grapes
4 mint leaves

Make certain all rough outer skin is removed from pineapple slices. Cut into star shapes. Remove hard center core. Place 2 berries or grapes in center of each slice and top with mint leaf. Overlap 2 thin slices per serving.

Serves 4.

Nutritive values per serving:	CHO (gm)	PRO (gm)	FAT (gm)	NA (mg)	CAL
	18	.5	0	2	74
Food exchanges per serving:	2 fruit				

JAPAN—MENU 4
TAIRAGAI NO SANSHO YAKI (SEA SCALLOPS WITH
JAPANESE PEPPER)
KURI GOHAN (CHESTNUT RICE)
ASPARAGUS NO MISO-AE
AWAYUKI-KAN (STRAWBERRY WHIP)

TAIRAGAI NO SANSHO YAKI
(SEA SCALLOPS WITH JAPANESE PEPPER)

16 sea scallops (1 pound)
¼ cup low-sodium soy sauce
6 tablespoons sake or dry sherry
1 tablespoon concentrated frozen apple juice
Dash cayenne
4 curly lettuce leaves
1 lime, sliced thin
2 red radishes, sliced thin

Wash and dry scallops and cut in half horizontally. Combine soy, sake, and apple juice in small pan and slowly bring to boil. Remove from heat and cool. Add scallops and marinate for 5 minutes. Remove scallops. Thread onto metal skewers and broil for 1 minute 4 inches under preheated broiler. Paint with marinade and turn; broil 1 minute. Sprinkle with pepper. Divide scallops among lettuce leaves. Decorate with lime and radish slices.

Serves 4.

Nutritive values per serving:	CHO (gm)	PRO (gm)	FAT (gm)	NA (mg)	CAL
	11	13.5	.5	738	103
Food exchanges per serving:	1 fruit + 2 lean meat				

KURI GOHAN
(CHESTNUT RICE)

½ cup long-grain brown rice
10-11 chestnuts, cooked and peeled (or canned)
1 tablespoon sake or dry sherry
1½ cups water

Wash rice until water runs clear. Let soak for 1 hour. Drain. Meanwhile, cook chestnuts (see Chapter 20). If chestnuts are large, cut into quarters. Add chestnuts to rice (if using canned chestnuts, begin at this point), along with sake or sherry. Cover with 1½ cups water. Bring to boil. Cover, reduce heat, and cook for 25–30 minutes. Do not stir during cooking. Remove from heat and let steam, covered, until all water is absorbed. When rice is cooked, remove cover, fluff with fork, and serve.

Serves 4.

Nutritive values per serving:	CHO (gm)	PRO (gm)	FAT (gm)	NA (mg)	CAL
	27	2	1	2	125
Food exchanges per serving:	2 bread				

ASPARAGUS NO MISO-AE

1 pound fresh asparagus
2 tablespoons miso (bean paste)
2 tablespoons dry sherry
2 tablespoons concentrated frozen apple juice

Trim asparagus and break off hard ends. Cut on diagonal into 2-inch pieces. Drop into boiling water and cook until tender but still firm, about 3 minutes. Quickly run under cold water. Drain. Meanwhile, in small pan, combine bean paste, sherry, and apple juice. Cook over low heat until mixture is warmed but not boiling. Mix with drained asparagus and serve.

Serves 4.

Nutritive values per serving:	CHO (gm)	PRO (gm)	FAT (gm)	NA (mg)	CAL
	7	2.5	0	142	38
Food exchanges per serving:	1 vegetable + ¼ fruit				

AWAYUKI-KAN
(STRAWBERRY WHIP)

1 egg white
⅛ teaspoon cream of tartar
2 tablespoons fructose
½ teaspoon pure vanilla extract
3 cups fresh strawberries

Whip egg white and cream of tartar until frothy. Gradually add fructose and vanilla extract, beating in well. Continue beating until peaks form. Mash berries and fold into egg white. Save several whole berries for garnish. Pile whip into glass dessert dishes and top each with a whole berry. Serve at once or freeze 1–2 hours.

Serves 4.

Nutritive values per serving:	CHO (gm)	PRO (gm)	FAT (gm)	NA (mg)	CAL
	15.5	1.5	0	13	68
Food exchanges per serving:	1½ fruit				

Menu 1

KONG-NA-MOOL KUK
Bean Sprout Soup

KIM CHEE
Pickled Cabbage

BUL-KO-KEE
Barbecued Beef

SONG I PAHB
Brown Rice and Vegetables

WHASHAI
Fruit Cup

Menu 2

SANSUHN JIM
Fish with Vegetables

GREEN SALAD

VERMICELLI
Chinese Noodles

SPICED FRUIT

12

KOREA

Little known until recently in this country, Korean food often borrows from its neighboring cuisines. With Japan it shares soy sauce, rice, tofu, and miso, but it does have a spicy flavor all its own.

The sea is a valuable source of protein for the Koreans. A long coastline offers a wealth of marine life—fish, shellfish, and seaweeds rich in iodine, minerals, and vitamins. Meat, too, is part of the Korean diet. The Koreans like sesame seeds sprinkled over everything—ground to release the oils or just toasted. As in Japan, the meal is not a sequence of separate courses, but rather a simultaneous presentation of many dishes. One-pot meals are common, and rice is always served. Desserts, while not traditional, are apt to be fresh fruit.

Korea is predominantly agricultural, and the people love fresh vegetables. *Kim chee* is the national dish, made of Chinese cabbage, red peppers, pears, and hot spices. Steeped in pickle pots, it is on hand throughout the year. For sheer variety in taste and color, Korean sustenance is superb. *Monni dhu saeyo!* Eat well, eat a lot!

KOREA—MENU 1
KONG-NA-MOOL KUK (BEAN SPROUT SOUP)
KIM CHEE (PICKLED CABBAGE)
BUL-KO-KEE (BARBECUED BEEF)
SONG I PAHB (BROWN RICE AND VEGETABLES)
WHASHAI (FRUIT CUP)

KONG-NA-MOOL KUK
(BEAN SPROUT SOUP)

1 ounce lean beef, cut into very thin strips
2 cloves garlic, crushed
2 teaspoons ground roasted sesame seeds
2 scallions, chopped fine (green part only)
3 tablespoons low-sodium soy sauce
½ teaspoon pepper
1 tablespoon sesame oil
2 cups bean sprouts
5 cups water

Mix beef, garlic, and sesame seeds with half the scallions. Add half the soy sauce and the pepper. Heat sesame oil in a nonstick saucepan. Add meat mixture and brown. Then add bean sprouts and stir-fry for 3 minutes. Add water and remaining soy sauce. Cover and simmer over low heat for 30 minutes. Stir in remaining scallions and simmer 5 minutes more.

Serves 4.

Nutritive values per serving:	CHO (gm)	PRO (gm)	FAT (gm)	NA (mg)	CAL
	7	5	5	393	93
Food exchanges per serving:	1½ vegetable + ¼ lean meat + 1 fat				

KIM CHEE
(PICKLED CABBAGE)

2 tablespoons salt
1 small Chinese cabbage (about 2 cups), quartered
2 teaspoons dried red pepper flakes (less if this is too strong)
1 clove garlic, crushed
2 scallions, chopped
1 small onion, chopped
1 small carrot, chopped
2 tablespoons concentrated frozen apple juice
1-inch piece fresh gingerroot, peeled and julienned

Sprinkle salt over cabbage. Cover and set in refrigerator in covered bowl to release water overnight. Rinse cabbage in cold water and squeeze to remove all water. Shred. Place all ingredients in a deep bowl, mix, and cover with heavy weight. Let pickle at least 1–2 weeks before using. This is a traditional Korean accompaniment, but it takes time to cook itself! It will keep in the pickle pot for some time.

Serves 4.

Nutritive values per serving:	CHO (gm)	PRO (gm)	FAT (gm)	NA (mg)	CAL
	8	1	0	2964	36
Food exchanges per serving:	1 vegetable + ⅓ fruit				

BUL-KO-KEE
(BARBECUED BEEF)

1 pound top round beef, sliced into thin strips
½ cup low-sodium soy sauce
Pepper
2 tablespoons sesame oil
1 clove garlic, crushed
2 scallions, sliced thin (green part only)
4 tablespoons toasted sesame seeds, divided

Mix beef, soy, pepper, oil, garlic, scallions, and half the sesame seeds. Let marinate at room temperature for 2 hours. Turn periodically. Preheat broiler and arrange beef on foil-lined grill. Broil for about 4–5 minutes 4 inches below heat source. Remove from broiler. Sprinkle with remaining sesame seeds and serve.

Serves 4.

Nutritive values per serving:	CHO (gm)	PRO (gm)	FAT (gm)	NA (mg)	CAL
	7	37	33	1010	473
Food exchanges per serving:	½ vegetable + ⅓ fruit + 5 medium-fat meat + 1 fat				

SONG I PAHB
(BROWN RICE WITH VEGETABLES)

½ cup long-grain brown rice, rinsed until water runs clear
1 cup water
1 cup sliced mushrooms
½ cup chopped carrots
1 cup finely chopped celery
2 scallions, sliced
2 tablespoons low-sodium soy sauce
1 tablespoon dry sherry
½ cup green peas

Place all ingredients except peas in saucepan with rice and cover with water. Bring to boil. Cover and let simmer 30 minutes over low heat. Add peas 5 minutes before done. Do not stir. Remove from heat and let steam another 10 minutes, until liquid is absorbed.

Serves 4.

Nutritive values per serving:	CHO (gm)	PRO (gm)	FAT (gm)	NA (mg)	CAL
	27	4	1	302	135
Food exchanges per serving:	1½ bread + 1 vegetable				

WHASHAI
(FRUIT CUP)

1 cup orange juice
1 cup water
1 cinnamon stick
1 tangerine, sectioned, peeled, pulp removed
1 peach, peeled and sliced
1 cup strawberries
1 ripe pear, peeled, cored, and sliced
2 tablespoons chopped blanched almonds

Cook orange juice, water, and cinnamon into a syrup. Let cool. Discard cinnamon stick. Combine all fruit with the cooled syrup and chill 1 hour. (Other seasonal fruits may be substituted, such as apples, grapes, melons, etc.) Sprinkle with almonds and serve.

Serves 4.

Nutritive values per serving:	CHO (gm)	PRO (gm)	FAT (gm)	NA (mg)	CAL
	23.5	2	2	8	120
Food exchanges per serving:	2½ fruit + 1 fat				

KOREA—MENU 2
SANSUHN JIM (FISH WITH VEGETABLES)
GREEN SALAD
VERMICELLI (CHINESE NOODLES)
SPICED FRUIT

SANSUHN JIM
(FISH WITH VEGETABLES)

4 ounces chuck steak, cut into thin strips
1 cup canned button mushrooms, drained
3 stalks celery, trimmed and chopped
1 pound daikon (Japanese radish) or turnips, peeled and
    chopped
2 carrots, sliced
1 pound fish fillets, cut into bite-size chunks
4 scallions, chopped
2 small green chilis, chopped (take care not to burn fingers
    on seeds or veins)
3 tablespoons low-sodium soy sauce

MARINADE

1 tablespoon rice wine vinegar
Pepper
2 cloves garlic, minced
3 tablespoons sesame oil
1 tablespoon toasted sesame seeds
1 teaspoon concentrated frozen apple juice
2 tablespoons low-sodium soy sauce

Mix the marinade ingredients together in a bowl and add
beef strips. Let marinate at room temperature ½ hour, turning
periodically. Remove beef from marinade, reserving marinade,

and place in bottom of a flameproof casserole. Cover meat with mushrooms, then celery, daikon or turnips, then the carrots. Arrange fish pieces on top of vegetables and sprinkle half the scallions and chilis on top.

Pour in enough water to come to about halfway up ingredients. Add reserved marinade and soy sauce. Bring to boil on top of stove, then cover and place in preheated 350°F oven for 10–15 minutes, until fish is tender. Remove from oven, garnish with remaining scallions and chilis, and serve with Vermicelli (see recipe below).

Serves 4.

Nutritive values per serving:	CHO (gm)	PRO (gm)	FAT (gm)	NA (mg)	CAL
	19	26.5	18	817	344
Food exchanges per serving:	2 vegetable + ½ bread + 3 lean meat + 2 fat				

VERMICELLI
(CHINESE NOODLES)

6 ounces vermicelli
1 teaspoon sesame oil

In large kettle, bring 2 quarts water to boil. Drop in vermicelli and boil for about 3 minutes, until tender. Drain and rinse under hot running water. Return to kettle with sesame oil, toss, and serve with Sansuhn Jim (see recipe above).

Serves 4.

Nutritive values per serving:	CHO (gm)	PRO (gm)	FAT (gm)	NA (mg)	CAL
	34	2	1	5	153
Food exchanges per serving:	2⅓ bread				

GREEN SALAD

1 head boston or romaine lettuce, or a combination, washed and dried
1 cucumber, peeled and sliced thin
12 red radishes, trimmed and sliced thin
1 scallion, chopped
1 tablespoon rice wine vinegar
1 tablespoon low-sodium soy sauce
Juice of 1 lemon
1 tablespoon pine nuts, toasted, or sunflower seeds

Tear lettuce leaves into bite-size pieces; mix in bowl with cucumber slices, radishes, and scallion. In mixing bowl, whip together rice wine vinegar, soy, and lemon juice. When ready to serve salad, dress with this mixture and top with pine nuts or sunflower seeds.

Serves 4.

Nutritive values per serving:	CHO (gm)	PRO (gm)	FAT (gm)	NA (mg)	CAL
	5	1.5	1	140	35
Food exchanges per serving:	1 vegetable + ¼ fat				

SPICED FRUIT

1 kiwifruit, peeled and sliced
2 tangerines or oranges, peeled and sectioned
20 red grapes or 1 cup strawberries, hulled
½ cup sliced canned water chestnuts, drained
¼ teaspoon peeled and minced fresh gingerroot
½ teaspoon ground cinnamon
½ teaspoon ground allspice
½ teaspoon ground cloves
½ teaspoon almond extract
1 tablespoon toasted sesame seeds

Mix the fruit together with water chestnuts and spices and chill. Before serving, garnish with sesame seeds. (Other fruit combinations can be substituted.)

Serves 4.

Nutritive values per serving:	CHO (gm)	PRO (gm)	FAT (gm)	NA (mg)	CAL
	15	2	2	5	86
Food exchanges per serving:	1½ fruit + ½ fat				

Menu 1

GUACAMOLE Y TOSTADOS
Avocado and Corn Chips

PESCADO VERACRUZ
Red Snapper Veracruz

PAPAS PEREJILS
Parsley Potatoes

TEQUILA POMELAS AL HORNO
Baked Tequila Grapefruit

Menu 2

ENSALADA MIXTA
Mixed Salad

ARROZ CON POLLO
Chicken and Rice

FLAN AL CAFE
Baked Coffee Custard

Menu 3

ESPARRAGOS CON PIMIENTO
Asparagus with Pimiento

CAMARONES DE CORTES
Soused Shrimp

SOPA SECA DE ARROZ
Mexican Rice

POSTRE DE MANGO
Mango Frappe

Menu 4

SOPA DE ELOTE Y CHAYOTE
Corn and Squash Soup

CARNE DE PUERCO EN SALSA DE RAJAS
Pork in Coriander Sauce

FRIJOLES REFRITOS
Refried Beans

PLATO DE FRUTA
Fresh Fruit Platter

Menu 5

TACOS DE POLLO
Chicken Tacos

CREMA DE PAPAYA
Papaya Cream

13

MEXICO

In the United States, we tend to think of Mexican food as a combination platter of tacos, tortillas, and enchiladas. The reality is that Mexico's cuisine is delicate in flavor and healthful in variety. Our neighbors south of the border derive their cuisine from a history touched by many civilizations. Based on staples of its early Aztec and Mayan peoples, the region has absorbed foods brought to Mexico by its many conquerors— the French, English, Spanish, and even Danish. From Moctezuma to Maximilian, each invader left a mark.

Corn, beans, chilies, roots, limes, pineapples, and bananas mingle with vanilla beans and almonds. Spices and sesame and pumpkin seeds enliven the food, and about 100 different kinds of chilies are used. (Be wary in slicing fresh chilies; the seeds and veins burn the hand and lips when touched.) The Mexicans cook with lard, and much of their food is fried. We prefer to substitute vegetable oils and bake.

The tortilla is Mexico's bread, made from either corn or flour. We like the corn tortilla best and recommend steaming or crisping in the oven. To make a taco, just wrap a tortilla around a stuffing of your choice and bake. *A las comidas excelentes!*

MEXICO—MENU 1
GUACAMOLE Y TOSTADOS (AVOCADO AND CORN CHIPS)
PESCADO VERACRUZ (RED SNAPPER VERACRUZ)
PAPAS PEREJILS (PARSLEY POTATOES)
TEQUILA POMELAS AL HORNO (BAKED TEQUILA
GRAPEFRUIT)

GUACAMOLE Y TOSTADOS
(AVOCADO AND CORN CHIPS)

TOSTADOS

12 corn tortillas

Stack tortillas and cut into pie-shaped wedges. Spread out on cookie sheet and bake in 400°F oven until crisp, 15–20 minutes. Turn to bake evenly. (Some may also be baked whole to accompany fish.)

GUACAMOLE

1 small ripe avocado, peeled, pitted, and cut into chunks
1 tablespoon lime juice
½ cup peas (fresh or frozen)
½ cup chopped asparagus (2-inch pieces)
½ cup chopped broccoli (2-inch pieces)
½ cup peeled and chopped ripe tomatoes
½ cup chopped fresh coriander leaves
1 clove garlic, minced
1 chili, seeded and minced (wear rubber gloves when seeding to prevent burns)
2 tablespoons low-fat cottage cheese
2 tablespoons chopped onion
Lettuce leaves

Mash avocado chunks with fork in bowl with lime juice. Steam the peas, the asparagus, and the broccoli (or other green vegetables) and puree them in a blender. Mix together with avocados. Add tomatoes, coriander, garlic, chili, cottage cheese, and onion. Serve on bed of lettuce with tostadas.

Serves 6 (2 tortillas per serving).

Nutritive values per serving:	CHO (gm)	PRO (gm)	FAT (gm)	NA (mg)	CAL
	37	6	5.5	77	222
Food exchanges per serving:	2 bread + 1½ vegetable + 1 fat				

PESCADO VERACRUZ
(RED SNAPPER VERACRUZ)

1½ pounds red snapper fillets (cod, pollack, bass, or any other white fish may be used)
4 tablespoons fresh lime juice
1 teaspoon vegetable oil
1 medium onion, chopped
3 cloves garlic, minced
5 medium tomatoes, peeled and chopped
2 bay leaves
6 peppercorns
12 olives with pimientos, sliced
2 tablespoons capers, rinsed and drained
2 tablespoons chopped fresh coriander

Wash fish and marinate in lime juice for at least 30 minutes. In large nonstick saucepan, heat oil and cook onion and garlic in it until tender. Add tomatoes, bay leaves, and peppercorns and bring to boil. Reduce heat and simmer, uncovered, over low heat for 10 minutes. Place fish in saucepan, add olives and capers, and cover with the sauce. Cover and let simmer 10 minutes, until fish flakes easily. Discard bay leaves and garnish with coriander.

Serves 4.

Nutritive values per serving:	CHO (gm)	PRO (gm)	FAT (gm)	NA (mg)	CAL
	14	37	8	337	276
Food exchanges per serving:	2 vegetable + 5 lean meat; omits 1 fat				

PAPAS PERIJILS
(PARSLEY POTATOES)

8 medium new potatoes or 12 tiny ones, well scrubbed
2 tablespoons finely chopped fresh parsley
Pepper

Boil potatoes in their jackets until tender. Serve with dusting of parsley and a few grinds of fresh pepper.

Serves 4.

Nutritive values per serving:	CHO (gm)	PRO (gm)	FAT (gm)	NA (mg)	CAL
	17	2	0	1	58
Food exchanges per serving:	1 bread				

TEQUILA POMELAS AL HORNO
(BAKED TEQUILA GRAPEFRUIT)

**2 grapefruit (white or pink), peeled and sectioned, all
  membranes removed**
2 tablespoons concentrated frozen apple juice
2 tablespoons tequila
1 teaspoon cinnamon

Remove seeds from grapefruit sections. Douse fruit with apple juice and tequila and spread in a circle in round baking dish. Sprinkle with cinnamon. Bake in preheated 300°F oven for 10 minutes. Just before serving, place under broiler for 2 minutes, until brown.

Serves 4.

Nutritive values per serving:	CHO (gm)	PRO (gm)	FAT (gm)	NA (mg)	CAL
	14	.5	0	1	58
Food exchanges per serving:	1½ fruit				

MEXICO—MENU 2
ENSALADA MIXTA (MIXED SALAD)
ARROZ CON POLLO (CHICKEN AND RICE)
FLAN AL CAFE (BAKED COFFEE CUSTARD)

ENSALADA MIXTA
(MIXED SALAD)

3 tablespoons red wine vinegar
1 tablespoon prepared mustard
¼ cup lemon juice
Lettuce leaves
1 pound carrots, scraped and grated
1 pound beets, boiled, drained, peeled, and julienned
Beet tops
1 lime, sliced

Combine vinegar, mustard, and lemon juice. Line salad plates with lettuce leaves. Fill with equal portions of carrots and beets. Boil the beet tops and drain. Place a bit of these, too, in each lettuce cup. Garnish vegetables with a lime slice and serve with lemon mustard dressing.

Serves 4.

Nutritive values per serving:	CHO (gm)	PRO (gm)	FAT (gm)	NA (mg)	CAL
	27.5	4	.5	172	131
Food exchanges per serving:	¼ fruit + 5 vegetable				

ARROZ CON POLLO
(CHICKEN AND RICE)

1 pound skinless, boneless chicken breasts, cut into
   1-inch strips
1 medium onion, quartered
2 green peppers, chopped
1 jalapeño pepper, seeded and chopped (wear gloves to
   prevent burns)
3 cloves garlic, minced
2 tablespoons chopped fresh coriander
2 cups chicken stock
1 cup crushed and drained canned Italian plum tomatoes
1 teaspoon ground cumin
1 teaspoon chili powder
¾ cup long-grain brown rice
Pinch salt
Dash cayenne
1 cup green peas (fresh or frozen)
1 tablespoon sliced pimientos
1 tablespoon rinsed and drained capers

   Sauté chicken strips in nonstick skillet until white, about 5 minutes. Set aside and keep warm. In a large skillet, bring all other ingredients, except peas, pimientos, and capers, to a boil. Cover and simmer about 30 minutes, until rice has absorbed liquid. Add peas, remove from heat, and let steam. Arrange chicken and sauce over rice, garnished with pimientos and capers.

Serves 6.

Nutritive values per serving:	CHO (gm)	PRO (gm)	FAT (gm)	NA (mg)	CAL
	36	24	2.5	107	262
Food exchanges per serving:	2 bread + 1 vegetable + 3 lean meat; omits ½ fat				

FLAN AL CAFE
(BAKED COFFEE CUSTARD)

2 eggs (use only 1 yolk)
1 cup evaporated skim milk
1 teaspoon instant coffee
¼ teaspoon pure vanilla extract
1 tablespoon concentrated frozen orange juice
1 tablespoon grated orange rind
Ground cinnamon

Place eggs in blender and process. Add milk, coffee, vanilla extract, and orange juice. Blend. Pour mixture into ovenproof pan or individual custard cups. Then place in a larger baking dish into which hot water has been poured. Bake custard in this bath in preheated 350°F oven for 45–50 minutes. Test by inserting a knife into the middle of the custard. If it comes out clean, flan is ready. Remove from hot water and chill several hours. To remove flan from cups, run a knife around edges and invert. Garnish each serving with orange rind and sprinkle of cinnamon.

Serves 4.

Nutritive values per serving:	CHO (gm)	PRO (gm)	FAT (gm)	NA (mg)	CAL
	9	7	1	103	73
Food exchanges per serving:	½ skim milk + ⅕ fruit + ½ medium-fat meat				

MEXICO—MENU 3
ESPARRAGOS CON PIMIENTO (ASPARAGUS WITH PIMIENTO)
CAMARONES DE CORTES (SOUSED SHRIMP)
SOPA SECA DE ARROZ (MEXICAN RICE)
POSTRE DE MANGO (MANGO FRAPPE)

ESPARRAGOS CON PIMIENTO
(ASPARAGUS WITH PIMIENTO)

1 pound fresh asparagus or broccoli
½ cup cold water
2 tablespoons fresh lime juice
1 large pimiento, rinsed in cold water and cut into strips

Wash asparagus under cold water, snap off ends, and trim. (If using broccoli, cut into flowerets.) Place water in skillet large enough to hold all asparagus stalks. Cover and steam over moderate heat no longer than 5 minutes, just until stalks are bright green. Do not overcook. Drain, run quickly under cold water, and transfer to platter. Sprinkle with lime juice and decorate with crisscrosses of pimiento strips. Serve warm or chilled.

Serves 4.

Nutritive values per serving:	CHO (gm)	PRO (gm)	FAT (gm)	NA (mg)	CAL
	8.5	3	0	2	46
Food exchanges per serving:	2 vegetable				

CAMARONES DE CORTES
(SOUSED SHRIMP)

½ cup tarragon vinegar
½ teaspoon white horseradish, grated
2 tablespoons sharp mustard
3 tablespoons tomato paste
1 teaspoon chili powder (more if desired)
Pinch dried oregano
2 tablespoons sunflower seed oil
Juice of 2 limes
1 pound jumbo shrimp, boiled 2–3 minutes until pink,
    shelled, and deveined
1 small red onion, peeled and sliced thin
¼ cup pepitas (pumpkin seeds) or sunflower seeds,
    hulled and toasted
3 ripe tomatoes, sliced thin
1 lime, sliced

Blend all ingredients except the shrimp, onion, pepitas, tomatoes, and lime. Place cooked shrimp in a bowl and cover with this marinade mixture. Refrigerate at least 6 hours, turning a few times.

Chill red onion slices in cold water to crisp. Toast pumpkin seeds in 400°F oven for about 10 minutes, turning. Do not let burn.

When ready to serve, drain shrimp, reserving marinade. Place tomato slices on platter or on individual dishes. Arrange shrimp over tomatoes. Remove onions from water and pat dry. Place a few rings on top of shrimp and spoon 2 tablespoons of marinade over each portion of shrimp. Garnish with lime slices. Serve with side dish of pepitas.

Serves 4.

Nutritive values per serving:	CHO (gm)	PRO (gm)	FAT (gm)	NA (mg)	CAL
	19	28	16	320	332
Food exchanges per serving:	2 vegetable + 4 lean meat + 1 fat + ½ fruit				

SOPA SECA DE ARROZ
(MEXICAN RICE)

¾ cup long-grain brown rice
2 cups water
1 teaspoon corn oil
1 clove garlic, mashed into a paste with a little salt
1 onion, chopped
2 cups chicken broth (see index)
2 tablespoons chopped parsley
½ teaspoon dried marjoram or oregano
2 small green chilies (canned or fresh), seeded if fresh, and
    cut into strips
¼ cup grated low-fat Jack cheese

Soak rice in 2 cups water for 15 minutes. Drain and let dry for 1 hour. In large nonstick saucepan, heat oil. Add rice, cook over medium heat, stirring, until brown. Add garlic paste and onion and cook until onion is tender. Add chicken broth, parsley, marjoram or oregano, and chilies. Cover and simmer until liquid is absorbed. Do not stir. Remove from heat and let steam for ½ hour. Just before serving, add cheese and toss lightly with a fork.

Serves 4.

Nutritive values per serving:	CHO (gm)	PRO (gm)	FAT (gm)	NA (mg)	CAL
	33.5	9	3	107	220
Food exchanges per serving:	2 bread + 1 vegetable + 1 lean meat				

POSTRE DE MANGO
(MANGO FRAPPE)

1 large ripe mango, peeled, pitted, and cut into chunks
8 ounces unsweetened, evaporated skim milk
½ teaspoon rum extract
1 envelope unflavored gelatin
2 tablespoons concentrated frozen apple juice
2 tablespoons chopped walnuts
½ teaspoon ground cinnamon

Combine mango chunks, milk, and rum extract in blender and puree. In measuring cup, sprinkle gelatin over apple juice and let stand 5 minutes to soften. Place cup in bowl of hot water to dissolve gelatin. Add to mango mixture and blend. Pour into bowl or directly into dessert dishes and refrigerate until set. Top with walnuts and sprinkle with cinnamon.

Serves 5.

Nutritive values per serving:	CHO (gm)	PRO (gm)	FAT (gm)	NA (mg)	CAL
	15	6	2	61	102
Food exchanges per serving:	1 fruit + ½ skim milk + ½ lean meat				

MEXICO—MENU 4
SOPA DE ELOTE Y CHAYOTE (CORN AND SQUASH SOUP)
CARNE DE PUERCO EN SALSA DE RAJAS
(PORK IN CORIANDER SAUCE)
FRIJOLES REFRITOS (REFRIED BEANS)
PLATO DE FRUTA (FRESH FRUIT PLATTER)

SOPA DE ELOTE Y CHAYOTE
(CORN AND SQUASH SOUP)

SOUP

2 cups corn kernels, scraped and cut from 1 large ear of corn
1 large stalk celery, chopped fine
2 cloves garlic, minced
3 scallions, chopped (white part only)
3 cups chicken stock
⅓ cup scraped and diced carrots
1 tablespoon ground coriander
Dash cayenne
1 cup chayote or zucchini, steamed briefly and cubed
1 cup Salsa Mexicana (see recipe below)

In nonstick saucepan, place corn, celery, garlic, scallions, and ¼ cup of the chicken stock. Sauté 10 minutes. Add carrot, remainder of stock, coriander, and cayenne. Bring to boil, lower heat, and cover. Let simmer 40 minutes. Add cooked chayote or zucchini and heat through. Serve in soup bowls with salsa on the side.

SALSA MEXICANA

2 ripe tomatoes, chopped, *or* **1 13-ounce can Italian plum
    tomatoes, drained, chopped**
**2 jalapeño peppers, seeded and chopped (wear rubber gloves
    to prevent burns)** *or* **3 canned serrano peppers**
¼ cup finely chopped cilantro leaves
1 clove garlic, minced
1 medium onion, chopped
¼ cup fresh lime juice
1 tablespoon chopped fresh oregano or ¼ tablespoon dried
¼ teaspoon pepper

Combine all ingredients and set aside for at least 1 hour.

Serves 6.

Nutritive values per serving:	CHO (gm)	PRO (gm)	FAT (gm)	NA (mg)	CAL
	21	5	1	19	113
Food exchanges per serving:	⅔ bread + 2½ vegetable				

CARNE DE PUERCO EN SALSA DE RAJAS
(PORK IN CORIANDER SAUCE)

1 pound lean pork, cubed, all fat removed
1 cup chicken broth (see index)
1 clove garlic
Pepper
1 large onion, chopped
1 8-ounce can Italian plum tomatoes, drained and chopped
1 teaspoon coriander seeds, crushed and soaked in 1
    tablespoon water
½ teaspoon crushed rosemary
1 green chili cut into strips and seeded (wear rubber gloves to
    prevent burns)
½ cup drained, herbed yogurt (see Chapter 20)
Salsa Mexicana (see preceding recipe)
¼ cup chopped green pepper

Simmer meat in chicken broth with garlic and pepper until liquid is absorbed. Discard garlic. Sauté meat in ungreased nonstick pan until lightly browned. Add onion and continue cooking until onion is soft. Add tomatoes. Drain water from coriander seeds and add to meat with rosemary and chili. Cover and cook over low heat for 1 hour, until pork is tender. To serve, place 2 tablespoons of drained yogurt alongside the meat serving and on top of each drizzle a little ribbon of the salsa and some chopped green peppers.

Serves 4.

Nutritive values per serving:	CHO (gm)	PRO (gm)	FAT (gm)	NA (mg)	CAL
	9	38.5	13	253	424
Food exchanges per serving:	5 medium-fat meat + 2 vegetable				

FRIJOLES REFRITOS
(REFRIED BEANS)

8 ounces dried pinto beans
2 quarts water
1 small onion, minced
5 tablespoons tomato paste
1 teaspoon hot chili powder
1 teaspoon ground coriander
4 cloves garlic, chopped fine
1 teaspoon ground cumin
1 jalapeño pepper, seeded and chopped (wear gloves to
    prevent burns)
1 tablespoon low-sodium soy sauce

Soak the beans overnight in water to cover. Drain several times. Cook beans in 2 quarts water with remaining ingredients for about 2 hours. Add more water if necessary. When tender and thick, mash well.

Serves 6.

Nutritive values per serving:	CHO (gm)	PRO (gm)	FAT (gm)	NA (mg)	CAL
	30	10	1	77	169
Food exchanges per serving:	1⅔ bread + 1 vegetable + ½ lean meat				

PLATO DE FRUTA
(FRESH FRUIT PLATTER)

1 small fresh pineapple
1 navel orange, peeled and sliced
1 cup peeled, seeded, and cubed honeydew or cantaloupe
12 fresh strawberries, stems left intact
½ cup fresh lime juice

Quarter the pineapple and remove hard core, leaving on spikes. Separate pulp from the shell and cut pineapple into cubes. Arrange pineapple shells on platter so that the green spikes form a colorful arrangement. Contrasting their colors, arrange assorted fruit over the shells. Place orange slices and strawberries on top. Sprinkle with lime juice and serve chilled.

Serves 6.

Nutritive values per serving:	CHO (gm)	PRO (gm)	FAT (gm)	NA (mg)	CAL
	20	1	0	6	84
Food exchanges per serving:	2 fruit				

MEXICO—MENU 5
TACOS DE POLLO (CHICKEN TACOS)
CREMA DE PAPAYA (PAPAYA CREAM)

TACOS DE POLLO
(CHICKEN TACOS)

12 corn tortillas
1 pound whole chicken breast, skinned
1 onion, sliced
1 bay leaf
8 peppercorns
2 cups water
1 medium onion, chopped
1 tablespoon chopped ripe olives
1 small jalapeño pepper, chopped (wear gloves
    to prevent burns)
Enchilada Sauce (see recipe below)

CHICKEN FILLING

Combine chicken breasts, sliced onion, bay leaf, pepper-corns, and water. Bring to boil, reduce heat, and cover. Let simmer ½ hour until chicken is tender. Let cool in broth (broth may be used in Enchilada Sauce). Separate chicken from bones and shred meat, discarding bones and any fat. In another nonstick skillet, sauté the chopped onion. When translucent, stir in the chicken, ¾ cup of Enchilada Sauce, olives, and jalapeño pepper. Simmer together 10 minutes. Place in earthen-ware serving bowl and let guests fill their own tacos with chicken and condiments.

TORTILLAS

Wrap tortillas in damp, clean dishcloth and then in aluminum foil and place in preheated 350°F oven for 10 minutes until soft and warm. Remove and serve (2 per person).

ENCHILADA SAUCE

2 cloves garlic, minced
1 teaspoon corn oil
1 tablespoon chili powder
1 cup chicken stock (use stock from recipe above)
1 cup tomato sauce
1 tablespoon tomato paste
½ teaspoon dried oregano
¼ teaspoon ground cumin

Heat all enchilada sauce ingredients together for 15 minutes at simmer. Use ¾ cup of this sauce to moisten chicken taco filling. Makes 2 cups.

Serves 6.

Nutritive values per one taco:	CHO (gm)	PRO (gm)	FAT (gm)	NA (mg)	CAL
	16	11	2	110	127
Food exchanges per serving:	1 bread + 1 lean meat				

CONDIMENTS

2 cups iceberg lettuce, shredded
¼ cup Monterey Jack cheese, shredded
½ cup chopped onion
1 cup chopped tomatoes
1 cup chopped parsley

Place each of the condiments in an individual bowl and pass with tortillas and chicken. Each person may fill tacos with ½ cup chicken, 1 tablespoon cheese, and as much of the other garnishes as desired.

Serves 6.

Nutritive values of condiments:	CHO (gm)	PRO (gm)	FAT (gm)	NA (mg)	CAL
	5.5	3	1.5	40	48
Food exchanges per serving:	1 vegetable + ¼ medium-fat meat				

CREMA DE PAPAYA
(PAPAYA CREAM)

1 papaya, peeled and seeded (reserve seeds)
1 cup plain low-fat yogurt
½ teaspoon pure vanilla extract
1 teaspoon lemon juice
1 teaspoon grated orange rind
Sprinkling cinnamon
2 tablespoons peeled and chopped pistachios

Place cut papaya in blender or food processor and puree with yogurt. Add vanilla, lemon juice, and orange rind. Pour into ice tray and freeze for about 1–2 hours. Serve in individual dessert dishes, topped with sprinkling of cinnamon and pistachio nuts. This may be served at once rather than freezing. Garnish with papaya seeds.

Serves 4.

Nutritive values per serving:	CHO (gm)	PRO (gm)	FAT (gm)	NA (mg)	CAL
	13	4	3	42	95
Food exchanges per serving:	1 fruit + ⅓ skim milk + ½ fat				

GREECE

Menu 1

SANTORINI SPINACH APPETIZER
Stuffed Mushrooms

PSARI PLAKI
Baked Snapper with Clams

CHICK-PEA SALAD

METAXA BRANDIED PEACHES

Menu 2

AVGOLEMONO SOUP
Lemon and Egg Soup

MOUSSAKA
Eggplant and Lamb Casserole

TSISIKI SALAD
Cucumber Yogurt Salad

COMPOSTA LAMPSA CRETE
Sliced Oranges

Menu 3

YALANTZI DOLMADAKIA CORFU
Steamed Grape Leaves

STIFADO
Veal Stew

LEGUMES A LA GREQUE
PITA BREAD

MELON WITH YOGURT ALMONDS

TURKEY

Menu 1

TAVUK TSHORBASI YOGURTLU
Chicken Soup with Yogurt

KABABE MAHI
Baked Stuffed Fish (Iran)

HUNKAR BEGENDI
Sultan's Delight Eggplant Puree

WHOLE WHEAT PITA BREAD

POMEGRANATE SORBET

Menu 2

ANATOLIAN SOUP
Barley Chicken Soup

SIS KEBAB
Chicken or Turkey Kebabs

BORANI ESFANAJ
Spinach and Nut Salad (Iran)

IRMIK HELVASI
Semolina with Almonds and Milk

LEBANON

SHORABAT KAREI
Pumpkin Soup

TABBOULEH
Cracked Wheat Salad

SAMAK MAKLI
Fish with Herbs

YAOUTOPITA
Yogurt Fruit Cream

14

EASTERN MEDITERRANEAN

More than the sparkling sea and the shimmering sunshine, the Eastern Mediterranean lands share the golden harvest that climate produces. Greece, Turkey, Lebanon, and Iran all produce tomatoes, eggplants, olives, peppers, and many herbs. Healthful and flavorful garlic is the essence of the Middle East, and olive oil is used for cooking. Dates, apricots, pomegranates, oranges, lemons, and melons abound. Sherbet originated in Persia (Iran) and was made of these perfumed juices. Walnuts and pine nuts, almonds and filberts, pistachios and sesame seeds offer rich flavorings.

Memory takes me back to a sun-drenched beach at Mykonos. Lunch there was a freshly caught and perfectly grilled fish; a salad of olives, peppers, and the inimitable Greek feta cheese; and dessert a succulent fresh fruit to quench the thirst of a sun worshipper.

The Middle East is also the home of the chick-pea (it goes back to biblical times). Along with lentils and beans, they are protein-rich and used in soups and stews. Hummus is made of chick-peas and sesame paste. The kebab is the hot dog of the Middle East. In Greece, it's souvlaki—meat or fish skewered, lemon-soaked, and broiled, and paired with fresh vegetables. From aubergine to zucchini, the riches of these lands will please all who partake. As the Greeks say, *kali orexi!*

GREECE—MENU 1

SANTORINI SPINACH APPETIZER (STUFFED MUSHROOMS)
PSARI PLAKI (BAKED SNAPPER WITH CLAMS)
CHICK-PEA SALAD
METAXA BRANDIED PEACHES

SANTORINI SPINACH APPETIZER
(STUFFED MUSHROOMS)

½ cup chopped onions
½ pound fresh leaf spinach or ½ package frozen
¼ cup chopped fresh dill
¼ cup part-skim ricotta cheese
1 teaspoon ground nutmeg
Pinch salt
⅛ teaspoon pepper
8 large mushrooms
2 tablespoons lemon juice

Sauté onions in nonstick pan. Boil and drain spinach and chop very fine. Add sautéed onions, fresh dill, ricotta cheese, nutmeg, salt, and pepper and mix thoroughly. Remove stems from mushrooms and wash carefully. Spoon filling into each cap and sprinkle with lemon juice. Bake for 25 minutes in preheated 350°F oven.

Serves 4.

Nutritive values per serving:	CHO (gm)	PRO (gm)	FAT (gm)	NA (mg)	CAL
	8.5	5.5	2	71	74
Food exchanges per serving:	1½ vegetable + ½ medium-fat meat				

PSARI PLAKI
(BAKED SNAPPER WITH CLAMS)

**1 snapper or bass (3½ pounds), cleaned, split,
    head and tail intact**
½ cup chopped parsley
2 tablespoons tomato paste
½ cup chopped scallions
2 bay leaves, crushed
1 teaspoon dried oregano
½ teaspoon cayenne
2 teaspoon fresh basil or ½ teaspoon dried
Vegetable spray
1½ cups dry white wine
8 cherrystone clams, well scrubbed

Rinse snapper in cold water and score with diagonal
slashes on one side. Mix parsley, tomato paste, scallions, bay
leaves, oregano, cayenne, and basil and stuff into cavity of fish.
Pin together with skewers. Place in baking pan lightly coated
with vegetable spray. Pour wine over the fish and bake in
preheated 350°F oven for 45 minutes. Add clams to pan,
distributing around the fish, and add more wine if needed.
Continue baking another few minutes until clams open.

Serves 4.

Nutritive values per serving:	CHO (gm)	PRO (gm)	FAT (gm)	NA (mg)	CAL
	9	52	7	81	307
Food exchanges per serving:	2 vegetable + 7 lean meat; omits 3 fat				

CHICK-PEA SALAD

1 8-ounce can chick-peas (garbanzos), drained
½ cup plain low-fat yogurt
2 tablespoons red wine vinegar
2 cloves garlic, minced
⅛ teaspoon cayenne
3 tablespoons chopped fresh mint, or 1 teaspoon dried
Dash salt
4 lettuce leaves
Few leaves fresh mint for garnish

Mix drained chick-peas with yogurt, vinegar, garlic, cayenne, salt, and mint. Chill in covered dish for 1 hour. Divide among lettuce leaves and garnish with fresh mint.

Serves 4.

Nutritive values per serving:	CHO (gm)	PRO (gm)	FAT (gm)	NA (mg)	CAL
	21	8	2	23	134
Food exchanges per serving:	1⅖ bread + ½ vegetable + ½ lean meat				

METAXA BRANDIED PEACHES

1 cup fresh blueberries
¼ cup Metaxa brandy
4 fresh peaches, peeled, pitted, and sliced

Puree blueberries in blender. Add brandy, transfer to small saucepan, and bring to a boil. Let cool. Arrange peach slices on dessert plates and spoon blueberry sauce over each serving.

Serves 4.

Nutritive values per serving:	CHO (gm)	PRO (gm)	FAT (gm)	NA (mg)	CAL
	15	1	0	1	64
Food exchanges per serving:	1½ fruit				

GREECE—MENU 2
AVGOLEMONO SOUP (LEMON AND EGG SOUP)
MOUSSAKA (EGGPLANT AND LAMB CASSEROLE)
TSISIKI SALAD (CUCUMBER YOGURT SALAD)
COMPOSTA LAMPSA CRETE (SLICED ORANGES)

AVGOLEMONO SOUP
(LEMON AND EGG SOUP)

4 cups chicken broth (see index)
½ cup orzo
3 tablespoons fresh lemon juice
2 eggs (use only 1 yolk), beaten until frothy
2 teaspoons finely chopped fresh mint

In saucepan, bring broth to boil and add orzo. Simmer for 10–15 minutes, until orzo is tender but not mushy. Lower heat. Add lemon juice to beaten eggs and slowly add to broth when it has stopped boiling. Simmer gently until soup is thick enough to coat spoon. Do not let soup boil. Serve in bowls with mint.

Serves 4.

Nutritive values per serving:	CHO (gm)	PRO (gm)	FAT (gm)	NA (mg)	CAL
	20	9	2	59	134
Food exchanges per serving:	1⅓ bread + ½ medium-fat meat				

MOUSSAKA
(EGGPLANT AND LAMB CASSEROLE)

1 large eggplant
Salt
⅓ **cup corn oil**
½ **teaspoon olive oil**
1 **medium onion, chopped**
1 **cup tomato sauce**
½ **cup chopped parsley**
¾ **pound ground lamb**
½ **cup red wine**
¼ **teaspoon ground cinnamon**
½ **cup plain low-fat yogurt**
½ **teaspoon ground nutmeg**
Vegetable spray
½ **cup whole wheat bread crumbs**
¼ **cup grated sapsago or Parmesan cheese**

Cut eggplant into ¼-inch-thick slices. Lightly salt and let stand on paper towel for ½ hour. Pat dry and brush with corn oil. Broil until golden on each side. Remove from broiler and set aside. Heat olive oil in nonstick skillet and sauté onion in it. Add tomato sauce and parsley and set aside. In another skillet, brown the ground lamb and add the wine, cinnamon, yogurt, nutmeg, and tomato sauce mixture. Lightly coat a baking pan with vegetable spray. Layer the eggplant, then the lamb mixture, until both eggplant and lamb are used up. Sprinkle top with bread crumbs and grated cheese and bake in preheated 350°F oven for 35 minutes.

Serves 4.

Nutritive values per serving:	CHO (gm)	PRO (gm)	FAT (gm)	NA (mg)	CAL
	26	30	19	588	395
Food exchanges per serving:	3½ vegetable + ½ bread + 3 medium-fat meat + 1 fat				

TSISIKI SALAD
(CUCUMBER YOGURT SALAD)

4 medium cucumbers, peeled, seeded, and chopped fine
Salt
8 cloves garlic, peeled and minced
1 tablespoon plain low-fat yogurt
½ tablespoon part-skim ricotta cheese
Dash pepper
½ cup chopped mint leaves or 2 tablespoons dried

Let chopped cucumbers sit in salt for 1 hour. Rinse and dry. Mix with garlic and yogurt to bind along with ricotta. Serve chilled with fresh pepper and garnish of mint leaves.

Serves 4.

Nutritive values per serving:	CHO (gm)	PRO (gm)	FAT (gm)	NA (mg)	CAL
	5.5	1.5	0	15	28
Food exchanges per serving:	1 vegetable				

COMPOSTA LAMPSA CRETE
(SLICED ORANGES)

Rind from 1 orange, cut into slivers
4 navel oranges
4 teaspoons concentrated frozen orange juice
2 tablespoons peeled and crushed pistachios

Place orange rind slivers in a saucepan and cover with cold water. Bring to boil. Remove from heat and let steep 15 minutes, then drain. Section the oranges, removing any pulp and pits. Place in glass serving bowl. Add concentrated orange juice and mix. Sprinkle with orange slivers and garnish with pistachios.

Serves 4.

Nutritive values per serving:	CHO (gm)	PRO (gm)	FAT (gm)	NA (mg)	CAL
	22	2.5	2	1	116
Food exchanges per serving:	2 fruit + ⅓ high-fat meat				

GREECE—MENU 3
YALANTZI DOLMADAKIA CORFU (STEAMED GRAPE LEAVES)
STIFADO (VEAL STEW)
LEGUMES A LA GREQUE
PITA BREAD
MELON WITH YOGURT ALMONDS

YALANTZI DOLMADAKIA CORFU
(STEAMED GRAPE LEAVES)

¾ cup finely chopped onions
2 tablespoons vegetable oil, divided
⅓ cup Basmati rice, well washed
1¼ cups water
1 tablespoon pine nuts
Freshly ground black pepper
1 tablespoon raisins
15 small grape leaves
2 tablespoons cold water
Lemon wedges

Sauté onions in 1 tablespoon oil in a nonstick skillet. Add uncooked rice and stir until grains are coated. Pour in 1¼ cups water and bring to boil. Reduce heat to low and simmer until rice is tender and water absorbed. Add more water if needed. Lightly brown pine nuts in nonstick pan and add to rice along with pepper and raisins.

Blanch grape leaves in boiling water and separate. Place on paper towels, dull side up. Stuff each leaf with rice mixture, forming small bundles. Fold so that grape leaf is wrapped around rice. Stack bundles seam side down in a large casserole. Add cold water and dot with 1 tablespoon vegetable oil. Cover and simmer for 50 minutes. Serve at room temperature with lemon wedges.

Serves 5.

Nutritive values per serving:	CHO (gm)	PRO (gm)	FAT (gm)	NA (mg)	CAL
	16	2	7.5	73	140
Food exchanges per serving:	⅔ bread + 1 vegetable + 1½ fat				

STIFADO
(VEAL STEW)

2 pounds lean veal, all fat removed, cubed
Salt and pepper to taste
2 cloves garlic, minced
½ teaspoon dried cinnamon
2 tablespoons red wine vinegar
1 cup red wine
20 small white onions
2 tablespoons tomato paste
1½ cups peeled, seeded and chopped tomatoes
½ cup chicken broth (see index)
½ teaspoon dried oregano
1 bay leaf
½ cup feta cheese

In ovenproof casserole, combine veal, salt, pepper, garlic, and cinnamon. Cover and cook for 10 minutes over medium heat. Add vinegar and wine and place in 350°F oven. Bake for 1 hour. Peel and trim onions and boil 3 minutes. Drain and add to casserole along with tomato paste and remaining ingredients except cheese. Crumble feta cheese on top and bake for ½ hour more.

Serves 6.

Nutritive values per serving:	CHO (gm)	PRO (gm)	FAT (gm)	NA (mg)	CAL
	8	34	17	402	321
Food exchanges per serving:	1½ vegetable + 5 lean meat + ⅓ fat				

LEGUMES A LA GREQUE

MARINADE

1 cup chicken stock (see index)
1 cup dry white wine
1 tablespoon olive oil
½ cup fresh lemon juice
3 sprigs parsley
2 cloves garlic, minced
⅛ teaspoon dried thyme
5 peppercorns

VEGETABLES

4 cups onions, zucchini, yellow squash, string beans, celery
    hearts, cucumbers, red peppers, carrots, or any firm
    vegetable combination
1 lemon, sliced

Stir all marinade ingredients together in enamel or stainless steel saucepan. Bring to boil and simmer 45 minutes. Discard parsley sprigs.

Cook each vegetable in marinade, starting with the hardest vegetable (carrots). Softest vegetable (mushrooms) should be last. Let cool. Cover dish and let vegetables marinate in refrigerator for at least 4 hours. Remove from marinade with slotted spoon and serve with lemon slices.

Serves 4.

Nutritive values per serving:	CHO (gm)	PRO (gm)	FAT (gm)	NA (mg)	CAL
	15	3	3.5	39	104
Food exchanges per serving:	2 vegetable + ½ fruit + ⅔ fat				

PITA BREAD

2 large or 4 small whole wheat pita loaves

Serve warmed whole wheat pita bread with main course. Wrap pita in foil and heat in moderate oven.

Serves 4.

Nutritive values per serving:	CHO (gm)	PRO (gm)	FAT (gm)	NA (mg)	CAL
	13	4	1	—	160
Food exchanges per serving:	1 bread				

MELON WITH YOGURT ALMONDS

Ground cinnamon
2½ cups plain low-fat yogurt
4 slices honeydew melon, seeded and chopped
2 tablespoons chopped almonds

Mix cinnamon with yogurt and strain in cheesecloth for 2 hours or until it is quite firm. In a small bowl, mix honeydew melon, almonds, and firm yogurt, chill, and serve.

Serves 4.

Nutritive values per serving:	CHO (gm)	PRO (gm)	FAT (gm)	NA (mg)	CAL
	22	9	5	92	170
Food exchanges per serving:	1 fruit + 1 skim milk + 1 fat				

TURKEY—MENU 1
TAVUK TSHORBASI YOGURTLU (CHICKEN SOUP
WITH YOGURT)
KABABE MAHI (BAKED STUFFED FISH) (Iran)
HUNKAR BEGENDI (SULTAN'S DELIGHT EGGPLANT PUREE)
WHOLE WHEAT PITA BREAD
POMEGRANATE SORBET

TAVUK TSHORBASI YOGURTLU
(CHICKEN SOUP WITH YOGURT)

4 cups chicken broth (see index)
½ cup raw Basmati rice, washed until water runs clear
Freshly ground pepper
1 cup plain low-fat yogurt
2 eggs (use only 1 yolk), beaten with fork
1 tablespoon chopped fresh mint or ¼ tablespoon dried
1 tablespoon chopped parsley

Bring broth to boil in saucepan. Add rice and pepper. Cover and simmer 20 minutes, until rice is tender. Stir yogurt into the beaten eggs and mix well. Add to this ¼ cup of the soup and blend together. Return this to the soup, stirring. Do not let boil. Serve in soup bowls, topped with mint and parsley.

Serves 6.

Nutritive values per serving:	CHO (gm)	PRO (gm)	FAT (gm)	NA (mg)	CAL
	18	7	2	46	118
Food exchanges per serving:	1 bread + ¾ lean meat + ⅙ skim milk				

KABABE MAHI
(STUFFED BAKED FISH) (Iran)

1 striped bass (about 3½ pounds), cleaned and scaled, head
    and tail left intact
2 tablespoons walnut oil, plus oil for brushing fish
1 tablespoon soaked, drained, and finely chopped dried
    apricots
3 tablespoons chopped walnuts
2 tablespoons chopped shelled pistachios
Freshly ground pepper
Pinch saffron or turmeric
¼ teaspoon ground cardamom
Pinch ground cinnamon
Grated peel of 1 orange (no white pith)
Vegetable spray
1 tablespoon lemon juice
1 lemon, sliced thin
1 tablespoon chopped parsley

Wash fish under cold running water. Heat walnut oil in
nonstick skillet and add all ingredients except the fish, vegetable spray, lemon juice, lemon slices, and parsley. Sauté over
low heat for 4 minutes, mixing well. Stuff the fish with this
mixture and pin openings together with skewers. Coat baking
pan with vegetable spray and arrange fish in pan. Brush fish
with lemon juice and some of the walnut oil. Cover baking dish
with aluminum foil and bake in preheated 375°F oven for 25
minutes. Uncover and bake another 15 minutes. Transfer to
warm serving platter and garnish with lemon slices and
parsley.

Serves 4.

Nutritive values per serving:	CHO (gm)	PRO (gm)	FAT (gm)	NA (mg)	CAL
	7	45	19	5	379
Food exchanges per serving:	½ fruit + ½ vegetable + 6½ lean meat				

HUNKAR BEGENDI
(SULTAN'S DELIGHT EGGPLANT PUREE)

2 eggplants (about 2 pounds)
Juice of 1 lemon
1 tablespoon sunflower seed oil
2 cloves garlic, crushed
Pinch salt
Dash cayenne
4 ounces Creative Cream Cheese (see index)
Lettuce leaves
Pomegranate seeds
4 black olives, pitted
Parsley sprigs

Prick eggplants with a fork and place on baking dish in preheated 350°F oven. Bake 1 hour, until soft. Halve lengthwise when cool and scoop out the pulp. Place pulp in blender and puree. Add lemon juice, oil, garlic, salt, cayenne, and cream cheese. Process until smooth. Transfer to bowl and chill a few hours. Serve on lettuce leaves, garnished with pomegranate seeds (reserved from dessert), olives, and parsley sprigs.

Serves 4.

Nutritive values per serving:	CHO (gm)	PRO (gm)	FAT (gm)	NA (mg)	CAL
	11	5	9	122	145
Food exchanges per serving:	2 vegetable + 2 fat				

WHOLE WHEAT PITA

2 large or 4 small whole wheat pita loaves

Serve whole wheat pita bread, toasted lightly and cut into quarters, with Hunkar Begendi.

Serves 4.

Nutritive values per serving:	CHO (gm)	PRO (gm)	FAT (gm)	NA (mg)	CAL
	13	4	1	7	77
Food exchanges per serving:	1 bread				

POMEGRANATE SORBET

2 pomegranates (reserve some seeds)
Juice of 1 lemon
4-6 ice cubes
Mint leaves or lime slices

Cut fruit in half and scrape out seeds. Place seeds in food mill and grind out juice. Mix juice with lemon juice and puree in blender with 4-6 ice cubes. Pour into ice tray and freeze for 2-3 hours, stirring with a fork every 20 minutes or so to break up crystals. Serve in sherbet dishes, topped with mint leaf or lime slice. (If pomegranates are not available, this may be made with watermelon, strawberries, melon, orange juice, or grape juice).

Serves 4.

Nutritive values per serving:	CHO (gm)	PRO (gm)	FAT (gm)	NA (mg)	CAL
	13	0	0	3	52
Food exchanges per serving:	1⅓ fruit				

TURKEY—MENU 2
ANATOLIAN SOUP (BARLEY CHICKEN SOUP)
SIS KEBAB (CHICKEN OR TURKEY KEBABS)
BORANI ESFANAJ (SPINACH AND NUT SALAD) (Iran)
IRMIK HELVASI (SEMOLINA WITH ALMONDS AND MILK)

ANATOLIAN SOUP
(BARLEY CHICKEN SOUP)

½ cup pearl barley, well rinsed
1 teaspoon Creative Butter (see index)
1 onion, chopped
4 cups chicken broth (see index)
Freshly ground black pepper
½ cup plain low-fat yogurt
2 tablespoons chopped fresh parsley
1 tablespoon chopped fresh mint or 1 teaspoon dried

Boil the barley in water to cover. Remove from heat and set aside for 1 hour. Drain. In nonstick saucepan, heat the butter and sauté onion in it for 5 minutes, until soft. Add broth. Bring to boil and add drained barley and pepper. Simmer 45 minutes, until barley is tender. Add a few tablespoons of hot broth to the yogurt and mix until well blended. Add to soup when ready to serve. Reheat but do not boil. Serve in warm soup bowls with garnish of parsley and mint.

Serves 4.

Nutritive values per serving:	CHO (gm)	PRO (gm)	FAT (gm)	NA (mg)	CAL
	26.5	7.5	2	35	154
Food exchanges per serving:	2 vegetable + 4 lean meat; omits ⅔ fat				

SIS KEBAB
(CHICKEN OR TURKEY KEBABS)

**1 pound boneless, skinless chicken or turkey cutlet, cut into
    1-inch cubes, all fat removed**
2 tablespoons safflower oil
¼ cup fresh lemon juice
Pinch salt
½ teaspoon freshly ground black pepper
½ teaspoon dried thyme
1 onion, quartered
1 green pepper, seeded, ribs removed
12 cherry tomatoes

Place turkey or chicken pieces in a bowl and mix with all ingredients but the last three. Separate the quartered onion leaves and slice peppers into 1-inch squares. Place in bowl with the meat and the marinade and mix to coat everything. Cover and refrigerate several hours. When ready to prepare, alternate meat, onions, peppers, and tomatoes on skewers. Place skewers on broiler pan. Preheat broiler and place pan at least 8 inches from heat source so that kebabs don't burn. Turn and baste with marinade until done, about 10 minutes. Kebabs may also be cooked on a barbecue.

Serves 4.

Nutritive values per serving:	CHO (gm)	PRO (gm)	FAT (gm)	NA (mg)	CAL
	10	28.5	9.5	68	240
Food exchanges per serving:	2 vegetable + 4 lean meat; omits ⅔ fat				

BORANI ESFANAJ
(SPINACH AND NUT SALAD) (Iran)

1 pound fresh spinach
1 small onion, chopped
1 tablespoon walnut oil
½ cup plain low-fat yogurt
1 tablespoon chopped fresh mint or ¼ tablespoon dried
Pinch salt
Freshly ground pepper
1 clove garlic, minced
1 tablespoon chopped walnuts

Wash spinach leaves well. Remove stems. Chop fine. Combine with onion and place in large saucepan. Cook over low heat, stirring until water clinging to leaves evaporates. Drain. Add walnut oil and toss. Transfer to serving bowl. Add yogurt, mint, salt, pepper, and garlic. Chill 2 hours. Garnish with walnuts.

Serves 4.

Nutritive values per serving:	CHO (gm)	PRO (gm)	FAT (gm)	NA (mg)	CAL
	9.5	6	5.5	103	112
Food exchanges per serving:	2 vegetable + ⅓ lean meat				

IRMIK HELVASI
(SEMOLINA WITH ALMONDS AND MILK)

2 teaspoons walnut oil
½ cup blanched almonds
⅓ cup semolina
1½ cups skim milk
3 teaspoons fructose
½ teaspoon pure vanilla extract
2 tablespoons raisins, plumped in hot water

In large nonstick saucepan, heat walnut oil over low heat. Sauté almonds in oil for 2–3 minutes. Add semolina and cook a few minutes, stirring until lightly browned. Meanwhile, in another saucepan, bring to boil skim milk and fructose. Pour into semolina and almond mixture and stir. Simmer until thick. This takes only a few minutes. Add vanilla extract and raisins and serve warm in dessert dishes.

Serves 4.

Nutritive values per serving:	CHO (gm)	PRO (gm)	FAT (gm)	NA (mg)	CAL
	23	7	10	50	210
Food exchanges per serving:	½ bread + ½ skim milk + 1 fruit + 2 fat				

LEBANON—MENU 1
SHORABAT KAREI (PUMPKIN SOUP)
TABBOULEH (CRACKED WHEAT SALAD)
SAMAK MAKLI (FISH WITH HERBS)
YAOUTOPITA (YOGURT FRUIT CREAM)

SHORABAT KAREI
(PUMPKIN SOUP)

**2 acorn or butternut squash to equal 3 cups (these squash
have more taste than pumpkin, but pumpkin is fine)**
1 onion, chopped
3 cups water
½ teaspoon ground cinnamon
¼ teaspoon ground coriander
⅛ teaspoon turmeric
¼ teaspoon ground cumin
Freshly ground black pepper to taste
1 tablespoon vinegar
1 tablespoon low-sodium soy sauce
1 tablespoon chopped parsley

Cut squash or pumpkin in half and discard the seeds. (Seeds may be washed and roasted for other use.) Cut into slices. Place in steamer basket over boiling water and steam until tender, about 20 minutes. Let cool and peel. Place the squash in a large saucepan with the onion and water. Cook for ten minutes until tender. Pour into blender and puree. Return to saucepan and add spices, vinegar, and soy sauce. Bring to boil and simmer. Adjust seasoning and serve in warm bowls with sprinkling of parsley as garnish.

Serves 6.

Nutritive values per serving:	CHO (gm)	PRO (gm)	FAT (gm)	NA (mg)	CAL
	18	2.5	0	90	82
Food exchanges per serving:	1 bread + ½ vegetable				

TABBOULEH
(CRACKED WHEAT SALAD)

½ **cup bulgur**
½ **small onion**
2 scallions, chopped fine
1 small ripe tomato, peeled, seeded, and chopped
2 tablespoons chopped fresh mint or 1 teaspoon dried
¼ **cup finely chopped parsley**
Freshly ground black pepper to taste
⅛ **cup lemon juice**
½ **tablespoon sunflower seed oil**
4 lettuce leaves
2 black olives, sliced

Wash bulgur and pick over. Cover with 2 cups cold water and set aside to soak for 1 hour. Drain. (Save liquid—it makes a healthful soup base! In fact, it might be used for the pumpkin soup.)

Place bulgur in large bowl and add onion, scallions, tomato, mint, parlsey, and pepper. Toss well. Mix lemon juice and sunflower seed oil. Toss into salad and mix. Let chill a few hours before serving on lettuce leaves, topped with olives.

Serves 4.

Nutritive values per serving:	CHO (gm)	PRO (gm)	FAT (gm)	NA (mg)	CAL
	25.5	4	2.5	26	141
Food exchanges per serving:	1½ bread + ½ vegetable + ½ fat				

SAMAK MAKLI
(FISH WITH HERBS)

1½ pounds haddock, halibut, or other firm white fish
Pinch salt
1 tablespoon sunflower seed oil
2 onions, chopped
4 tablespoons chopped fresh coriander or parsley
1 clove garlic, crushed
1 cup clam juice
1 cup water
½ teaspoon ground cumin
3 tablespoons lemon juice
Dash cayenne
1 lemon, sliced thin

Wash fish and pat dry. Cut into 1-inch pieces. Sprinkle with salt and set aside 1 hour. Wipe salt off the fish. In nonstick skillet large enough to hold all fish slices, brown fish quickly on both sides, about 2 minutes. Remove from skillet and set aside, keeping warm. In same skillet, heat sunflower seed oil and add onions, 3 tablespoons of coriander leaves or parsley, and garlic. Cook together about 5 minutes. Place in bottom of ovenproof casserole and place fish over this bed. Add clam juice, water, and cumin. Poach in preheated 350°F oven for 15 minutes. Add lemon juice, sprinkle with cayenne, and garnish with lemon slices and 1 tablespoon coriander or parsley. Serve when cool.

Serves 4.

Nutritive values per serving:	CHO (gm)	PRO (gm)	FAT (gm)	NA (mg)	CAL
	9.5	34	4	115	210
Food exchanges per serving:	1 vegetable + 4½ lean meat + ⅓ fruit; omits 2 fat				

YAOUTOPITA
(YOGURT FRUIT CREAM)

1 ripe persimmon
1 cup plain low-fat yogurt
1 teaspoon pure vanilla extract
1 tablespoon grated lemon rind
1 teaspoon ground cinnamon
¼ teaspoon freshly grated nutmeg
1 tablespoon crushed pistachios

Persimmon should be soft to touch, but not mushy. If not, let ripen in paper bag with an apple. Then cut off a slice and remove pulp. Place in blender with the yogurt. Process until smooth. Fold in vanilla extract and lemon rind and pour into ice tray. Place in freezer for about 2–3 hours, but do not let freeze solid. When ready to serve, pile into dessert glasses and top with sprinkling of cinnamon, nutmeg, and pistachios.

Note: Almost any fruit can be used in place of the persimmon—bananas, mango, papaya, cantaloupe, etc.

Serves 4.

Nutritive values per serving:	CHO (gm)	PRO (gm)	FAT (gm)	NA (mg)	CAL
	12	3.5	2	41	80
Food exchanges per serving:	½ fruit + ½ skim milk + ½ fat				

PORTUGAL

Menu 1

LOMBO DE PORCO COM PIMENTA
MALAGUETA
Pork with Red Peppers

ABOBORA COZIDA
Baked Squash with Oranges

PUDIM AO PORTO
Flan

Menu 2

BACALHAU
Baked Codfish with Onions and Tomatoes

SALADA DE ENDIVAS
Endive Salad

ARROZ AMARELO
Saffron Rice

FIGOS RECHEADOS
Stuffed Figs

Menu 3

CANJA
Chicken Soup with Lemon and Mint

VATAPA
Steamed Shrimp

SALADA DE VAGEM
Green Bean Salad

ARROZ DOCE
Rice Pudding

Menu 4

CALDO VERDE
Kale Soup

ROUXINOL
Chicken with Almonds

LEGUMES
Grilled Vegetables

MOLHO DE MACA
Applesauce

SPAIN

Menu 1

GAZPACHO
Cold Vegetable Soup

PAVO A LA SEVILLANO
Sauteed Turkey

CACEROLA DE PAPAS
Anchovy Potato Casserole

NEBLINA DE NARANJA
Orange Mist

Menu 2

PAELLA
Chicken, Shellfish, and Rice

ENSALADA VERDE
Chicory Salad

MANZANAS AL HORNO
Baked Apples

Menu 3

SOPA DE AJO
Garlic Soup

PARILLA DE SALMON ROMESCU
Grilled Salmon

VERDURAS AL HORNO
Baked Vegetables

POSTRE DE VALENCIA
Chocolate Cream Dessert

Menu 4

POLLO JEREZ
Chicken in Sherry

PAPAS EN SALSA VERDE
Potatoes in Green Sauce

ENSALADA DE PIMIENTOS ASADOS
Roasted Bell Pepper Salad

LAS FRUTAS CAMORRAS
Broiled Fruit Barcelona

15

PORTUGAL AND SPAIN

Portugal and Spain are bounded by the Mediterranean and the Atlantic. They share the sun and the bounty of the seas. It is difficult to define what is especially Spanish or Portuguese food. A profusion of produce grows in both lands—olives, almonds, garlic, onions, and peppers. The authentic Spanish dishes go back to the cuisine of the peasant and fisherman. To this, the Romans and Moors brought the tomato, saffron (the world's most expensive spice), pepper, cumin, nutmeg, lemons, and oranges. One can never forget the perfumed aroma of the oranges of Seville and the gardens of the Alhambra!

Both nations cook by slow simmering methods, using locally crafted earthenware pottery. Simple spicing—just a touch of thyme or a bit of bay leaf or some cayenne, paprika, and parsley—turns out a tasty sauce.

The Spaniards are great snackers, and their main meal is the *comida,* eaten around two in the afternoon; *cena,* dinner, is eaten much later at night. No wonder a *siesta* is required!

In Spain, foods change with the seasons and are often occasions for festivities. A fond summer remembrance is of the tiny town of Aranjuez celebrating the white asparagus season—bunches of it hung everywhere!

In Catalonia, baby octopus, tripe in tomato sauce, owl meat, and fried chicken blood are delicacies. These treats are not for us! The Basques pride themselves on perfectly cooked fish. Andalusia is the land of *gazpacho*—but there are as many recipes for this as one can count. But Spain is perhaps best known for its *Paella Valenciana,* although there's some form of *paella* in every corner of the country. *Flan,* a delicious custard dessert, is ubiquitous. We've taken out the caramel but left an appealing pudding.

We hope our Iberian introduction captures the flavor and spirit of some old traditions. *Buen gusto!*

PORTUGAL—MENU 1

LOMBO DE PORCO COM PIMENTA MALAGUETA (PORK WITH
RED PEPPERS)
ABOBORA COZIDA (BAKED SQUASH WITH ORANGES)
PUDIM AO PORTO (FLAN)

LOMBO DE PORCO COM PIMENTA MALAGUETA
(PORK WITH RED PEPPERS)

1 tablespoon finely chopped garlic
1 teaspoon salt (preferably coarse)
1 teaspoon freshly ground black pepper
1½ pounds boneless pork, cut into ¼-inch slices
1 tablespoon corn oil
4 medium sweet red peppers, seeded, deribbed, and cut
    lengthwise into ½-inch strips
1 cup dry white wine
½ cup chicken stock (see index)
1 lemon, cut into 8 wedges

Using a mortar and pestle, or the back of a heavy spoon, mash the garlic, salt, and pepper into a smooth paste. Lightly spread the pork slices with the paste and place them in a bowl, turning. Cover and marinate at room temperature for 2–3 hours, or in refrigerator for 6 hours, turning the pork from time to time.

In a large nonstick skillet, brown pork slices, turning with tongs to cook evenly. Transfer meat slices to warm plate as they brown. Add corn oil to pan and cook peppers for 5 minutes, stirring so they are coated with oil. Transfer to meat platter. Pour off any excess oil, add wine and stock, and bring to rapid boil. Return pork and peppers to the skillet, cover, and reduce heat to low. Simmer 20 minutes, until pork is tender. Transfer pork and peppers to a deep platter. Boil and reduce sauce over high heat, stirring until it thickens. Season, pour over meat, garnish with lemon, and serve.

Serves 4.

Nutritive values per serving:	CHO (gm)	PRO (gm)	FAT (gm)	NA (mg)	CAL
	14	45	18	618	398
Food exchanges per serving:	1¾ vegetable + ½ fruit + 6 lean meat				

ABOBORA COZIDA
(BAKED SQUASH WITH ORANGES)

2 large acorn squash
2 teaspoons ground cinnamon
Salt
Pepper to taste
4 thin orange slices, peeled
1 teaspoon Creative Butter (see index)

Cut squash in half. Bake in preheated 375°F oven for 45 minutes, until tender. Remove from oven, discard seeds, and then carefully scoop out pulp. Mix pulp in large bowl with all other ingredients except oranges and butter. Stuff mixture back into shells and bake another 10–15 minutes. While heating, sauté orange slices in Creative Butter until they begin to caramelize. Arrange a slice of orange over each squash half and serve.

Serves 4.

Nutritive values per serving:	CHO (gm)	PRO (gm)	FAT (gm)	NA (mg)	CAL
	27.5	3.5	3	22	151
Food exchanges per serving:	⅓ fruit + 1⅔ bread + ½ fat				

PUDIM AO PORTO
(FLAN)

2 eggs (use only 1 yolk), beaten
1 cup evaporated skim milk
¼ teaspoon pure vanilla extract
2 teaspoons port wine

Blend eggs with evaporated milk. Add vanilla extract and port and blend again. Pour into ovenproof baking dish. Place this in a larger pan of hot water and bake in preheated 350°F oven for 40 minutes. Insert knife into middle of pudding. If it comes out clean, custard is done. If not, cook until ready. Let cool and serve at room temperature.

Serves 4.

Nutritive values per serving:	CHO (gm)	PRO (gm)	FAT (gm)	NA (mg)	CAL
	7	7	1	97	65
Food exchanges per serving:	½ skim milk + ½ lean meat				

PORTUGAL—MENU 2
BACALHAU (BAKED CODFISH WITH ONIONS AND TOMATOES)
SALADA DE ENDIVAS (ENDIVE SALAD)
ARROZ AMARELO (SAFFRON RICE)
FIGOS RECHEADOS (STUFFED FIGS)

BACALHAU
(BAKED CODFISH WITH ONIONS AND TOMATOES)

1 tablespoon olive oil
2 cloves garlic, minced
1 large onion
1½ pounds fresh cod fillets
1 herb bouquet (1 bay leaf, 2 tablespoons parsley, and 1
    tablespoon thyme tied in cheesecloth)
½ tablespoon tomato paste
1½ cups canned Italian plum tomatoes
½ cup dry white wine
Freshly ground pepper to taste
1 tablespoon capers, rinsed and dried
1 lemon, sliced thin

Heat the oil in a large, flat, ovenproof dish. Sauté the garlic
and onions in the oil. Arrange cod fillets over onions and add
the herb bouquet, tomato puree, tomatoes, and white wine.
Season with pepper. Cover and bake in preheated 350°F oven
for 20 minutes. Serve in the same dish, garnished with capers
and lemon slices.

Serves 4.

Nutritive values per serving:	CHO (gm)	PRO (gm)	FAT (gm)	NA (mg)	CAL
	10	32	4	232	204
Food exchanges per serving:	⅕ fruit + 1⅔ vegetable + 4½ lean meat; omits 2 fat				

SALADA DE ENDIVAS
(ENDIVE SALAD)

4 medium endives, leaves separated
¼ cup lemon juice
2 tablespoons walnut oil
2 black olives, minced

Arrange endive leaves on 4 plates. In a small bowl, whisk lemon juice and oil until blended and spoon over endives. Garnish with minced olives.

Serves 4.

Nutritive values per serving:	CHO (gm)	PRO (gm)	FAT (gm)	NA (mg)	CAL
	5.5	2	8	124	102
Food exchanges per serving:	1 vegetable + 1½ fat				

ARROZ AMARELO
(SAFFRON RICE)

¾ cup long-grain brown rice
1½ cups boiling water
1 teaspoon olive oil
1 clove garlic, minced
1 onion, sliced
Pinch saffron, soaked 30 minutes in 2 tablespoons
**   boiling water**
Dash cayenne

Rinse rice well. Place in saucepan and cover with 1½ cups boiling water. Simmer, covered, 30 minutes. Remove from heat. Do not stir. Let stand about 10 minutes to absorb water. Meanwhile, heat olive oil in small nonstick skillet and sauté garlic and onion in it. Stir into rice, add saffron with water, and toss lightly to fluff. Season with dash of cayenne.

Serves 4.

Nutritive values per serving:	CHO (gm)	PRO (gm)	FAT (gm)	NA (mg)	CAL
	31	3	2	6	154
Food exchanges per serving:	½ vegetable + 2 bread				

FIGOS RECHEADOS
(STUFFED FIGS)

4 large fresh figs
8 almonds, blanched
¼ cup Creative Cream Cheese (see index)

Cut stems off figs and split lengthwise. Stuff each with 2 almonds and pinch closed. Arrange on cookie sheet and bake 10 minutes in a preheated 325°F oven. Serve at room temperature, each with 1 tablespoon of Creative Cream Cheese.

Note: Eight dried figs or 4 fresh peaches may be used.

Serves 4.

Nutritive values per serving:	CHO (gm)	PRO (gm)	FAT (gm)	NA (mg)	CAL
	11	2.5	4	54	90
Food exchanges per serving:	1 fruit + ⅔ fat + ⅓ lean meat				

PORTUGAL—MENU 3

CANJA (CHICKEN SOUP WITH LEMON AND MINT)
VATAPA (STEAMED SHRIMP)
SALADA DE VAGEM (GREEN BEAN SALAD)
ARROZ DOCE (RICE PUDDING)

CANJA

(CHICKEN SOUP WITH LEMON AND MINT)

4 cups chicken broth (see index)
4 lemon slices, scored
4 teaspoons chopped fresh mint or 1 teaspoon dried

Heat chicken broth and garnish each serving with a slice of lemon and 1 teaspoon of chopped fresh mint.

Serves 4.

Nutritive values per serving:	CHO (gm)	PRO (gm)	FAT (gm)	NA (mg)	CAL
	3	3.5	.5	30	31
Food exchanges per serving:	½ vegetable + ¼ lean meat				

VATAPA
(STEAMED SHRIMP)

1 tablespoon olive oil
1 onion, chopped
1 green pepper, chopped
1 red pepper, chopped
3 cloves garlic, minced
2 small bay leaves
1 teaspoon paprika
½ teaspoon dried red pepper flakes
¼ teaspoon freshly ground pepper
1 teaspoon Durkee's Imitation Bacon Chips
½ cup peeled and chopped tomatoes
1½ cups dry white wine
1 pound shrimp, cleaned and deveined
½ cup chopped parsley

Heat olive oil in nonstick skillet and in it sauté onion, red and green peppers, garlic, bay leaves, paprika, pepper flakes, pepper, and bacon chips. Stir over heat until soft. Add tomatoes and wine and bring to a boil. Add shrimp, cover, and steam about 3–5 minutes, until shrimp turn pink. Remove bay leaves, garnish with fresh parsley, and serve.

Serves 4.

Nutritive values per serving:	CHO (gm)	PRO (gm)	FAT (gm)	NA (mg)	CAL
	16	25	5	295	209
Food exchanges per serving:	3 vegetable + 3 lean meat; omits 1 fat				

SALADA DE VAGEM
(GREEN BEAN SALAD)

1 pound fresh string beans, trimmed
2 tablespoons fresh lemon juice
3 tablespoons minced shallots
2 tablespoons olive oil
1 tablespoon snipped fresh dill or ½ teaspoon dried

Drop beans into boiling water and cook for 5 minutes, until tender. Refresh in cold water and drain. In a bowl, mix lemon juice, shallots, oil, and beans. Toss and serve with a garnish of dill.

Serves 4.

Nutritive values per serving:	CHO (gm)	PRO (gm)	FAT (gm)	NA (mg)	CAL
	10	2.5	7	9	113
Food exchanges per serving:	2 vegetable + 1⅓ fat				

ARROZ DOCE
(RICE PUDDING)

1 cup cooked brown rice
1 small banana, mashed
½ cup nonfat milk
1 teaspoon pure vanilla extract
½ teaspoon ground cinnamon
½ teaspoon freshly grated nutmeg
¼ cup frozen concentrated apple juice
1 teaspoon raisins
2 egg whites, beaten stiff

Mix all ingredients together except the egg whites. When blended, fold in egg whites and pour into baking pan. Bake in middle of preheated 350°F oven until top is brown and pudding is set, about 1 hour.

Serves 4.

Nutritive values per serving:	CHO (gm)	PRO (gm)	FAT (gm)	NA (mg)	CAL
	20	4	0	146	96
Food exchanges per serving:	¾ bread + 1 fruit				

PORTUGAL—MENU 4
CALDO VERDE (KALE SOUP)
ROUXINOL (CHICKEN WITH ALMONDS)
LEGUMES (GRILLED VEGETABLES)
MOLHO DE MACA (APPLESAUCE)

CALDO VERDE
(KALE SOUP)

½ pound fresh kale or Swiss chard
4 cups chicken broth (see index)
Pinch salt
¼ teaspoon freshly ground pepper
3 medium potatoes, peeled and sliced
1 teaspoon safflower oil
2 cloves garlic, minced
4 slices lemon

Wash kale or chard and discard any discolored leaves. Shred as fine as possible. In saucepan, mix chicken stock, salt, pepper, and potatoes and cook until potatoes are tender. Remove and mash. Return to broth, add oil, garlic, and bring to rolling boil. Add kale or chard and boil, uncovered, for 5 minutes. Serve with lemon slices.

Serves 4.

Nutritive values per serving:	CHO (gm)	PRO (gm)	FAT (gm)	NA (mg)	CAL
	21.5	8.5	2	76	138
Food exchanges per serving:	¾ bread + 2 vegetable + ½ lean meat				

ROUXINOL
(CHICKEN WITH ALMONDS)

2½ ounces blanched almonds
1 cup dry white wine
2 cloves garlic, crushed
½ teaspoon corn oil
1 medium onion, chopped
1½ teaspoons chili powder
½ teaspoon cayenne
1 pound skinless, boneless chicken breasts, cut into 4 pieces
Pinch salt
Pepper to taste
2 bay leaves

Crush almonds with a mortar and pestle or between 2 sheets of wax paper. In a small bowl, mix almonds, wine, and crushed garlic. Cover and let stand 1 hour. In a nonstick skillet, heat oil and sauté onion in it until soft. Add chili powder and cayenne and sauté 5 minutes more. Add the chicken breasts, season with salt and pepper, and reduce heat to low. Cover and cook, turning chicken occasionally, for 10 minutes. Add almonds and bay leaves and cook 5–10 minutes more, until sauce is slightly thickened. Remove bay leaves before serving.

Serves 4.

Nutritive values per serving:	CHO (gm)	PRO (gm)	FAT (gm)	NA (mg)	CAL
	7	26.5	19	128	305
Food exchanges per serving:	1½ vegetable + 4 lean meat + 1 fat				

LEGUMES
(GRILLED VEGETABLES)

¼ pound whole, medium-size mushrooms (wiped clean, with
  ¼ of stem removed)
2 zucchini, cut into 1½-inch pieces
1 green pepper, seeded and quartered
¼ cup olive oil
¼ cup red wine vinegar
2 tablespoons fresh lemon juice
½ teaspoon Dijon mustard
½ teaspoon dried oregano
½ teaspoon dried tarragon
½ teaspoon salt
¼ teaspoon freshly ground black pepper

Place the mushrooms, zucchini, and green pepper in a
bowl and set aside. Mix together the remaining ingredients in a
bowl and pour over the vegetables. Refrigerate for 6 hours or
overnight, turning occasionally. Spear vegetables onto bamboo
skewers and grill for 10 minutes, brushing occasionally with
reserved marinade. (These are good left over, cold, as a snack.)

Serves 8.

Nutritive values per serving:	CHO (gm)	PRO (gm)	FAT (gm)	NA (mg)	CAL
	7	2	7.5	174	104
Food exchanges per serving:	1½ vegetable + 1½ fat				

MOLHO DE MACA
(APPLESAUCE)

4 Granny Smith or MacIntosh apples, cored and quartered
½ cup water
¼ teaspoon ground nutmeg
½ teaspoon ground cinnamon
¼ teaspoon ground allspice
¼ teaspoon lemon juice

Cook apples, covered, with ½ cup of water until soft. Place in food mill and sieve into a bowl. Add spices and lemon juice, mix, and serve warm.

Serves 4.

Nutritive values per serving:	CHO (gm)	PRO (gm)	FAT (gm)	NA (mg)	CAL
	22	0	0	1	88
Food exchanges per serving:	2 fruit				

SPAIN—MENU 1
GAZPACHO (COLD VEGETABLE SOUP)
PAVO A LA SEVILLANA (SAUTEED TURKEY)
CACEROLA DE PAPAS (ANCHOVY POTATO CASSEROLE)
NEBLINA DE NARANJA (ORANGE MIST)

GAZPACHO
(COLD VEGETABLE SOUP)

SOUP

1 large cucumber, peeled and chopped
3 medium tomatoes, peeled and chopped
1 large onion, chopped
1 small green pepper, seeded and chopped
1 teaspoon minced garlic
3 cups unsweetened tomato juice
¼ cup red wine vinegar
Pinch salt
2 tablespoons olive oil
¾ tablespoon tomato paste

GARNISH

¼ cup whole wheat bread croutons
½ cup chopped onion
½ cup chopped green pepper

In a blender, combine cucumber, tomatoes, onion, green pepper, garlic, and tomato juice until blended into a smooth puree. Pour into a bowl and whisk in the vinegar, salt, olive oil, and tomato paste. Cover and chill in the refrigerator for at least 2 hours. Whisk again just before serving and pass the dishes of garnishes.

Serves 4.

Nutritive values per serving:	CHO (gm)	PRO (gm)	FAT (gm)	NA (mg)	CAL
	26	5	9	417	205
Food exchanges per serving:	⅓ bread + 4¼ vegetable + 1¼ fat				

PAVO A LA SEVILLANA
(SAUTEED TURKEY)

1 pound turkey cutlet, cut into 4 pieces, pounded thin
¼ pound mushrooms, sliced
1 tablespoon blanched and pulverized almonds
1 tablespoon minced garlic
¼ teaspoon salt
1 teaspoon cayenne
1 cup dry sherry
½ cup water
4 green olives

Sauté turkey in a nonstick skillet, turning, until browned, about 10 minutes. Remove turkey and set aside. In the same pan, quickly sauté mushrooms, almonds, garlic, salt, and cayenne. Add sherry and water and cook down until thickened. Add the turkey and olives. Simmer until turkey is tender, about 10 minutes.

Serves 4.

Nutritive values per serving:	CHO (gm)	PRO (gm)	FAT (gm)	NA (mg)	CAL
	5.5	29	11	277	237
Food exchanges per serving:	1 vegetable + 4½ lean meat				

CACEROLA DE PAPAS
(ANCHOVY POTATO CASSEROLE)

Vegetable spray
4 new potatoes, sliced thin
3 anchovy fillets, rinsed, drained, and chopped
½ teaspoon dried thyme
Pinch cayenne
½ cup Creative Cream Cheese (see index)
3 tablespoons grated sapsago or Romano cheese

Coat small baking dish with vegetable spray and layer potatoes in bottom. Sprinkle with anchovies. Sprinkle with thyme and pepper and spread cream cheese over the top. Cover with foil and place in preheated 350°F oven. Bake until potatoes are tender, about 35 minutes. Remove from oven, sprinkle with grated cheese, and pass under broiler to brown. Remove and let rest 30 minutes before serving.

Serves 4.

Nutritive values per serving:	CHO (gm)	PRO (gm)	FAT (gm)	NA (mg)	CAL
	6.5	5	6	157	100
Food exchanges per serving:	⅖ bread + ¾ medium-fat meat + ½ fat				

NEBLINA DE NARANJA
(ORANGE MIST)

1 teaspoon grated orange zest
1 cup fresh orange juice
2 teaspoons lemon juice
¾ cup evaporated skim milk

In a small bowl mix zest, orange juice, and lemon juice. Pour into ice tray and freeze for about 1½ hours. Pour evaporated milk into a bowl and place in freezer, along with beaters, until crystals form around edges, about 1 hour. Remove from freezer and beat until milk stands in stiff peaks. Remove orange juice mixture from freezer and beat for 1 minute. Fold into whipped milk and return to freezer until ready to serve.

Serves 4.

Nutritive values per serving:	CHO (gm)	PRO (gm)	FAT (gm)	NA (mg)	CAL
	12	4	0	53	64
Food exchanges per serving:	½ fruit + ½ skim milk				

SPAIN—MENU 2
PAELLA (CHICKEN, SHELLFISH, AND RICE)
ENSALADA VERDE (CHICORY SALAD)
MANZANAS AL HORNO (BAKED APPLES)

PAELLA
(CHICKEN, SHELLFISH, AND RICE)

1½ pound skinless, boneless chicken breasts, cut into 6 pieces
4½ cups chicken broth (see index)
6 mussels, well scrubbed
6 clams, well scrubbed
1 cup brown rice
Vegetable spray
¾ cup chopped onions
1 cup cubed tomatoes
2 cloves garlic
2 teaspoons paprika
¼ teaspoon saffron strands, soaked in 2 tablespoons
    hot water
1 cup cooked peas
6 large shrimp, cooked, peeled, and deveined
6 lemon wedges

Poach chicken pieces in broth until tender, about 5–10 minutes. Remove from broth and set aside, keeping warm. Cook mussels and clams in boiling water until they open. If any do not open, discard them. Bring 2 cups of broth back to boil and add rice. Cook for 20 minutes, covered. Remove from heat and let steam for 10 minutes.

In a large nonstick pan or a paella dish coated with vegetable spray, sauté onions, tomatoes, and garlic until onions are soft. Season with paprika and saffron and add the rice, any remaining chicken broth, and the peas. Cook over high heat for

10 minutes, stirring. Arrange chicken and shellfish over the rice. Lower heat and cook without stirring until rice is tender and all broth is absorbed, about 10 minutes. Add cooked shrimp and let stand covered for 10 minutes before serving with lemon wedges.

Serves 6.

Nutritive values per serving:	CHO (gm)	PRO (gm)	FAT (gm)	NA (mg)	CAL
	11	25	6	130	198
Food exchanges per serving:	1 vegetable + ⅓ bread + 2½ lean meat				

ENSALADA VERDE
(CHICORY SALAD)

2 tablespoons walnut oil
3 tablespoons wine vinegar
Pinch salt
Dash pepper
4 cloves garlic, minced
8 almonds, blanched, toasted, and chopped
1 small chili pepper, seeded and chopped (wear gloves to prevent burns)
1 large head chicory, washed and dried

Combine oil, vinegar, salt, and pepper and shake well. In blender, puree garlic, almonds, and chili pepper. Gradually add dressing and blend again. Tear chicory into pieces and toss with dressing.

Serves 6.

Nutritive values per serving:	CHO (gm)	PRO (gm)	FAT (gm)	NA (mg)	CAL
	2	.5	5.5	1	60
Food exchanges per serving:	½ vegetable + 1 fat				

MANZANAS AL HORNO
(BAKED APPLES)

6 medium cooking apples, cored
Vegetable spray
2 tablespoons raisins, plumped
½ cup port wine, brought to a boil to burn off alcohol
2 egg whites

Place apples in a baking dish lightly coated with vegetable spray. Fill hollowed apples with raisins, cover with wine, and bake for 40 minutes in preheated 325°F oven. While apples are baking, beat egg whites until stiff. Remove apples from oven and spoon egg whites over the top of each one. Return to oven for 10 minutes or until meringue is browned. Serve at room temperature.

Serves 6.

Nutritive values per serving:	CHO (gm)	PRO (gm)	FAT (gm)	NA (mg)	CAL
	26	1.5	1	20	119
Food exchanges per serving:	2½ fruit + ⅓ lean meat				

SPAIN—MENU 3
SOPA DE AJO (GARLIC SOUP)
PARILLA DE SALMON ROMESCU (GRILLED SALMON)
VERDURAS AL HORNO (BAKED VEGETABLES)
POSTRE DE VALENCIA (CHOCOLATE CREAM DESSERT)

SOPA DE AJO
(GARLIC SOUP)

1 tablespoon olive oil
2 tablespoons minced garlic
1 cup whole wheat bread crumbs
4 cups chicken stock (see index)
½ teaspoon cayenne
½ teaspoon paprika
Salt to taste
2 eggs (use only 1 yolk), beaten
2 tablespoons chopped parsley

In nonstick saucepan, heat olive oil and sauté garlic in it until soft. Add bread crumbs, stock, pepper, and paprika and stir. Add salt and bring to a boil. Reduce heat and simmer, uncovered, for 20 minutes. Remove from heat. Place a small amount of soup in a bowl and slowly add to it the beaten egg, stirring constantly. Keep adding soup and then finally pour back into original saucepan. Adjust seasoning. Heat but do not let boil. Garnish with parsley.

Serves 4.

Nutritive values per serving:	CHO (gm)	PRO (gm)	FAT (gm)	NA (mg)	CAL
	20	9	6	222	170
Food exchanges per serving:	1 vegetable + 1 bread + 1 lean meat + ½ fat				

PARILLA DE SALMON ROMESCU
(GRILLED SALMON)

¼ cups blanched and crushed almonds
1 teaspoon minced garlic
¼ cup vinegar
½ tablespoon corn oil
Pinch salt
Dash pepper
4 salmon steaks (1 pound total weight)

Combine almonds, garlic, vinegar, oil, salt, and pepper. Beat until sauce is thick and creamy. Preheat broiler and broil salmon 4 inches from heat, 4 minutes on each side. Serve with sauce.

Serves 4.

Nutritive values per serving:	CHO (gm)	PRO (gm)	FAT (gm)	NA (mg)	CAL
	2.5	23.5	24	52	320
Food exchanges per serving:	½ vegetable + 3 lean meat + 3 fat				

VERDURAS AL HORNO
(BAKED VEGETABLES)

1 large leek, washed well to remove all sand
1 onion, sliced thick
1 eggplant, peeled and sliced
1 tablespoon olive oil
Freshly ground pepper to taste

Trim leek and split. In foil-lined baking dish, place leek, onion, and eggplant slices. Brush with oil and bake until onions are tender, about 40 minutes. Season with pepper and serve.

Serves 4.

Nutritive values per serving:	CHO (gm)	PRO (gm)	FAT (gm)	NA (mg)	CAL
	9.5	2	4	5	82
Food exchanges per serving:	2 vegetable + ¾ fat				

POSTRE DE VALENCIA
(CHOCOLATE CREAM DESSERT)

1 teaspoon unflavored gelatin
¼ cup cold water
3 tablespoons carob powder
1 cup evaporated skim milk, divided
1 egg yolk, beaten
½ teaspoon pure vanilla extract
Pinch salt

Sprinkle gelatin over cold water. Then place in bowl of hot water to dissolve. In saucepan, combine carob, salt, dissolved gelatin, and ½ cup milk and mix until blended. Add egg yolk and cook over low heat until thickened, stirring. Stir in vanilla, using wire whisk. Remove from heat and let cool. Meanwhile, chill the second ½ cup of evaporated skim milk in freezer, along with beaters. When frosty around edges (about 1 hour), beat until stiff. Fold carob mixture into whipped milk. Beat together if necessary to make peaks. Serve at once in sherbet dishes or place in freezer compartment for 1 hour before serving.

Serves 4.

Nutritive values per serving:	CHO (gm)	PRO (gm)	FAT (gm)	NA (mg)	CAL
	13	5.5	1	73	83
Food exchanges per serving:	½ skim milk + ⅔ fruit + ¼ lean meat				

SPAIN—MENU 4
POLLO JEREZ (CHICKEN IN SHERRY)
PAPAS EN SALSA VERDE (POTATOES IN GREEN SAUCE)
ENSALADA DE PIMIENTOS ASADOS (ROASTED BELL
PEPPER SALAD)
LAS FRUTAS CAMORRAS (BROILED FRUIT BARCELONA)

POLLO JEREZ
(CHICKEN IN SHERRY)

1 pound skinless, boneless chicken breasts
1 bay leaf
Pinch salt
Dash pepper
2 cloves garlic, minced
2 onions, chopped
½ teaspoon chili powder
⅔ cup dry sherry
8 green olives
2 tablespoons cornstarch
2 tablespoons water

Cut chicken into 4 pieces and place in flameproof casserole. Add enough water to cover. Add bay leaf, salt, and pepper and bring to a slow boil over a low flame; simmer for 5 minutes. Add garlic, onions, and chili powder and simmer for another 10 minutes. Stir in sherry and olives and simmer 8 minutes more. In a small cup, blend cornstarch and water to a smooth paste. Add 2 tablespoons of warm sauce from the chicken, then return to the casserole and stir to blend. Serve when sauce has thickened. Remove bayleaf.

Serves 4.

Nutritive values per serving:	CHO (gm)	PRO (gm)	FAT (gm)	NA (mg)	CAL
	13	24	12	250	256
Food exchanges per serving:	⅓ bread + 1¾ vegetable + 3½ lean meat				

PAPAS EN SALSA VERDE
(POTATOES IN GREEN SAUCE)

½ teaspoon olive oil
3 cloves garlic, minced fine
4 medium red potatoes, peeled and sliced thin (about 3 cups)
4 tablespoons peas
3 tablespoons chopped parsley

Heat oil in a nonstick saucepan and brown garlic in it. Spread the sliced potatoes over the garlic and shake to blend. Add 3 tablespoons of water and continue cooking. Slowly add enough hot water to cover potatoes. Cover saucepan and simmer 20 to 30 minutes until potatoes are tender. Add peas. Shake to blend, sprinkle with parsley, and serve.

Serves 4.

Nutritive values per serving:	CHO (gm)	PRO (gm)	FAT (gm)	NA (mg)	CAL
	22	3	1	8	109
Food exchanges per serving:	1⅓ bread + ¼ vegetable + ¼ fat				

ENSALADA DE PIMIENTOS ASADOS
(ROASTED BELL PEPPER SALAD)

1 medium red pepper
1 large green pepper
3 tablespoons red wine vinegar
1 tablespoon safflower oil
2 anchovy fillets, rinsed and chopped
¼ teaspoon pepper
2 teaspoons capers, rinsed

Place peppers under broiler and char on all sides. Remove from oven and place in brown paper bag to steam. When cool enough to handle, peel and cut into strips. In separate bowl, mix vinegar, oil, anchovy fillets, and pepper and whisk until thoroughly blended. Arrange peppers on a platter in a decorative circle and pour dressing over peppers. Garnish with capers and serve.

Serves 4.

Nutritive values per serving:	CHO (gm)	PRO (gm)	FAT (gm)	NA (mg)	CAL
	4	1	4	5	56
Food exchanges per serving:	¾ vegetable + ¾ fat				

LAS FRUTAS CAMORRAS
(BROILED FRUIT BARCELONA)

½ cup peeled and cubed fresh pineapple
1 banana, cut into 1-inch slices
1 orange, peeled, sectioned, and seeded
1 teaspoon ground cinnamon
¼ cup orange liqueur, simmered 3 minutes

Thread fruit on skewers, alternating the pineapple, banana, and orange. Sprinkle with cinnamon and place in foil-lined pan. Broil until lightly browned (about 3–5 minutes). Remove from skewers and spoon orange liqueur over each serving.

Serves 4.

Nutritive values per serving:	CHO (gm)	PRO (gm)	FAT (gm)	NA (mg)	CAL
	18	1	0	1	76
Food exchanges per serving:	2 fruit				

Menu 1
SALAT IZ OGURTSOV
Cucumber Salad
SHASHLYK IZ BARANINY
Lamb Shish Kebeb
KASHA PLOV
Buckwheat Groats with Mushrooms, Onions, Turnips
RHUBARB KISSEL
Rhubarb Dessert

Menu 2
TSYPLIATA NA MAHER RIABCHOKOV
Spring Chicken Cooked to Taste Like Grouse
LOBIA IZ GRESKIKH OREKHOV
String Beans with Walnut Sauce
LAPSHEVNIK
Noodle Pudding
KHOLODETS IZ KLUBNIKI ILI MALINY
Raspberry Compote

Menu 3
KHOLOKNYI BORSCHT
Cold Beet Soup
SALIVNAIA RYBA
Fish in Aspic
KREM IZ VZBITYKH SLIVOK
Whipped Cream Dessert

Menu 4
BEF STROGANOV
Beef Strogonoff
TUSHONAIA MORKOV'
Braised Carrots
PECHONYI KARTOFEL'
Baked Potatoes
IABLONCHNYI PIROG
Apple Pie

Menu 5
CUTLETI
Veal Patties
BALALAIKA PERLOVOI
Barley with Green Butter
KAPUSTA SO SMETANOI V LUK
Brussels Sprouts in Onion Cream
KESSEL
Grape Sponge

16

RUSSIA

No nation exists that is as vast as the USSR in the territory and climate it encompasses. From the frozen Siberian tundra to the steppes of Central Asia to the subtropical shores of the Black Sea, each region offers different foods and cooking methods. And neighboring culinary patterns have been absorbed, from Armenia, Scandinavia, Germany, and Turkey.

Root vegetables—cabbage, potatoes, beets—are the staples that sustain the Russians during the long, cold winters. The growing season in the North is painfully short, so these vegetables are stored, or pickled. In the South, fresh salad ingredients are plentiful, along with vegetables. A visit to the sunny seashore resort of Sochi is memorable—everyone had an armful of flowers and a large bag of fresh oranges. One can never forget the many dishes of cucumber salad and the vodka! Yogurt is enjoyed almost as much as the ubiquitous and sinful sour cream.

Russians are reputedly prodigious eaters. Each meal, in former days, was preceded by a meal in itself—an assortment of *zakuski*, or appetizers, that included smoked and pickled fish, meats, pâtés, pickles, *piroshkis*, and caviar. We haven't included any caviar (because of salt and prices!), but a dab of it on a baked potato shell is marvelous!

Fish, lamb, chicken, and some beef figure in our menus, rather than organ meats. Served with the traditional glass of tea, guests at our Russian repasts will wish each other a warm *priiyatnavo apetita!*

RUSSIA—MENU 1
SALAT IZ OGURTSOV (CUCUMBER SALAD)
SHASHLYK IZ BARANINY (LAMB SHISH KEBAB)
KASHA PLOV (BUCKWHEAT GROATS WITH MUSHROOMS,
ONIONS, TURNIPS)
RHUBARB KISSEL (RHUBARB DESSERT)

SALAT IZ ORGUTSOV
(CUCUMBER SALAD)

4 Kirby cucumbers, peeled and sliced
4 scallions, chopped
2 teaspoons chopped fresh dill or ½ teaspoon dried
1 tablespoon safflower oil
Dash pepper
½ cup fresh lemon juice
Several sprigs fresh dill for garnish

Combine all ingredients except garnish and toss well. Chill
and serve with fresh dill sprigs as garnish.

Serves 4.

Nutritive values per serving:	CHO (gm)	PRO (gm)	FAT (gm)	NA (mg)	CAL
	7.5	1	4	8	70
Food exchanges per serving:	1 vegetable + 1 fat				

SHASHLYK IZ BARANINY
(LAMB SHISH KEBAB)

1 pound boneless lamb (leg or shoulder), cubed
2 medium onions, quartered, leaves separated
4 scallions
12 cherry tomatoes
1 lemon, quartered

MARINADE

¼ cup fresh lemon juice
¼ cup red wine vinegar
1 tablespoon corn oil
1 tablespoon minced parsley
1 tablespoon chopped fresh basil or ½ teaspoon dried
1 teaspoon freshly ground black pepper

Remove all fat from lamb and cut into 1½-inch cubes. Combine meat with onion in bowl along with marinade. Cover and refrigerate 4 hours. When ready to prepare, preheat broiler or prepare barbecue. Drain and reserve marinade. Thread meat onto skewers, alternating with onions. Brush some of the marinade on meat and broil about 15 minutes, turning and brushing several times. Outdoor grilling will take a few minutes longer. Remove from skewers and garnish with tomatoes, scallions, and lemon quarters.

Serves 4.

Nutritive values per serving:	CHO (gm)	PRO (gm)	FAT (gm)	NA (mg)	CAL
	12	55	14	163	394
Food exchanges per serving:	2 vegetable + 7 lean meat; omits 1 fat				

KASHA PLOV
(BUCKWHEAT GROATS WITH MUSHROOMS, ONIONS, TURNIPS)

1 tablespoon sunflower seed oil
2 medium turnips, pared and grated (about 2 cups)
1 medium onion, minced
1 cup sliced mushrooms
½ cup buckwheat groats
1 cup skim milk
2 tablespoons minced fresh dill or ½ tablespoon dried

Heat sunflower seed oil in nonstick saucepan and sauté the vegetables in it. Wash groats, drain, then add to vegetable medley. Mix. Transfer to ovenproof casserole. Pour milk over mixture and sprinkle with dill. Cover and bake in preheated 350°F oven for 1 hour or until groats are tender. Fluff and serve.

Serves 7.

Nutritive values per serving:	CHO (gm)	PRO (gm)	FAT (gm)	NA (mg)	CAL
	16	4	3	55	107
Food exchanges per serving:	¾ bread + ½ vegetable + ¼ skim milk + ½ fat				

RHUBARB KISSEL
(RHUBARB DESSERT)

1 pound rhubarb, washed and peeled
¼ cup concentrated frozen apple juice
1 tablespoon arrowroot
2 tablespoons cold water

Soak rhubarb in cold water for 10 minutes. Drain and slice into chunks. Place in saucepan with apple juice and 2 tablespoons of water. Simmer for 10–15 minutes until soft and stringy. Thicken with arrowroot, which has been dissolved in 2 tablespoons of cold water. Chill and serve.

Serves 4.

Nutritive values per serving:	CHO (gm)	PRO (gm)	FAT (gm)	NA (mg)	CAL
	7	.5	0	3	30
Food exchanges per serving:	¾ fruit				

RUSSIA—MENU 2
TSYPLIATA NA MAHER RIABCHIKOV (SPRING CHICKEN
COOKED TO TASTE LIKE GROUSE)
LOBIA IZ GRESKIKH OREKHOV (STRING BEANS
WITH WALNUT SAUCE)
LAPSHEVNIK (NOODLE PUDDING)
KHOLODETS IZ KLUBNIKI ILI MALINY (RASPBERRY COMPOTE)

TYSPLIATA NA MAHER RIABCHIKOV
(SPRING CHICKEN COOKED TO TASTE LIKE GROUSE)

2 Rock Cornish hens
2 tablespoons juniper berries, crushed in blender
½ tablespoon ground allspice
1 tablespoon Creative Butter (see index)
¼ cup fresh lemon juice
1 tablespoon Durkee's Imitation Bacon Chips
Vegetable Spray
¼ cup plain low-fat yogurt
2 tablespoons whole wheat bread crumbs

Wash hens and wipe dry. Mix juniper berries and allspice together and rub hens inside and out with this mixture. Wrap birds in large piece of foil and refrigerate 24 hours. Rinse hens, pat dry, rub on butter, and drizzle with lemon juice. Sprinkle half of Imitation Bacon Chips into cavities and half on top of breasts. Preheat oven to 375°F and place birds breast side up in roasting pan coated lightly with vegetable spray. Roast 35–40 minutes, until tender, basting legs and wings with pan juices at intervals. Remove hens from oven and cut in half. Remove skin. Cover each half with yogurt, sprinkle with bread crumbs, and place under broiler a few minutes, until tops are golden.

Serves 4.

Nutritive values per serving:	CHO (gm)	PRO (gm)	FAT (gm)	NA (mg)	CAL
	5	23.5	10.5	205	209
Food exchanges per serving:	3 lean meat + ⅓ bread + ⅓ fat				

LOBIO IZ GRESKIKH OREKHOV
(GREEN BEANS WITH WALNUT SAUCE)

½ **cup shelled walnuts**
1 **clove garlic, minced**
½ **cup chopped scallions**
¼ **cup minced parsley**
¼ **cup red wine vinegar or fresh lemon juice**
Dash cayenne
1 **teaspoon Dijon mustard**
1 **pound string beans, washed and trimmed**

Grind nuts and garlic together in blender or food processor. Add remaining ingredients except beans and stir together. Steam green beans until tender, about 4–8 minutes, and drain. Mix with walnut sauce in warm saucepan.

Serves 4.

Nutritive values per serving:	CHO (gm)	PRO (gm)	FAT (gm)	NA (mg)	CAL
	13.5	6	9.5	30	164
Food exchanges per serving:	3 vegetable + 2 fat				

LAPSHEVNIK
(NOODLE PUDDING)

8 ounces fettucini
1 cup skim milk
1 egg (use only ½ yolk)
1 tablespoon concentrated frozen apple juice
1 tablespoon whole wheat bread crumbs
1 tablespoon Creative Butter (see index)
1 tablespoon caraway seeds

Cook noodles in boiling water for 12–14 minutes, until tender but not too soft. Drain. Place in baking pan. Combine milk, egg, and apple juice and pour over the noodles. Sprinkle top with bread crumbs, Creative Butter, and caraway seeds. Bake in preheated 375°F oven for 15 minutes or until golden.

Serves 6.

Nutritive values per serving:	CHO (gm)	PRO (gm)	FAT (gm)	NA (mg)	CAL
	31	8	3	45	183
Food exchanges per serving:	2 bread + ½ lean meat + ⅓ fat				

KHOLODETS IZ KLUBNIKI ILI MALINY

(RASPBERRY COMPOTE)

1 cup hulled fresh strawberries
2 tablespoons concentrated frozen apple juice
Juice of ½ lemon
2 tablespoons plain low-fat yogurt
3 cups fresh raspberries
1 tablespoon grated lemon rind

Puree strawberries in blender with apple and lemon juices and the yogurt. Place raspberries in compote dish or glass dessert dishes and pour sauce over each portion. Sprinkle with lemon rind and serve chilled.

Serves 4.

Nutritive values per serving:	CHO (gm)	PRO (gm)	FAT (gm)	NA (mg)	CAL
	17.5	2	1	6	87
Food exchanges per serving:	2 fruit				

RUSSIA—MENU 3
KHOLODNYI BORSCHT (COLD BEET SOUP)
SALIVNAIA RYBA (FISH IN ASPIC)
KREM IZ VZBITYKH SLIVOK (WHIPPED CREAM DESSERT)

KHOLODNYI BORSCHT
(COLD BEET SOUP)

1 pound beets, peeled and sliced
6 cups boiling water
2 teaspoons apple cider vinegar
½ pound potatoes, boiled, skinned, and diced
1 small cucumber, peeled, seeded, and diced
1 teaspoon Dijon mustard
¼ cup minced scallions
2 tablespoons plain low-fat yogurt
2 tablespoons chopped fresh dill or ½ teaspoon dried

Place beets in boiling water with apple cider vinegar. Simmer 45 minutes, until beets are cooked through. Drain beet broth and chill. Reserve beets. Puree beets, potatoes, and cucumber in blender with mustard. Add to chilled beet broth with scallions. Add yogurt and stir together. Serve in soup bowls, garnished with chopped dill.

Serves 4.

Nutritive values per serving:	CHO (gm)	PRO (gm)	FAT (gm)	NA (mg)	CAL
	30	4.5	.5	94	143
Food exchanges per serving:	1 bread + 3 vegetable				

SALIVNAIA RYBA
(FISH IN ASPIC)

**1 pound fish fillets (salmon, haddock, perch, or any mixture
   of boneless, thick fish)**
Juice of 1 lemon

COURT BOUILLON AND ASPIC

6 cups water
1 bay leaf
6 allspice berries
1 carrot
2 ounces celery root
1 onion, quartered
2 tablespoons unflavored gelatin
¼ cup cold water

GARNISH

1 lemon, sliced thin, then cut into quarters
¼ cup cornichons or unsweetened pickle slices
4 black olives, halved
Fresh parsley leaves
1 dozen cherry tomatoes, cut in half
½ cup Creative Mayonnaise with dill (see index)

Cut fish into 12 pieces, about 1 inch thick. Sprinkle with
lemon juice and let sit for 30 minutes. Place in saucepan 6 cups
water and add all spices, carrot, celery root, and onion. Bring to
boil and simmer 30 minutes, uncovered. Add fish after draining
off lemon juice and return to boil. Simmer over low heat 5
minutes or just until fish is done. Remove fish.

Dissolve gelatin in ¼ cup cold water. Strain 4 cups of the broth into another saucepan and add gelatin mixture. Stir until dissolved. Refrigerate until this begins to gel. Remove carrot from strainer and cut into thin rounds. Arrange fish on deep serving dish and artfully decorate with carrot slices, lemon, slices of pickles, olives, parsley leaves, and tomato halves. Cover carefully with the aspic so that the design is not disturbed. Refrigerate for several hours. Serve with dill mayonnaise. Extra gelatin may be diced and strewn around dish. A good pumpernickel bread or rye bread would complement this meal (see index).

Serves 4.

Nutritive values per serving:	CHO (gm)	PRO (gm)	FAT (gm)	NA (mg)	CAL
	12.5	29	14	355	292
Food exchanges per serving:	2 vegetable + 4 lean meat + ½ fat				

KREM IZ VZBITYKH SLIVOK
(WHIPPED CREAM DESSERT)

1 pound apples, cored and sliced
½ teaspoon ground cinnamon
½ teaspoon freshly grated nutmeg
1 cup water
1 teaspoon lemon juice
½ cup evaporated skim milk
1 teaspoon vanilla extract
¼ cup unsweetened grape juice

Place apple slices in saucepan with cinnamon and nutmeg. Add 1 cup water and lemon juice. Bring to a boil and let simmer, covered, for 10 minutes, stirring a few times. Let cool. Pour into food mill and puree. Pour evaporated skim milk into a metal bowl and place in freezer along with beaters. Chill until milk begins to freeze, about 1 hour. When ready, whip with electric beaters until the milk is stiff. Place applesauce in large bowl and add vanilla and grape juice. Stir. Into this mixture, whisk half of the whipped milk and then fold in the remainder. Place in freezer for about 2 hours (not much longer or this will solidify). Serve in dessert glasses.

Serves 4.

Nutritive values per serving:	CHO (gm)	PRO (gm)	FAT (gm)	NA (mg)	CAL
	23	2.5	1	37	111
Food exchanges per serving:	2 fruit + ¼ skim milk				

RUSSIA—MENU 4
BEF STROGANOV (BEEF STROGONOFF)
TUSHONAIA MORKOV' (BRAISED CARROTS)
PECHONYI KARTOFEL' (BAKED POTATOES)
IABLONCHNYI PIROG (APPLE PIE)

BEF STROGANOV
(BEEF STROGONOFF)

1 pound filet mignon or lean top sirloin, cut into thin strips
1 tablespoon Creative Butter (see index)
1 cup chopped onion
3 cups sliced mushrooms
⅔ cup beef stock (see index)
⅓ cup dry sherry
1 bay leaf
2 teaspoons Dijon mustard
2 teaspoons tomato paste
½ cup plain low-fat yogurt
¼ cup chopped fresh parsley
Dash cayenne

Trim off any fat from meat and slice thin. Using a nonstick skillet, brown meat in Creative Butter a little at a time, no more than 2 minutes for each batch. Transfer meat to a platter and keep warm as the remaining meat is browned. Then, to the same skillet, add onions, mushrooms, stock, sherry, bay leaf, mustard, and tomato paste. Stir with a wooden spoon. Simmer for 5 minutes. If too thin, let sauce cook down. Return meat to skillet for a minute to warm. Remove from heat and stir in yogurt. Garnish with parsley and sprinkle of cayenne.

Serves 4.

Nutritive values per serving:	CHO (gm)	PRO (gm)	FAT (gm)	NA (mg)	CAL
	12.5	35	10	38	280
Food exchanges per serving:	2 vegetable + 4 lean meat				

TUSHONAIA MORKOV'
(BRAISED CARROTS)

**1 pound carrots, scraped, trimmed, and cut into
    ½-inch rounds
1 cup chicken stock (see index)
1 tablespoon concentrated frozen apple juice
2 tablespoons chopped fresh dill or 1 teaspoon dried
2 tablespoons chopped parsley
2 tablespoons Madeira wine**

Place carrots in saucepan and cover with stock. Add apple juice. Bring to boil; then simmer, covered, for 15 minutes. Add half of dill and parsley, the Madeira, and cook another 5–10 minutes, until carrots are tender. Drain. Garnish with remaining dill or parsley and serve.

Serves 4.

Nutritive values per serving:	CHO (gm)	PRO (gm)	FAT (gm)	NA (mg)	CAL
	13	2	0	56	60
Food exchanges per serving:	2½ vegetable				

PECHONYI KARTOFEL'
(BAKED POTATOES)

4 medium baking potatoes, well scrubbed
¼ cup drained plain low-fat yogurt (see index)
1 tablespoon chopped fresh dill or parsley

Prick potatoes in several places with a fork and place in preheated 475°F oven. Bake on middle rack for 1–1½ hours. When ready to serve, cut a cross in the top of each potato and pinch to open. Dot each with a bit of yogurt and sprinkle with dill or parsley. Potatoes will be very crisp on outside and supersoft inside.

Serves 4.

Nutritive values per serving:	CHO (gm)	PRO (gm)	FAT (gm)	NA (mg)	CAL
	18	2	0	50	80
Food exchanges per serving:	1⅕ bread				

IABLOCHNYI PIROG
(APPLE PIE)

1 Whole Wheat Pie Crust (see index)
2 egg whites, beaten stiff
3 large tart apples (Granny Smith or greening)
1 tablespoon fresh lemon juice
Freshly grated rind of ½ lemon
1 teaspoon ground cinnamon
½ teaspoon freshly grated nutmeg
½ teaspoon ground coriander
¼ cup concentrated frozen apple juice
¼ teaspoon cream of tartar

Coat crust with a little egg white and bake for 5 minutes at 350°F. Remove from oven. Meanwhile, peel and core apples and slice into thin pieces. Drop apple slices into bowl of cold water with 1 tablespoon lemon juice. Drain and dry before using. Mix apple slices with half the lemon rind, cinnamon, nutmeg, coriander, and apple juice concentrate. Turn into pie shell. Place in oven and bake for 12–15 minutes at 350°F. Meanwhile, whip 2 egg whites until stiff peaks form. Add ½ teaspoon lemon rind and ¼ teaspoon cream of tartar. Continue beating until thick. Remove pie from oven, pile meringue on top of it in decorative swirls, top with remaining lemon rind, and return to oven. Bake for 5–7 minutes more until meringue is golden. Serve warm or let cool.

Serves 8.

Nutritive values per serving:	CHO (gm)	PRO (gm)	FAT (gm)	NA (mg)	CAL
	24	2.5	4	50	142
Food exchanges per serving:	½ bread + 1½ fruit + 1 fat				

RUSSIA—MENU 5
CUTLETI (VEAL PATTIES)
BALALAIKA PERLOVOI (BARLEY WITH GREEN BUTTER)
KAPUSTA SO SMETANOI V LUK (BRUSSELS SPROUTS IN
ONION CREAM)
KISSEL (GRAPE SPONGE)

CUTLETI
(VEAL PATTIES)

2 slices whole wheat bread
¾ pound lean ground veal
1 egg (use only ½ yolk)
1 small onion, grated
2 tablespoons grated sapsago or Parmesan cheese
Pepper to taste
3 tablespoons Wheatena

Moisten bread and squeeze to remove water. Work into small pieces and add to ground veal in a mixing bowl. Add the egg, onion, cheese, and pepper and mix together. Shape into flat patties. Pat on Wheatena and make X-marks on both sides. Heat nonstick skillet large enough to hold 4 cutlets. Sauté patties about 5 minutes on each side, until brown.

Serves 4.

Nutritive values per serving:	CHO (gm)	PRO (gm)	FAT (gm)	NA (mg)	CAL
	14	21	10	178	230
Food exchanges per serving:	1 bread + 3 lean meat				

BALALAIKA PERLOVOI
(BARLEY WITH GREEN BUTTER)

½ cup pearl barley, well washed
2 cups water
1 tablespoon grated onion
1 teaspoon Creative Butter (see index)
4 tablespoons chopped parsley
1 teaspoon dried marjoram
1 teaspoon dried sage
¼ teaspoon dried thyme
Pepper

Cover barley with water and bring to boil. Remove from heat, cover, and set aside 1 hour. When ready to start meal, drain and then place in saucepan with 2 cups water. Bring to boil, reduce heat, and simmer until tender, about 40 minutes. Drain and rinse with hot water. Return to pan, cover, and keep warm. Meanwhile, sauté onion in butter (this may be done at same time as onions for sprouts). To the cooked onion, add parsley, seasonings, and lemon juice. Stir to mix, add to warm barley, fluff, and serve.

Serves 4.

Nutritive values per serving:	CHO (gm)	PRO (gm)	FAT (gm)	NA (mg)	CAL
	14	1.5	2	15	75
Food exchanges per serving:	1 bread				

KAPUSTA SO SMETANOI V LUK
(BRUSSELS SPROUTS IN ONION CREAM)

1 pound brussels sprouts, trimmed
¼ cup chopped onion
1 teaspoon corn oil
½ cup plain low-fat yogurt

Cut stems off sprouts and wash. Steam over boiling water for 10–15 minutes, until tender. Meanwhile, sauté onion in oil until translucent. Mix together with drained sprouts. Remove from heat, stir in yogurt, and serve.

Serves 4.

Nutritive values per serving:	CHO (gm)	PRO (gm)	FAT (gm)	NA (mg)	CAL
	2	7	2	37	94
Food exchanges per serving:	1 bread + 3 lean meat				

KISSEL
(GRAPE SPONGE)

1 envelope unflavored gelatin
¼ cup cold water
1 tablespoon fructose
½ cup hot water
1 cup unsweetened grape juice
1½ tablespoons lemon juice
2 egg whites, beaten until stiff

Soften gelatin in cold water. Add fructose and hot water and stir until dissolved. Add grape juice and lemon juice. Refrigerate until mixture begins to stiffen, then beat until frothy. Fold in stiffly beaten egg white. Turn into sherbet glasses and serve immediately or place in freezer for a short time.

Serves 4.

Nutritive values per serving:	CHO (gm)	PRO (gm)	FAT (gm)	NA (mg)	CAL
	14	3	0	25	68
Food exchanges per serving:	1½ fruit				

DENMARK

ARTER
Yellow Pea Soup

FISKE MUSTARD
Haddock with Mustard

MOSEDE PASTINAKKER
Pureed Parsnips

PRESSGURKA
Cucumber and Cherry Tomato Salad

ROM CUSTARD
Custard with Rum

FINLAND

KESAEKEITTO
Summer Soup

TILLILIEMESSAKEITEYKAKAARYLEGT
Rolled Sole Fillets

SIENIMUREKE
Baked Mushrooms

VATKATTU MARJAPUURO
Cranberry Pudding

NORWAY

FAAR I KAAL
Lamb in Cabbage

VARM POTETSALAT
Hot Potato Salad

BRINGEBAER
Raspberries Bergen

SWEDEN

INLAGDA RODBETOR
Pickled Green Beans

KOTTBULLAR
Swedish Meatballs

POTATIS
parsley Potatoes

FRUKTSOPPA
Fruit Soup

17

SCANDINAVIA

Denmark, Finland, Norway, and Sweden are washed by the cold waters of the Baltic, North Sea, Arctic Ocean, the Kattegat, and the Skagerrak. An abundance of fish is thus the mainstay of the Scandinavian diet. The histories of these neighbors are intertwined, and they share some Germanic traditions in language, habits, and food. Sweden has become a fertile agricultural land, and Denmark and Finland are noted for fine dairy farming. Finnish *lappi* and Danish *tivoli danalette* are but two excellent low-fat cheeses (more are listed in Chapter 20).

An eye-popping display appears at a Swedish *smorgasbrod*. Literally a groaning board of every kind of fish, salad, sliced meat, pickled vegetables, hot and cold dishes, fresh breads, cheeses, and fruits, in it all Scandinavian foods are represented. We give just a hint of these wonderful dishes—because of space we can't do it all!

The Danes are fond of open-faced sandwiches and warm, filling soups, and fresh berries provide dessert ideas. The Norwegians don't necessarily wish each other a hearty appetite, for they usually have one. But they do have a nice practice of automatically saying *"takk for maten"* as they get up from the table. Thanks so much for the food!

DENMARK
ARTER (YELLOW PEA SOUP)
FISKE MUSTARD (HADDOCK WITH MUSTARD)
MOSEDE PASTINAKKER (PUREED PARSNIPS)
PRESSGURKA (CUCUMBER AND CHERRY TOMATO SALAD)
ROM CUSTARD (CUSTARD WITH RUM)

ARTER
(YELLOW PEA SOUP)

½ cup dried yellow peas
2 quarts water, divided
4 cups beef broth (see index)
2 tablespoons chopped onion
1 teaspoon chopped fresh thyme or ¼ teaspoon dried
Pinch salt
1 teaspoon Durkee's Imitation Bacon Chips
1 tablespoon vinegar
Pepper to taste

Soak peas in quart of water overnight. Remove any shells. Drain. In large kettle, heat broth and 1 quart of water with onion, thyme, salt, and drained peas. Simmer 2 hours or until peas are tender. Puree in blender and return to pot. Stir in vinegar and add more water if puree is too thick. Ladle into bowls and garnish with bacon chips.

Serves 4.

Nutritive values per serving:	CHO (gm)	PRO (gm)	FAT (gm)	NA (mg)	CAL
	18	10.5	1	162	123
Food exchanges per serving:	1 bread + ½ vegetable + ¾ lean meat				

FISKE MUSTARD
(HADDOCK WITH MUSTARD)

1½ pounds haddock fillets
3 tablespoons Dijon mustard
4 teaspoons skim milk
1 tablespoon juniper berries
Dash white pepper
2 tablespoons chopped parsley

Rinse haddock fillets several times in cold water, pat dry, and place on a large piece of foil. Mix mustard and milk together to make a smooth sauce. Place equal parts of this sauce on top of each fillet and add juniper berries and dash of white pepper. Fold foil to form an envelope and place in preheated 450°F oven. Bake for 10–12 minutes or until fish can be easily flaked with a fork. Unfold package, garnish each fillet with parsley, and serve.

Serves 4.

Nutritive values per serving:	CHO (gm)	PRO (gm)	FAT (gm)	NA (mg)	CAL
	1	32	1	253	141
Food exchanges per serving:	4½ lean meat; omits 2⅓ fat				

MOSEDE PASTINAKKER
(PUREED PARSNIPS)

7 medium parsnips, peeled and trimmed
¼ teaspoon mace
½ teaspoon Creative Butter (see index)

Place parsnips in saucepan, cover with water, and cook until tender, about 20 minutes. Drain and puree in blender until smooth. Add a bit of the cooking water if parsnips seem too thick. Add mace and butter.

Serves 4.

Nutritive values per serving:	CHO (gm)	PRO (gm)	FAT (gm)	NA (mg)	CAL
	25	2.5	1	7	119
Food exchanges per serving:	1⅔ bread				

PRESSGURKA
(CUCUMBER AND CHERRY TOMATO SALAD)

2 tablespoons wine vinegar
2 tablespoons water
Pinch pepper
1 tablespoon walnut oil
1 large cucumber, peeled and sliced very thin
8 cherry tomatoes

Mix vinegar, water, pepper, and oil together. Arrange cucumber and tomatoes on individual plates and spoon dressing over each serving.

Serves 4.

Nutritive values per serving:	CHO (gm)	PRO (gm)	FAT (gm)	NA (mg)	CAL
	5	1	3.5	4	56
Food exchanges per serving:	1 vegetable + ½ fat				

ROM CUSTARD
(CUSTARD WITH RUM)

2 eggs (use only 1 yolk)
¼ teaspoon pure vanilla extract
1 cup evaporated skim milk
2 tablespoons rum, brought to a boil to reduce alcohol
Pinch salt

Beat eggs and vanilla in blender at low speed for 20 seconds. Add milk and rum for 5 seconds. Pour into custard cups and set in pan with 1½ inches hot water. Bake in preheated 325°F oven for 40 minutes or until set. Custard is done when knife inserted in center comes out clean.

Serves 4.

Nutritive values per serving:	CHO (gm)	PRO (gm)	FAT (gm)	NA (mg)	CAL
	7	7	1	97	65
Food exchanges per serving:	½ skim milk + ⅓ lean meat				

FINLAND
KESAEKEITTO (SUMMER SOUP)
TILLILIEMESSAKEITEYKAKAARYLEGT (ROLLED
SOLE FILLETS)
SIENIMUREKE (BAKED MUSHROOMS)
VATKATTU MARJAPUURO (CRANBERRY PUDDING)

KESAEKEITTO
(SUMMER SOUP)

Salt to taste
½ cup peeled and diced potatoes
½ cup sliced carrots
½ cup chopped fresh spinach
½ cup shelled fresh peas or 5 ounces frozen peas
½ cup cauliflower flowerets
1 tablespoon arrowroot
1½ cups skim milk, divided
¼ teaspoon cayenne
1 tablespoon minced parsley

To 2 cups of boiling water, add a pinch of salt, potatoes, and carrots. Cover and cook 10 minutes. Add the remaining raw vegetables and cook for another 10 minutes. In a small cup, make a paste of arrowroot and 3 tablespoons of milk. When smooth, add this with remaining milk to the vegetables, add cayenne, and simmer for 5 minutes, until vegetables are tender. Serve in individual bowls, sprinkled with parsley.

Serves 4.

Nutritive values per serving:	CHO (gm)	PRO (gm)	FAT (gm)	NA (mg)	CAL
	16.5	6	0	111	90
Food exchanges per serving:	½ bread + 2 vegetable				

TILLILIEMESSAKEITEYKAKAARYLEGT
(ROLLED SOLE FILLETS)

1½ pounds fillet of sole
2 tablespoons minced fresh dill
2 tablespoons minced fresh parsley
¼ teaspoon ground allspice
1 teaspoon cayenne
Salt to taste
½ cup plain low-fat yogurt
1 hard-boiled egg, sliced (white only)
Minced fresh dill for garnish

Cut fillets into even strips and sprinkle them with a mixture of the dill and parsley. Roll each strip and secure with a toothpick. Place in shallow baking dish and cover with water. Simmer for 15 minutes. Drain. In separate pan, mix allspice, cayenne, salt, and yogurt. Heat, but do not allow to boil. Pour over fillets. Sprinkle with extra dill and garnish with egg slices.

Serves 4.

Nutritive values per serving:	CHO (gm)	PRO (gm)	FAT (gm)	NA (mg)	CAL
	3.5	28	2	130	140
Food exchanges per serving:	4 lean meat + ¼ skim milk; omits 2 fat				

SIENIMUREKE
(BAKED MUSHROOMS)

½ teaspoon Creative Butter (see index)
2 small onions, chopped
1 egg (use only ½ yolk)
½ cup whole wheat bread crumbs, toasted
½ cup skim milk
2 tablespoons part-skim ricotta cheese
Pinch salt
⅛ teaspoon pepper
¾ pound mushrooms, cleaned and sliced

Heat Creative Butter in nonstick skillet and sauté onions in it until tender. In 1-quart casserole, beat egg and mix with bread crumbs, milk, ricotta, salt, and pepper. Add mushrooms and onions. Bake in preheated 350°F oven for 1 hour, until set.

Serves 4.

Nutritive values per serving:	CHO (gm)	PRO (gm)	FAT (gm)	NA (mg)	CAL
	20	7	3	72	86
Food exchanges per serving:	½ bread + 2½ vegetable + ¼ lean meat				

VATKATTU MARJAPUURO
(CRANBERRY PUDDING)

2 cups fresh cranberries
2 cups water
4 tablespoons concentrated frozen apple juice
¼ cup uncooked Cream of Wheat (instant farina)
4 tablespoons skim milk
1 egg white, beaten stiff
4 thin lemon slices

Cook the cranberries in the water with apple juice and crush against side of pan. Stir for about 10 minutes. Add Cream of Wheat and cook 3–4 minutes. Stir until mixture becomes a puree. Remove from heat, transfer to a large bowl, and add the milk. With electric beaters, whip at high speed for 10–15 minutes until pudding turns light pink. Fold the beaten egg white into the cranberry mixture. Spoon into individual dessert dishes and top with sliced lemon.

Serves 4.

Nutritive values per serving:	CHO (gm)	PRO (gm)	FAT (gm)	NA (mg)	CAL
	21	3	.5	21	101
Food exchanges per serving:	1⅕ fruit + ½ bread + ¼ lean meat				

NORWAY
FAAR I KAAL (LAMB IN CABBAGE)
VARM POTETSALAT (HOT POTATO SALAD)
BRINGEBAER (RASPBERRIES BERGEN)

FAAR I KAAL
(LAMB IN CABBAGE)

1¼ pounds lamb shoulder
3 cups water
1 tablespoon dry white wine
1 small head cabbage
2 tablespoons arrowroot
½ teaspoon nutmeg
1 teaspoon crushed black peppercorns
¼ teaspoon ground cardamom
1 cup skim milk

Cut lamb into cubes and cook in water seasoned with wine for 20 minutes. Meanwhile, discard outer leaves of cabbage, cut into 1-inch squares, and place half of them in saucepan. When meat is tender, layer half the meat over the cabbage. Mix arrowroot, nutmeg, peppercorns, cardamom, and skim milk. Blend until smooth. Pour over lamb and cabbage. Add another layer of cabbage and lamb and pour the remaining sauce over this. Cover and cook over low heat for 1 hour or until tender.

Serves 4.

Nutritive values per serving:	CHO (gm)	PRO (gm)	FAT (gm)	NA (mg)	CAL
	13	25	34	135	458

Food exchanges per serving: ¼ bread + ¼ skim milk + 1¼ vegetable + 4 high-fat meat

VARM POTETSALAT
(HOT POTATO SALAD)

2 pounds potatoes
¼ onion, chopped
2 teaspoons cider vinegar
2 tablespoons drained low-fat yogurt
1 teaspoon cayenne
Pinch salt
2 tablespoons chopped parsley

Boil the potatoes until tender. Peel and slice. In a separate bowl, mix together onion, vinegar, yogurt, cayenne, and salt. Blend with warm potato slices, garnish with parsley, and serve.

Serves 4.

Nutritive values per serving:	CHO (gm)	PRO (gm)	FAT (gm)	NA (mg)	CAL
	31	4	0	8	140
Food exchanges per serving:	2 bread				

BRINGEBAER
(RASPBERRIES BERGEN)

1 cup fresh or thawed frozen raspberries
2 tablespoons fresh lemon juice
1 package unflavored gelatin
¼ cup cold water
6 tablespoons plain low-fat yogurt
½ teaspoon pure vanilla extract
2 egg whites, beaten stiff

Put raspberries in bowl, saving a few whole berries for garnish, and add lemon juice. Mash together. Sprinkle gelatin over ¼ cup cold water and then place cup in a bowl of hot water to dissolve. Mix yogurt and vanilla with raspberries and then stir in the gelatin. Fold beaten egg whites into mixture and spoon into serving bowl. Place in freezer for 1-2 hours and decorate with a few whole berries before serving.

Serves 4.

Nutritive values per serving:	CHO (gm)	PRO (gm)	FAT (gm)	NA (mg)	CAL
	8	5	1	39	61
Food exchanges per serving:	¾ fruit + ½ lean meat				

SWEDEN
INLAGDA RODBETOR (PICKLED GREEN BEANS)
KOTTBULLAR (SWEDISH MEATBALLS)
POTATIS (PARSLEY POTATOES)
FRUKTSOPPA (FRUIT SOUP)

INLAGDA RODBETOR
(PICKLED GREEN BEANS)

1 pound green beans
½ cup cider vinegar
½ cup reserved bean liquid
1 clove
½ medium onion, sliced and separated into rings

Wash beans, remove ends, and cook until tender. Drain, but reserve ½ cup liquid. Blend vinegar, reserved bean liquid, and clove. Pour over beans and onions. Marinate in refrigerator for several hours, until ready to serve.

Serves 4.

Nutritive values per serving:	CHO (gm)	PRO (gm)	FAT (gm)	NA (mg)	CAL
	11	2	0	9	52
Food exchanges per serving:	2 vegetable				

KOTTBULLAR
(SWEDISH MEATBALLS)

MEATBALLS

½ cup whole wheat bread crumbs
¼ pound ground round beef
¼ pound ground veal
1 tablespoon water
¼ cup wheat germ
1 egg (use only ½ yolk)
¼ teaspoon ground ginger
¼ teaspoon ground nutmeg
¼ teaspoon ground allspice
¼ teaspoon pepper
¼ teaspoon fructose
Pinch salt

In a large bowl, mix half the bread crumbs, both meats, water, wheat germ, and egg. After thoroughly blended, add ginger, nutmeg, allspice, pepper, fructose, and salt. Mix again and form into 1-inch balls. Roll balls in the extra bread crumbs. Brown in skillet and cook covered for 15 minutes. Drain off any fat.

SAUCE FOR MEATBALLS

2 tablespoons arrowroot
1 cup beef broth (see index)
½ cup plain low-fat yogurt

Blend arrowroot with 4 tablespoons water and stir. Mix into broth, stirring until smooth. Add yogurt and blend. Add browned meatballs, blend, and serve.

Serves 4.

Nutritive values per serving:	CHO (gm)	PRO (gm)	FAT (gm)	NA (mg)	CAL
	19.5	18	11	87	249
Food exchanges per serving:	⅕ skim milk + 1 bread + 2 medium-fat meat				

POTATIS
(PARSLEY POTATOES)

1 tablespoon Creative Butter (see index)
¾ pound new potatoes, boiled and pared
2 tablespoons minced parsley

In a nonstick suacepan, melt butter and add potatoes. Sprinkle with parsley and shake skillet until potatoes are coated.

Serves 4.

Nutritive values per serving:	CHO (gm)	PRO (gm)	FAT (gm)	NA (mg)	CAL
	11	1.5	3	23	77
Food exchanges per serving:	¾ bread + ½ fat				

FRUKTSOPPA
(FRUIT SOUP)

3 cups blueberries
2 tablespoons concentrated frozen apple juice
2 tablespoons minute tapioca
1 teaspoon lemon zest

Cook blueberries with apple juice for several minutes. Stir in tapioca and bring to a rolling boil. Lower heat and simmer a few minutes. Serve in soup bowls, warm or at room temperature, garnished with lemon zest.

Serves 4.

Nutritive values per serving:	CHO (gm)	PRO (gm)	FAT (gm)	NA (mg)	CAL
	24	1	5	1	105
Food exchanges per serving:	⅓ bread + 2 fruit				

THANKSGIVING DINNER
RELISH TRAY
Celery, Radishes, Olives
CREAM OF CAULIFLOWER SOUP
MINI MUFFINS
ROAST TURKEY
SWEET POTATO SOUFFLE
GREEN PEAS WITH CHESTNUTS
CRANBERRY RELISH
FRUIT TART
APPLE CRISP

18

UNITED STATES

Food in the USA has come a long way since the arrival of the first English colonists. America's resources and technology have produced everything from native corn, pumpkins, and squash to the cultivation of lush tropical fruits and vegetables in the sunshine states, vast fields of wheat, grain and legumes, and prime poultry, meat, fish, and nuts and seeds of all kinds.

Each new immigrant wave brings with it another culture, another cuisine that is soon absorbed into an already rich heritage. Today, the United States is a veritable melting pot of food from all nations. From Cajun to downhome New England cookin' to Tex Mex and California *nouvelle*, every conceivable kind of cuisine is prepared in our country, creating a food landscape of infinite variety.

But perhaps the most representative repast of all has a long historic tradition. For our one American meal, we've chosen a contemporary Thanksgiving feast. We hope you'll enjoy it with friends and family, whatever your ethnic background. To your very good health!

THANKSGIVING DINNER
RELISH TRAY (CELERY, RADISHES, OLIVES)
CREAM OF CAULIFLOWER SOUP
MINI MUFFINS
ROAST TURKEY
SWEET POTATO SOUFFLE
GREEN PEAS WITH CHESTNUTS
CRANBERRY RELISH
FRUIT TART
APPLE CRISP

RELISH TRAY

1 bunch celery, washed and trimmed
12 radishes, cut into rose shapes (see Chapter 20) and chilled
   in water
10 olives (5 red, 5 green), rinsed
10 cherry tomatoes

Arrange relishes decoratively on a platter.

Serves 6.

Nutritive values per serving:	CHO (gm)	PRO (gm)	FAT (gm)	NA (mg)	CAL
	9	2	.5	300	49
Food exchanges per serving:	2 vegetable				

CREAM OF CAULIFLOWER SOUP

1 head cauliflower, broken into flowerets
1 tablespoon Creative Butter (see index)
⅓ cup minced onion
1 clove garlic, minced
½ cup minced green pepper
½ teaspoon peeled and minced fresh gingerroot
¼ teaspoon curry powder
1 cup skim milk
1 tablespoon finely chopped fresh parsley
Dash cayenne
Chopped parsley and dash cayenne for garnish

Drop cauliflower flowerets into 6 cups of boiling water. Cook, covered, for 5 minutes. Drain, reserving 2 cups of liquid. Meanwhile, heat Creative Butter in nonstick skillet and sauté onion, garlic, green pepper, and ginger until soft. Add curry powder and cook another minute, blending. Pour the cauliflower into a blender or food processor with 2 cups of liquid. Puree. Stop blender while vegetables are still a bit chunky. Turn puree into a saucepan and add the milk, parsley, and cayenne. Heat gently and stir until hot, being careful not to let boil. Garnish with chopped parsley and dash of cayenne in center of each bowl.

Serves 8.

Nutritive values per serving:	CHO (gm)	PRO (gm)	FAT (gm)	NA (mg)	CAL
	9	4	2	43	70
Food exchanges per serving:	2 vegetable + ⅓ fat				

MINI MUFFINS

Vegetable spray
½ cup rye flour
⅓ cup unbleached all-purpose flour
¾ teaspoon baking powder
¼ teaspoon baking soda
⅛ teaspoon salt
1 teaspoon caraway seeds
1 teaspoon poppy seeds
3 tablespoons chopped walnuts
½ cup buttermilk
1 egg
1 tablespoon walnut oil
1 tablespoon concentrated frozen apple juice

Coat muffin pan with vegetable spray. Blend together the first 8 dry ingredients. In another mixing bowl, blend the buttermilk, egg, oil, and apple juice. Turn this into the dry ingredients and blend with a fork. Divide batter among muffin tins and bake in middle rack of preheated 400°F oven for 15 minutes, until brown. Turn onto rack to cool. Serve warm. These may be made ahead and frozen. Allow an hour or so to defrost. May be reheated at low temperature.

Makes 12 muffins.

Nutritive values per serving:	CHO (gm)	PRO (gm)	FAT (gm)	NA (mg)	CAL
	6	2	3	60	59
Food exchanges per serving:	½ bread + ½ fat				

ROAST TURKEY

1 8- to 10-pound fresh turkey (do not use self-basting
   varieties; if frozen turkey is used, thaw first)
1 teaspoon dried marjoram
1 teaspoon dried thyme
1 teaspoon pepper
1 apple, peeled
1 lemon, quartered
1 onion, quartered
1 tablespoon corn oil
1 teaspoon paprika
Bunch watercress, washed

Wash turkey and pat dry. Sprinkle cavity with marjoram, thyme, and some of the pepper. Insert apple, lemon, and onion into cavity and truss, tying up legs. Brush skin of turkey with corn oil and dust with pepper and paprika. Place breast side up on rack in roasting pan. Insert meat thermometer into leg joint, but do not let it touch the bone. Preheat oven to 400°F. Place bird, covered with aluminum foil tent, on middle rack. After 15 minutes, reduce heat to 350°F. Fresh bird should cook nicely at 350°F, giving it 20 minutes to the pound. A 10-pound bird should therefore cook in 3½ hours. Turkey is cooked when meat thermometer reads 185°F or when juices run clear when leg is pricked with a fork. Remove foil tent for last 20 minutes of cooking so that breast browns. Baste. Transfer to large platter and let stand 20 minutes before carving.

Discard stuffing and skin. Carve and arrange thin turkey slices on platter with watercress garnish.

Serves 12-14.

Nutritive values per 1 ounce serving:	CHO (gm)	PRO (gm)	FAT (gm)	NA (mg)	CAL
	0	9	2	37	54

Food exchanges per serving: 1 lean meat
(Choose amount according to your own
meal plan. If, for example, you wish 3
ounces, multiply by 3.)

GRAVY

1 cup chicken broth (see index)
1 cup dry white wine
1 carrot, chopped
Turkey neck and giblets
1 tablespoon arrowroot, mixed with 2 tablespoons water

Cook chicken broth, wine, carrot, turkey neck, and giblets in saucepan over low heat for about 1 hour. Discard neck, chop giblet fine, then return to saucepan. Add arrowroot mixture to saucepan, stirring. Skim any fat off turkey drippings. Add gravy to turkey pan and heat.

Makes 2 cups.

Nutritive values per 2 tablespoon serving:	CHO (gm)	PRO (gm)	FAT (gm)	NA (mg)	CAL
	2.5	3	2	5	40
Food exchanges per serving:	⅓ vegetable + ½ lean meat				

GREEN PEAS WITH CHESTNUTS

2 pounds fresh green peas or 2 10-ounce packages frozen
1 cup cooked chestnuts, peeled and quartered (see
Chapter 20)
2 tablespoons grated lemon rind

Cook peas in ½ cup water just until tender, about 5 minutes. Do not overcook. Drain. Stir in chestnuts and lemon rind and serve.

Serves 12.

Nutritive values per serving:	CHO (gm)	PRO (gm)	FAT (gm)	NA (mg)	CAL
	16.5	.5	.5	4	91
Food exchanges per serving:	1 bread + ½ lean meat				

SWEET POTATO SOUFFLE

2 cups cooked, peeled, and mashed sweet potatoes (about 1
pound)
⅔ cup hot skim milk
1 tablespoon grated lemon rind
Cayenne
4 egg whites, beaten stiff
Vegetable spray

Place mashed sweet potatoes in large bowl. Add hot milk and beat until fluffy. Add lemon rind and cayenne. Fold in beaten egg whites. Pour into vegetable-sprayed casserole. Bake in preheated 400°F oven for 35 minutes.

Serves 8.

Nutritive values per serving:	CHO (gm)	PRO (gm)	FAT (gm)	NA (mg)	CAL
	18	3.5	0	41	86
Food exchanges per serving:	1⅕ bread				

CRANBERRY RELISH

2 cups fresh cranberries, rinsed, odd stems discarded
2 tablespoons raisins, plumped in apple juice
¼ cup concentrated frozen apple juice
¼ cup concentrated frozen orange juice
2 tablespoons fructose
1 orange, peeled, membranes removed, and chopped

Place all ingredients except chopped orange in a saucepan and bring to boil. Simmer on low heat for 20 minutes or until berries pop. Crush berries against side of saucepan. Remove from heat and stir in orange chunks. Refrigerate. Keeps well for up to 48 hours.

Makes 3 cups.

Nutritive values per ¼ cup serving:	CHO (gm)	PRO (gm)	FAT (gm)	NA (mg)	CAL
	9	.5	0	2	38
Food exchanges per serving:	1 fruit				

FRUIT TART

1 Whole Wheat Pie Crust (see index)
1 tangerine
¹⁄₂ cup red grapes, halved and seeded
¹⁄₂ cup green grapes, halved and seeded
¹⁄₂ cup strawberries, hulled and halved
¹⁄₂ cup blueberries
¹⁄₄ cup concentrated frozen apple juice
1 package unflavored gelatin
¹⁄₂ cup No-Cal ginger ale or flavored diet soda

Bake crust as in master recipe, painting bottom with egg white before baking. Wait until just before the meal to fill crust. In concentric circles, layer the fruit carefully, alternating colors and mounding blueberries in center. Put apple juice in measuring cup and sprinkle with gelatin. Then dissolve by placing cup in a bowl of hot water. Mix with No-Cal ginger ale or soda. Let set partially and then spoon over the fruit pie as a glaze. Refrigerate until ready to serve. If more servings are necessary, make 2 of these. The fruit can be varied (kiwifruit looks nice, but it prevents gelatin from setting).

Serves 6.

Nutritive values per serving:	CHO (gm)	PRO (gm)	FAT (gm)	NA (mg)	CAL
	26	3	5	50	161
Food exchanges per serving:	1 fruit + 1 bread + 1¼ fat				

APPLE CRISP
(ALTERNATE OR ADDITIONAL DESSERT)

Vegetable spray
4-5 apples, peeled, cored, and sliced
2 tablespoons raisins
¼ cup rolled oats
1 tablespoon wheat germ
¼ cup Grapenuts
1 tablespoon ground cinnamon
¼ teaspoon ground cloves
¼ teaspoon freshly grated nutmeg
2 tablespoons sunflower seeds
1 tablespoon sunflower seed oil
½ cup apple juice
½ cup part-skim ricotta cheese (optional)

Lightly coat a 9″ × 12″ baking dish with vegetable spray. Line pan with sliced apples. Mix together all other ingredients except apple juice and cheese and spread over apples. Slowly drizzle apple juice over crust and set aside 15 minutes. Preheat oven to 350°F and bake crisp 25–30 minutes until crust is brown. If desired, serve with a dab of ricotta cheese.

Serves 6.

Nutritive values per serving:	CHO (gm)	PRO (gm)	FAT (gm)	NA (mg)	CAL
	28	3	6	34	178
Food exchanges per serving:	⅓ bread + 2⅓ fruit + 1¼ fat				

19

BASICS

Certain recipes form integral parts of many different cuisines. The foundation of a good soup, stew, or sauce is often a basic beef or chicken stock. Final results for any dish will be achieved by adjusting seasonings—fine tuning for individual national flavors. Stocks may be prepared well ahead of time, measured, and stored in the freezer for up to six months.

Our low fat Creative Butter is better! A healthful compromise for flavorful cooking. Tasty treats on their own, Creative Cream Cheese and Creative Mayonnaise will enhance many a dish from far flung lands. Just add herbs and spices appropriate to those cuisines. Draining low fat yogurt will produce a delicious but sane sour cream or cheese.

Our whole wheat pie crust recipe crosses many boundaries and may be used for one whole pie shell or individual tarts for fruits and other fillings.

As for the staff of life, the bread recipes we offer are but two examples of the wholesome, delicious loaves that may be prepared by using concentrated fruit juice instead of sugar or honey.

BASIC BEEF STOCK/BROTH

3 pounds meaty beef shanks, sawed into 2-inch pieces
2 onions, peeled and quartered
3 cups carrots, peeled and chopped
4 stalks celery, chopped
2 bay leaves
3 cloves
4 sprigs parsley
11 peppercorns
1 clove garlic
½ teaspoon dried thyme
4 quarts water

Place beef shanks in large soup pot and cover with cold water. Bring to a rolling boil and simmer for 5 minutes. Pour off water and rinse off any scum that has accumulated. Add remaining ingredients and simmer for 3 hours. Skim off any fat or froth. Strain, removing all vegetables and spices. This stock can be kept in the freezer in containers for use as needed.

Makes 4 quarts.

Nutritive values per cup:	CHO (gm)	PRO (gm)	FAT (gm)	NA (mg)	CAL
	2	3.5	0	30	22

BASIC CHICKEN STOCK/BROTH

1 fryer chicken or stewing hen, skinned
4 cloves garlic, chopped
2 ribs celery with tops, chopped
6 sprigs parsley
1 bay leaf
6 peppercorns
2 medium onions, chopped
8 cups water

Bring all ingredients to a boil in a large kettle and cook, uncovered, on low heat for 15 minutes. Remove accumulated residue. Reduce heat and simmer, partially covered, for 2½–3 hours. Remove cover and let stand until cool.

Strain, pressing meat to draw out liquid. Save chicken pieces for use in salad and discard other solids. After stock has been refrigerated, remove any fat that has hardened on the top. Stock may be used within a few days or frozen for future use, stored in small containers.

Makes 6 cups.

Nutritive values per cup:	CHO (gm)	PRO (gm)	FAT (gm)	NA (mg)	CAL
	2	3	.5	30	25

CREATIVE CREAM CHEESE

1 tablespoon skim milk
2 tablespoons whipped butter
2 tablespoons corn oil
1 cup low-fat cottage cheese

Blend all ingredients together and refrigerate, covered. May be herbed as desired.

Makes 1 cup.

Nutritive values per tablespoon:	CHO (gm)	PRO (gm)	FAT (gm)	NA (mg)	CAL
	0	1.5	2	53	28

CREATIVE BUTTER

1 cup of any of the following oils or a mixture: safflower oil,
sunflower seed oil, corn oil, soybean oil, vegetable oil
1 cup whipped butter
½ teaspoon salt

Blend together well and store in refrigerator or freeze, covered. May be herbed with garlic, scallions, chives, mustard, tarragon, etc.

Makes 2 cups.

Nutritive values per tablespoon:	CHO (gm)	PRO (gm)	FAT (gm)	NA (mg)	CAL
	0	0	11.5	77	105

CREATIVE MAYONNAISE

1 cup 1 percent low-fat cottage cheese
2 tablespoons corn or safflower oil
1 tablespoon tarragon vinegar
½ teaspoon salt
Dash freshly ground pepper

Blend ingredients until smooth and then refrigerate, covered, for at least 24 hours before using. May be mixed with mustard, tomato paste, or herbs as desired.

Makes 1 cup.

Nutritive values per tablespoon:	CHO (gm)	PRO (gm)	FAT (gm)	NA (mg)	CAL
	.5	2	2	12	28

STRAINED YOGURT SOUR CREAM

Herbs as desired
16 ounces plain low-fat yogurt

Mix herbs (such as dill, tarragon, etc.) into yogurt. Place yogurt into a cheesecloth-lined sieve and let it drip for about 2 hours, until the yogurt has the consistency of sour cream. If the yogurt is allowed to drip for longer than the 2 hours, the result will be a fine yogurt cheese resembling the French herbed cheese, boursin.

Makes 8 ounces sour cream or 6 ounces cheese.

Nutritive values per tablespoon:	CHO (gm)	PRO (gm)	FAT (gm)	NA (mg)	CAL
	1	1	0	10	8

WHOLE WHEAT PIE CRUST

1 cup whole wheat pastry flour
⅛ teaspoon salt
2 tablespoons corn oil or walnut oil
2 tablespoons ice cold water (1 more if needed)
Egg white

Sift flour and salt together into mixing bowl. Stir in oil and water. Knead dough 3–4 times until moist and elastic. Roll into a ball, cover, and refrigerate for 10 minutes. Place between 2 sheets of wax paper. Roll dough into a 12-inch circle. Place in 8″ pie tin. Trim edges and finish by pressing with a fork. Poke a few holes in dough if cooking shell empty. Brush with egg white and refrigerate for 10 minutes. Bake in preheated 350°F oven for 10 minutes, until brown. The same dough may be used to make tartlets. To do so, cut rounds with a cup and place into muffin tins and bake as directed.

Serves 6.

Nutritive values per serving:	CHO (gm)	PRO (gm)	FAT (gm)	NA (mg)	CAL
	13	2	5	49	105
Food exchanges per serving:	1 bread + 1 fat				

PUMPERNICKEL RYE WITH CARAWAY SEEDS
(FOR RUSSIAN OR GERMAN MEALS)

1 package active dry yeast
½ cup water, 105°F–115°F
1 tablespoon concentrated frozen apple juice
⅔ cup evaporated skim milk
1 tablespoon Creative Butter (see index)
1 teaspoon salt
1 tablespoon caraway seeds
1 teaspoon poppy seeds
¼ teaspoon aniseed
1 cup rye flour
1 cup whole wheat flour
1 cup unbleached all-purpose flour
2 tablespoons coffee (or decaffeinated) powder
½ teaspoon corn oil
Vegetable spray

Dissolve yeast in warm water in a large bowl. Add apple juice and wait 5 minutes until yeast begins to foam. Add milk, butter, salt, seeds, and rye flour and coffee powder, and mix together. Add whole wheat flour and then the unbleached flour, one at a time, mixing well each time. When dough is stiff, turn onto floured bread board and let sit 15 minutes. Meanwhile, lightly grease a large bowl with oil and set aside. Knead the dough until it is smooth, about 10 minutes. Place in the greased bowl and turn to coat with oil. Cover and let rise in a warm place about 1–1½ hours, until doubled in bulk. Punch down dough and place on a vegetable-sprayed baking sheet. Flatten to about 2 inches thick, cover, and let rise again for 1 hour, until doubled. Preheat oven to 350°F. Bake for 1 hour or more, until brown. When done, bread sounds hollow if tapped with fingers. This recipe makes one large loaf which may be cut into quarters and frozen for future use.

Serves 12.

Nutritive values per 1 slice serving:	CHO (gm)	PRO (gm)	FAT (gm)	NA (mg)	CAL
	23	4.5	5	186	155
Food exchanges per serving:	1½ bread + 1 fat				

FRENCH BREAD/ITALIAN BREAD

This bread is adaptable for both French loaves and Italian. It is a whole wheat adaptation of the traditional French baguette.

1 package active dry yeast
1¼ cups warm water (105°F-115°F)
2 tablespoons concentrated frozen apple juice
Pinch ground cinnamon
Pinch ground coriander
1 teaspoon salt
1½ cups unbleached all-purpose flour
1½ cups whole wheat flour
2 teaspoons wheat germ
½ teaspoon corn oil
Vegetable spray
1 teaspoon cornmeal
1 teaspoon whole wheat flour

In a large bowl, dissolve the yeast in warm water with the apple juice and spices. Wait until the yeast begins to foam, about 5 minutes, then add salt and the unbleached flour. Mix well and then stir in the 1½ cups whole wheat flour and wheat germ until the dough becomes stiff. Turn onto a floured bread board and knead 10 minutes, until the dough is silky and springy. Lightly grease a large mixing bowl with oil and place the dough in it, turning to coat with oil. Cover and let rise in warm place until it is doubled in bulk, or for about 1 hour. When dough has risen, punch down and divide in half (or in quarters for 4 small loaves instead of 2). Shape into loaves that are long and thin. Lightly coat a 14" × 17" baking sheet with vegetable spray and then sprinkle with cornmeal. Place the loaves on the pan and make several slashes on the top of each with a sharp knife. Let rise again until doubled, about 45 minutes. Meanwhile, preheat the oven to 400°F. Brush top of each loaf with water and sprinkle with 1 teaspoon whole wheat flour. Bake in middle rack of oven for 30 minutes or more, until brown. Bread is done if it sounds hollow when tapped. Let cool on a wire rack. Loaves not used immediately may be frozen for future use.

Serves 12.

Nutritive values per 2 slice serving:	CHO (gm)	PRO (gm)	FAT (gm)	NA (mg)	CAL
	23	3.5	.5	164	111
Food exchanges per serving:	1½ bread				

20

HELPFUL HINTS:
INGREDIENTS AND RECIPE PREPARATION

Blanching

Plunge fruit, vegetables, or nuts into boiling water for 1 minute. Run under cold water to stop cooking process. Blanching facilitates peeling.

Bouquet Garni

Parsley, thyme, and bay leaves tied together in a cheesecloth perfumes soups and stews. Remove after cooking.

Bread

Almost any bread recipe can be changed to use frozen concentrated apple juice instead of sugar to prove the yeast. If purchasing bread, read the label and try to avoid brands with sugar, corn syrup, honey, and other sweeteners.

Bread Crumbs

The blender does a good job of making bread crumbs from whole wheat bread slices—day-old bread or toasted bread works best. Crumbs can be stored in a jar in the refrigerator.

Cheese

Place cheese in freezer before grating. The accompanying nutritional chart lists fat and sodium ratings for low-fat cheeses.

NUTRITIONAL CHART FOR SELECTED DIETARY CHEESES
(Based on 1 oz. serving, and compared with nondietary New York State Cheddar)

Cheese	Origin	Calories	Fat IDM**	Protein	Calcium	Cholesterol	Sodium	Carbohydrate
1. Tivoli Danalette	Den.	60	20%	8.7 gms.	224 mgs.	8.4 mgs.	.196 gm.	.28 gm.
Hand Kaese	Ger.	34	1.4%	7.6 gms.	70 mgs.	.32 mgs.	.32 gm.	.46 gm.
2. St. Otho	Switz.	50	9%	8.9 gms.	257 mgs.	N/A	.63 gm.	N.A
3. Uncle Otto Braided	U.S.	80	23%	7 gms.	210 mgs.	20 mgs.	.70 gm.	1 gm.
4. Sap Sago	Switz.	N/A	0	11.2 gms.	N/A	N/A	1.4 gms.	N/A
5. St. Felice	Switz.	50	13.5%	8.9 gms.	355 mgs.	N/A	.010 gm.	0
6. Lorraine Swiss	U.S.	131	53.2%	.67 gm.	200 mgs.	12.04 mgs.	.06 gm.	.75 gm.
7. New Holland	U.S.	90	47%	7 gms.	N/A	N/A	1 gm.	1 gm.
Low Sodium Gouda	Hol.	90	42%	7 gms.	225 mgs.	25 mgs.	less than .007 gm.	0
Uncle Otto's Yoghurt-Cheese Spread	U.S.	48	36%	2 gms.	40 mgs.	14.5 mgs.	.28 gm.	1 gm.
8. Lighter 'n Jack	U.S.	90	39.2%	8 gms.	N/A	14 mgs.	.067 gm.	1 gm.
Verde-Mont	U.S.	32	50%	3.2 gms.	28 mgs.	15 mgs.	.068 gm.	1.2 gms.
(for comparison)								
N.Y. State Cheddar	U.S.	114	53%	7.06 gms.	204 mgs.	30 mgs.	.176	.36 gm.

Special notes: Figures represent approximate values—N/A indicates "not available"
Numbered cheeses are described below.

*Courtesy of Otto Roth & Co., Inc., 14 Empire Blvd., Moonachie, NJ 07074; 39-43 Medford St., Somerville, MA 02143; Peacock Foods, Inc., 1961 La Cienega Blvd., Los Angeles, CA 90034; Monterey Cheese Co., 468 Littlefield Ave., PO Box 2487, South San Francisco, CA 94080.

**Refers to fat "in the dry matter," i.e., the percentage of butterfat that remains in the milk solids, such as the protein, once all the water has been removed.

1. *Tivoli Danalette.* A Danish cheese of Danbo-Tilsiter type. Semisoft, low-fat (89 percent fat-free).

2. *St. Otho.* 95 percent fat free. Resembles Appenzeller, muenster, and Port Salut. Good with fresh fruit.

3. *Uncle Otto Braided.* Armenian string cheese, with or without caraway seeds. Use as mozzarella. 70 percent fat-free.

4. *Sapsago.* Use grated over soups, pasta; a low-fat replacement for grated Parmesan, Romano.

5. *St. Felice.* Low-fat Swiss type with low salt content. Excellent as dessert cheese with fruit.

6. *Lorraine Swiss.* Available with or without jalapeño peppers, chives, and onions, and naturally smoked.

7. *New Holland.* Natural, with caraway, with garlic herbs. Produced by Fleur de Lait (New Holland, PA 17555).

8. *Lighter 'n Jack.* Also sold as Monterey Jack/Gold-N-Lite. Also available with jalapeño peppers, garlic, and chives.

Cooking at High Altitudes

In high mountainous regions where boiling point is lower, foods will take longer to boil, poach, or simmer.

Cottage Cheese

Use 1 percent low-fat cottage cheese. See recipes for Creative Cream Cheese and Creative Mayonnaise (see index).

Court Bouillon

A combination of water, white wine, herbs, peppercorns, celery, and carrots. Used for poaching.

Egg Whites

Whites will whip to larger volume and stiffen faster if beaten at room temperature. Make sure none of the yolk gets into the white. A whip or electric beater and stainless steel or copper bowls are the best utensils to use. Cream of tartar will help egg white to form peaks.

Eggs

To cut back on fat and cholesterol, use only ½ the yolk when 1 egg is called for; 1 yolk only if 2 eggs are used, etc.

Fish

Fresh fish is recommended. Frozen fish must be defrosted in refrigerator before cooking. Do not use breaded products. Fish generally is cooked for 8 minutes per inch of thickness. When cooked in liquid, it is done when flesh turns opaque. When baked, it should flake when pierced with a fork.

Fin Fish

Bluefish. Good baked or broiled.

Carp. For baking and poaching.

Cod, Croaker, Pollack, Haddock, Hake, and Ling. In the same family; best cooked moist.

Flounder, Fluke, and Sole. Good cooked whole or filleted.

Halibut. Sturdy fish good for broiling, steaming, and baking.

Mackerel. Best poached, grilled, or baked.

Monkfish. Sometimes called "poor man's lobster," good for kebabs.

Pompano. An expensive fish cooked often *en papillote* (in parchment).

Red Snapper. A juicy and mild, lean fish, good with sauces.

Salmon. Available in steaks, fillets, or whole. Broiling, baking, and poaching in court bouillon are common cooking methods.

Sea Bass. Much like snapper; good stuffed, baked, or broiled.

Shad. Specialty in some rivers during early spring. Excellent filleted (it has numerous bones) and stuffed.

Striped Bass. Lean and firm with good flavor. Like sea bass.

Swordfish. Lean and firm with distinct flavor. Available in steaks. Good broiled with light sauce or cooked in sauce.

Trout. Excellent baked or poached whole in white wine or broiled with sliced almonds.

Tuna. Available in steaks and fillets; like swordfish in texture.

Turbot. A thick white fish, best when fresh. Excellent poached in white wine.

Shellfish

Clams. Should be purchased live with shells tightly closed and washed in several waters before using. They may be steamed open in a little liquid, or by dropping into boiling water, or in a 350°F oven. Excellent in sauces with fish, rice, and pasta. Discard any that don't open.

Lobster. Prices and size vary according to season. Best live, cooked by dropping into boiling water, head first, until shell turns red. Everything in lobster is edible but the blackish intestinal tract. Lobster boiled for a couple of minutes may be split, then broiled quickly with a simple sauce. Do not overcook. Frozen lobster tails are also available and should be defrosted in refrigerator before cooking. Top and bottom shell should be slit down the middle to prevent curling.

Mussels. Care must be taken to purchase mussels from a reliable fishmonger. There are contaminated beds, but some mussels are raised in cultivated beds. They must be scrubbed well to remove beards, the trailing black strands on their shells. They can be placed in water with ½ cup of cornmeal per quart of cold water and refrigerated a day, then washed again and scrubbed. Best steamed open in very little liquid. Discard any that do not open.

Oysters. Rich in nutrients and minerals, many kinds are available, either alive in shells or shucked, packed in their juice. Should be cooked quickly in their own juice, or in stews and soups.

Scallops. Bay scallops or calicos are small and tender. Sea scallops are larger and tastier and can be sliced in half horizontally for faster cooking. Excellent with curries, au gratin, cold, and in Oriental dishes.

Shrimp. Available in small, medium, large, and jumbo sizes, fresh, canned, or frozen. Fresh are preferable. Contrary to former thinking, shrimp are low in fat and cholesterol. Care should be taken not to overcook, as they then become tough. To cook in shells, simply drop into boiling water with a little vinegar and lemon. Shrimp are done when water returns to boil and they turn pink. Remove and run under cold water. Shell and devein by removing black thread on upper curve with a sharp knife. To cook in a sauce, the raw cleaned shrimp need only be simmered for 1–3 minutes.

Garlic

More flavor is released if garlic is minced rather than crushed. To facilitate peeling, crush clove with flat side of a knife first.

Green Vegetables

Cook green vegetable uncovered in boiling water for only 5 minutes. Or steam over boiling water. Quick cooking retains vitamins and leaves vegetables crunchy. Water left after cooking may be saved and used for soup base. Many leafy green vegetables are interchangeable—Swiss chard, beet tops, spinach, escarole, kale—and all have high calcium content and are rich in vitamin A.

Herbs

Fresh herbs grown in the garden or purchased from a greengrocer are recommended. They may be frozen and kept for ready access. When available, such herbs as mint, basil, rosemary, oregano, and parsley may be stored this way. To keep a supply of basil, for example, pick leaves, place in blender with a little water, pour into a plastic ice cube tray, and freeze. Pop out cubes and store in plastic bags in the freezer. Dried herbs release more flavor if crushed in the hand before using or when soaked briefly in a teaspoon of boiling water.

To freeze, pick leaves off stems, spread on cookie sheet, and place in freezer. When frozen, store in containers.

Julienne

Cut vegetables into matchstick-shaped strips about ⅛ inch thick and 1–2 inches long.

Milk

Use nonfat powdered milk instead of cartons of skim milk. In the long run, it is less expensive, easy to store, and tastes just as good. If using skim milk, use only 1 percent fat-free milk. Unsweetened, evaporated skim milk is concentrated, and we use it whipped in many desserts, as a substitute for whipped cream. To whip, place milk in bowl and put in freezer until crystals form around edges—1–2 hours. Beaters should be cooled in freezer, too. Remove and beat until peaks form.

Nuts

Avoid raw nuts. Roast almonds or filberts with a little ground cinnamon for a crunchy, nutritious garnish. Sesame seeds and sunflower seeds are best toasted in a skillet. Pumpkin or squash seeds should be washed, fibers removed, and then roasted in the oven for 10 minutes at 400°F. Home-ground peanut or other nut butter or those from natural food stores are recommended, with no salt and no sugar. Watch out for dextrose, sucrose, corn syrup, and other sugar in commercial brands.

To blanch almonds or pistachios and other nuts, drop them into boiling water for a minute. Remove from water and, while they are still warm, pinch between thumb and index finger to slip off skins. Dry for 5–10 minutes in low oven.

Parboil

Blanch vegetables long enough to cook food partially so it may then be added to stews or grated, as with potatoes.

Pasta

Noodles, spaghetti, and other pasta products come in all shapes, sizes, and forms. Egg noodles are made in little squares, rounds, stars, penne, orzo, flakes, large curly lasagna noodles, angelhair, fettucini, elbows, ziti, rigatoni, linguine, shells, etc. Some are made of whole wheat (we prefer this type) and with spinach. Vegetable pastas are also available. They are pretty in their pastel colors but don't offer much more nutritionally. Buckwheat noodles are excellent (Japanese soba noodles are made of this grain, and some Italian pasta shops have them).

DeBoles Nutritional products distribute noodles made of soy and Jerusalem artichoke flours and are available in lasagna, spaghetti, shells, etc. They're good and are recommended as a wheat-free product. Hungarian egg noodles are available in New York City from H. Roth, and from Paprikas Weiss. (See Appendix II.) Egg barley, called *tarhonya*, is delicious. If not convenient to order, Goodman's makes a product that is similar.

Peppers

To facilitate peeling peppers, place under broiler until they begin to burn. Turn and, when seared, place in a brown paper bag to steam for 20 minutes. When cool, their skins will peel away easily.

Polyunsaturated

Polyunsaturated vegetable oils are those recommended in the recipes: corn oil, safflower oil, sesame oil, sunflower seed oil, walnut oil, and a good-quality olive oil in limited amounts are acceptable. Where a light coating is required to keep food from sticking, use a vegetable spray.

Poultry

Remove skin from poultry before serving, if roasting whole birds. In cooking soups or stews and in poaching, remove skin before cooking. Skin has a great deal of fat, and we try to avoid using it. Legs and thighs are very high in cholesterol. We prefer using chicken or turkey breasts. These are available as skinless and boneless cutlets and are used in many of our recipes.

Puree

Vegetables and fruits may be ground through a food mill or strainer to produce a fine pulp. Sometimes the blender may be used for this purpose, but it's not good for potatoes, which are best whipped with beaters or a potato ricer.

Reduce

Sauces are enhanced in flavor by reducing or cooking down the amount of liquid. Bring to boil and cook until liquid is halved.

Refresh

Run vegetables or fruit under cold water after boiling to stop cooking process. Also done with noodles, rice, or shrimp.

Rice and Grains

Different parts of the world produce different kinds of rice and grains. We recommend long-grain brown rice for most dishes because of the nutrients and the fiber. Natural food stores sell this variety. The only kind of white rice acceptable here is converted rice. Other white rice has all the vitamins processed out. Use twice as much water as the quantity of rice. While rice is cooking, it should not be stirred. When water is absorbed, the rice should be removed from the heat and left to steam, covered, for 10–15 minutes more. Then it may be fluffed. It is also good cooked in broth for added flavor.

Indian rice, called *Basmati,* also available in natural food stores or Indian food stores, is nutty in flavor and nutritious. It must be soaked in water and rinsed well to get rid of powder and other impurities. When water runs clear, the rice is ready to use. The Italian *Arborio* rice is similarly recommended. Wild rice takes a little longer to cook, and it is quite pricey. Other grains such as kasha (buckwheat groats), bulgur, barley, semolina, cornmeal, hominy, and couscous are excellent carbohydrate choices. Health food stores carry most of these grains.

Salt

We have used scant quantities of salt—just a pinch for taste. There's not much difference between sea salt and ordinary salt in these quantities. Most of the Oriental dishes call for soy sauce, which will increase the percentage of sodium. We recommend Kikkoman Shoyu, which has 47 percent less salt than ordinary soy sauces. Oyster sauce has even less sodium.

Soy can be further diluted with water. When anchovies or capers or other salted condiments are used, they should be rinsed first and drained.

Sauces

Puree vegetables with a little low-fat yogurt or skim milk for use as sauce over pasta, potatoes, salad, plain broiled fish.

Seasoning

Season vegetables with a squeeze of lime or lemon juice, a dash of red chili. This will eliminate the need for adding salt to food.

Serving

Use dishes that will just nicely accommodate smaller servings of food so that the meal does not look "lost" on the plate. Also arrange colors and servings attractively on each plate with a decoration such as a sliced curl of lemon or lime, a radish rose, or a scallion brush.

Soup

When making soup stocks such as chicken or beef (see index), remove scum that accumulates during the early cooking stage. Any fat that accumulates after refrigeration should be removed. Broth should be measured, poured into containers, and kept in freezer for later use, as desired. A squeeze of lemon or a dash of vinegar perks up the taste of soup. Chicken left over from cooking stock may be used in salads or in other dishes such as Chicken Tacos (see index). Any combination of vegetables, rice, pasta, and seasonings may be added to the broth to make vegetable bouillon or onion, lemon, yogurt, or barley soup. When adding eggs or yogurt to soups, mix a little of the soup into the mixture to be added before returning all of it to the soup kettle. When adding eggs or yogurt, do not bring back to a boil; just reheat (gently).

Spices

Fresh herbs and spices are recommended. Store in refrigerator, not on the shelf. Whole berries such as juniper, allspice, and cardamon may be ground.

Sweeteners

From bread baking to dessert making, a little frozen concentrated apple juice is an excellent sweetener, providing nutrients and flavor. Powdered fructose is used, but in small quantities. It carries the same power as plain sugar, but is not just empty calories. Use sparingly. We do not recommend cooking with any artificial sugar substitutes. Honey, molasses, and brown sugar are on our forbidden list.

Thickeners

We have avoided using flour as a thickener. Instead, we use arrowroot and in some cases cornstarch. Mix with a little water or milk and add to a soup, vegetable, or gravy, stirring into the sauce slowly. Mustard may also be added to thicken a meat sauce. Fine bread crumbs, farina, or a little instant tapioca will thicken soups, too. Peanut butter is also used to bind and thicken, particularly in African, Oriental, and Brazilian dishes.

2 tablespoons cornstarch = 1 bread exchange
1 tablespoon arrowroot = 1 bread exchange
1 teaspoon tapioca = 1 tablespoon flour

Tomato Sauce

DeBoles and Contadina make excellent sugar-free sauces. We also recommend using canned Italian plum tomatoes in puree for cooking. But in any canned products, read the label and avoid brands that list sugar and added salt.

Tomatoes

When recipes call for peeled, seeded, and diced tomatoes, follow these steps: *To peel tomatoes,* place ripe tomatoes in a bowl and cover with boiling water for 10 seconds; drain off water and run quickly under cold water. Skin will peel off readily. *To seed tomatoes,* slice off the top of the tomato (not the stem end) and flick out the core and seeds with a teaspoon or grapefruit cutter.

Utensils

We have specified nonstick pans for cooking. These might be Teflon or Silverstone pots and pans. No additional oils are required for searing meats, although we found that a drop of oil helps to sauté onions. A little water or stock may also be used for sautéing. Nothing sticks to these pans, however, so no deglazing is possible. A well-seasoned *wok* may be used for stir-frying as in Oriental recipes. A straw steamer or an ordinary stainless steel steamer basket in a kettle serves for cooking fish and vegetables and retaining flavors.

Vegetables

Fresh vegetables are recommended rather than frozen or canned. The more processing involved in food, the fewer the nutrients. Blanch or steam for best results. If frozen vegetables are used, they need to be cooked with just a little water for a short time to defrost.

Vinegar

White vinegar is fine for pickling and marinating meats such as lamb. But in salad dressings there is a wider choice of vinegars that truly make a flavor statement. Balsamic vinegar is delectable and different and will enhance an Italian or French vinaigrette. Tarragon or dill and wine vinegars are similarly more tasty. Raspberry vinegar is special! All are available in specialty food stores. Some can be made at home with fresh herbs.

Warming Food

Often our directions will say "set aside and keep warm." Place such foods in a warm dish, cover with aluminum foil, and leave in a warm place until ready to proceed.

Washing

All fruits and vegetables should be washed in warm water, even oranges. They have all been sprayed. If cucumbers are waxed, peel them.

Yogurt

Plain low-fat yogurt combines with nearly all fruits and vegetables, and it freezes well for dessert. To make your own frozen yogurt, mix together with a fruit or flavoring of your choice, add a little pure vanilla extract, perhaps some beaten egg whites, and freeze a few hours. A few sunflower seeds or chopped nuts make a nice topping for a refreshing, low-calorie dessert. Avoid prepackaged frozen yogurts and fruit yogurts, for these have added sugar.

Yogurt Sour Cream Substitute

Instead of sour cream, strain plain low-fat yogurt in a cheesecloth container and let the liquid drip out for 1–2 hours. Before doing this, the yogurt may be mixed with herbs for desired flavor such as dill or tarragon. Use where sour cream is called for in your favorite recipes. If the yogurt is allowed to drain overnight in the refrigerator, the result will be a delicious cheese, reminiscent of the forbiddingly fat French cheese, boursin. It is excellent with fruit for dessert.

FOREIGN FAVORITES

Bean Sprouts

Available in Oriental markets and some supermarkets, soy bean sprouts are also packed in cans. Sprouts should be kept in water, rinsed before using, and drained.

Cellophane Noodles

These have many names. They should be covered with boiling water for 10 minutes, then drained and added to the sauce in which it will be served. The Japanese call them *harusame.* Available in Oriental food stores.

Chayote

A Mexican vegetable for which zucchini may be substituted. Available in some supermarkets and in Hispanic food stores.

Chestnuts

To roast fresh chestnuts, slit the tops of each shell and spread chestnuts on a baking pan with a little water. Roast in preheated 375°F oven for 20 minutes. Peel chestnuts when cooked and use whole or sliced. They may also be boiled.

Chili Peppers

There are about 100 different kinds of chili peppers that range from mild to fiery hot. Jalapeño, serrano, and poblano are likely to be the most popular names of peppers found in supermarkets. When cutting and slicing them, be careful not to touch the seeds and veins. They are apt to burn your skin and lips!

Chinese Vermicelli

Vermicelli or rice sticks are made of rice flour and are cooked the same way as cellophane noodles. Available in Chinese markets.

Cilantro

Sometimes called *coriander,* this is also labeled *Chinese parsley.* It has a broader leaf than ordinary parsley and a slightly pungent flavor. It is used in many cuisines. Ground coriander, made from the seeds of the plant, has an entirely different taste.

Daikon

A mild, long, white radish used in Japanese cooking. Delicious raw as a snack or cooked. If not available, small white turnips may be substituted. Available in most supermarkets and Oriental food shops.

Dashi

Japanese soup stock made of nori and bonito flakes. Chicken stock may be substituted.

Durkee's Imitation Bacon Chips

These have a bacon flavor and are made of soybeans. They provide a smoky bacon taste without the fat. Use sparingly.

Ginger

A knobby root used in many countries. Peel away the outer skin and rough pulp and mince fine. To keep, store in refrigerator or drop into a jar of sherry.

Juniper Berries

Available in natural food stores and specialty shops. Used in German, Scandinavian, and Russian cookery.

Kiwifruit

A wonderful and beautiful fruit that is grown in New Zealand and California but that originated in the Yangtze Valley in China. Brown and fuzzy on the outside, it is bright green and gaily patterned inside. Only 45 calories per kiwifruit, and packed with potassium and Vitamin C, this is a colorful dessert and decorating idea.

Kombu or Nori

Dried kelp, seaweed, used in Japanese recipes. Available in Oriental markets and natural food stores.

Mango

An exotic, tropical fruit that is best eaten raw. Fruit is ripe when it is soft to the touch. It will ripen at room temperature. Peel skin and discard pit. Good mixed with yogurt or whipped evaporated milk.

Mirin

A Japanese sherry used in cooking and in dipping sauces. Available in Oriental food markets and some supermarkets.

Miso

Fermented soy bean paste used for marinating foods, for sauces, and as a Japanese soup base when added to dashi. Available in Oriental markets and natural food stores.

Papaya

Also called *papaw*. Thin-skinned, tropical fruit with edible seeds. Fruit is ripe if it yields to pressure. Store in refrigerator. Noted for healthful attributes. Ripens at room temperature.

Persimmon

Bright red fruit, sometimes called *Sharon fruit*. Pulp may be eaten spooned out of shell or mixed with yogurt. Ripen in bag with an apple. Persimmons should be soft to the touch.

Plantain

Green plantains are used for baking, broiling, or sautéing. They are inedible raw. May be used instead of bananas in cooking.

Sake

Rice wine, similar to sherry, used in cooking and for marinating. Available in Oriental markets and wine/liquor stores.

Sesame Oil

Oriental foods may be sautéed in this flavorful oil for a distinct Japanese or Chinese taste. Available in Oriental markets and many supermarkets.

Sesame Seeds

Korean food and Turkish dishes use a great deal of these tasty seeds. They are best toasted and may be ground to release oils. They are also nice sprinkled on desserts. But use sparingly, as they do contain saturated fat.

Shrimp Paste

Used in Indonesian and some Oriental cooking. Available dried in specialty food stores such as H. Roth, in New York City.

Soba Noodles

Thin, brown, buckwheat noodles used in Japanese cooking. Drop into a cup of boiling water, add another cup of cold water, and return to boil, then add another cup of cold water. Repeat until noodles are tender. Available in Oriental markets.

Somen Noodles

Fine, white noodles that are cooked the same way as soba noodles. *Hiyamugi* noodles are similar. Available in Oriental markets.

Tofu

Bean curd is an excellent source of protein, with no fat or cholesterol. It is now available in most supermarkets and in all natural food stores, as well as Oriental markets. Used in soups, stews, omelets, and desserts, it has little flavor of its own but can be marinated for flavor. It is best to squeeze out the water a loaf retains by placing the tofu between paper towels and placing a weight over it. It will then cook better. Mashed with fruit and flavored with vanilla, tofu makes an excellent dessert.

Try experimenting with bananas or a little ricotta cheese. Chill or freeze.

Udon Noodles

Thick noodles made of white flour, similar to spaghetti. Available in Oriental markets.

DECORATING FOODS WITH COLORFUL TOUCHES

Flowers

Nasturtiums, pansies, and squash blossoms, if available, impart a festive look to a dish.

Radish Roses

Clean red radishes, cut off stems, and then on the other end make sharp slashes through the red skin. Place in a bowl of cold water and chill. Radish petals will open and make a decorative addition to any dish or on a relish tray.

Scallion Brushes

Trim off roots of scallions and uppermost greens. Slash the long way in both the white and green parts. Chill in ice water until they curl. These look attractive on top of any Oriental dish and with other foods.

Scoring

To score lemons or oranges, cut a thin line out of the skin, cutting away the white pulp. When the fruit is sliced, it will have a decorative scalloped edge. A slice made halfway through the round will enable it to be folded over in a twist or curl, which is also a nice garnish touch.

Cucumbers with unwaxed skin may be scored with a fork and then sliced thin—they, too, will have a more decorative look.

APPENDIX I: EQUIVALENTS

EQUIVALENT MEASUREMENTS

3 teaspoons	=	1 tablespoon
4 tablespoons	=	¼ cup
5⅓ tablespoons	=	⅓ cup
8 tablespoons	=	½ cup
12 tablespoons	=	¾ cup
16 tablespoons	=	1 cup
2 cups	=	1 pint
4 cups	=	1 quart
4 quarts	=	1 gallon
16 ounces	=	1 pound

UNITED STATES AND METRIC WEIGHTS AND MEASURES

Fluid Measurement Equivalents

Metric	United States
1 liter =	4¼ cups or 1 quart plus 2 ounces
½ liter (demiliter) =	2 cups (generous) or 1 pint

Weight Measurement Equivalents

Metric	United States
1 gram =	.035 ounce
28.35 grams =	1 ounce
100 grams =	3.5 ounces
114 grams =	4 ounces
226.78 grams =	8 ounces (1 cup)
500 grams =	1 pound, 1.5 ounces
1 kilogram =	2.21 pounds

OVEN TEMPERATURES

very low = 200°F
low = 300°F
moderately low = 325°F
moderate = 350°F
moderately hot = 375°F
hot = 400°F
very hot = 450°F
broil = 550°F

Metric Equivalents and Common Measures

Weight

kilogram = 1000 grams (slightly more than 2 pounds—about 2.2 pounds)
gram = 0.001 ($\frac{1}{1000}$) kilogram
milligram = 0.001 ($\frac{1}{1000}$) gram

Liquid Measure

1 liter = slightly more than 1 quart
1 deciliter = 0.1 ($\frac{1}{10}$) liter
1 milliliter = 0.001 ($\frac{1}{1000}$) liter

APPENDIX II: FOOD SOURCES

SUGARLESS DRINKS AND FRUIT CONSERVES

After the Fall
Box B
Newfane, VT 05345
Fruit juices

Hain Pure Food
13660 S. Figeroa St.
Los Angeles, CA 90061
Fruit juices, health food products

R. W. Knudson Family
Chico, CA 95926
Fruit drinks

Lakewood Products
Miami, FL 33242
Sparkling drinks

Sorrell Ridge
100 Markley St.
Pt. Reading, NJ 07064
Fruit conserves

Willow Farms
Willow, NY 12495
Fruit preserves, pickled vegetables

Winter Hill Juices
Highland, NY 12528
Fruit juices

SPICES, GRAINS, AND OTHER INGREDIENTS

Antones Import Co.
807 Taft St.
Houston, TX 77025
Indian and Indonesian

Asia Bazar
87–46 Parsons Blvd.
Jamaica, NY 11432
Oriental

Balducci
424 Sixth Ave.
New York, NY 10011
Fine imported foods

Bremen House
218 E. 86th St.
New York, NY 10028
German

Casa Moneo Imports
210 E. 14th St.
New York, NY 10011
Spanish, Mexican, and Caribbean

Dean & Deluca, Inc.
121 Prince St.
New York, NY 10012
All imported foods

Health Valley
700 Union St.
Montebello, CA 90640
Health foods and grains

Jamail's
3114 Kirby Dr.
Houston, TX 77001
Ceylonese and Mexican

Kalamata Foods Imports
38–03 Ditmars Blvd.
Astoria, NY 11105
Greek

Kalustian Orient Trading Corp.
123 Lexington Ave.
New York, NY 10016
Indian

Nyborg & Nelson
153 E. 53rd St.
New York, NY 10022
Scandinavian

Paprika Weiss Importer
1546 Second Ave.
New York, NY 10028
Hungarian spices, noodles, pickled foods

Pennyroyal Place
Country Herb Market
72 E. Main St.
Worcester, MA 01608
Herbs and grains

De Boles Nutritional Foods
2120 Jericho Turnpike
Garden City Park, NY 11004
Wheat-free pastas, tomato sauces

Eden Trading & Co.
1240 Hilltop Ln.
Annapolis, MD 21403
All European imports

Europa Grocery
321 S. Spring St.
Los Angeles, CA 90013
Middle Eastern

European Imports
23 N. Beniston St.
St. Louis, MO 63105
Greek and Italian

Greens & Grains
5705 Hickman St.
Des Moines, IA 50310
Herbs and grains

Haigs
642 Clement Ave.
San Francisco, CA 94118
Middle Eastern

H. Roth & Sons
1577 First Ave.
New York, NY 10028
Hungarian and international specialties

INDEX